# Other Works by Max Haines

Bothersome Bodies (1977)
Calendar of Criminal Capers (1977)
Crime Flashback #1 (1980)
Crime Flashback #2 (1981)
Crime Flashback #3 (1982)
The Murderous Kind (1983)
Murder & Mayhem  (1984)
The Collected Works of Max Haines Vol. I (1985)
That's Life (1986)
True Crime Stories (1987)
True Crime Stories Book II  (1988)
True Crime Stories Book III (1989)
True Crime Stories Book IV (1990)
The Collected Works of Max Haines Vol. II (1991)
True Crime Stories Book V (1992)
Doctors Who Kill (1993)
Multiple Murderers (1994)
Multiple Murderers II (1995)
The Collected Works of Max Haines Vol. III (1996)
Celebrity Murders (1996)

# MURDERS STRANGE BUT TRUE

## MAX HAINES

VIKING

VIKING
Published by the Penguin Group
Penguin Books Canada Ltd, 10 Alcorn Avenue, Toronto, Ontario,
Canada M4V 3B2
Penguin Books Ltd, 27 Wrights Lane, London W8 5TZ, England
Viking Penguin, a division of Penguin Books USA Inc., 375 Hudson Street,
New York, New York 10014, U.S.A.
Penguin Books Australia Ltd, Ringwood, Victoria, Australia
Penguin Books (NZ) Ltd, cnr Rosedale and Airborne Roads, Albany,
Auckland 1310, New Zealand

Penguin Books Ltd, Registered Offices: Harmondsworth,
Middlesex, England

First published 1997

1 3 5 7 9 10 8 6 4 2
Copyright © Max Haines Ltd, 1997

Printed and bound in the U.S.A.

**Canadian Cataloguing in Publication Data**

Haines, Max
Murders strange but true

ISBN 0-670-87588-0

1. Murder. I. Title.

HV6515.H34 1997    364.1523    C97-930162-9

Visit Penguin Canada's web site at **www.penguin.ca**

For Marilyn

# Acknowledgments

In writing true-crime stories, many individuals and organizations contribute to the final product.

I am deeply indebted to the Metropolitan Toronto Police, the Ontario Provincial Police, the Federal Bureau of Investigation and New Scotland Yard for their fine cooperation in sharing information with me. In many cases, the information I needed had to be dug out of the distant past and therefore was not easy to retrieve.

I would be remiss not to thank the many newspapers around the world which provided me with information on various crimes that occurred in their areas.

In particular, the news resource staff of my own paper, *The Toronto Sun*, have been invaluable. They are manager Julie Kirsh, assistant manager Kathy Webb Nelson and their staff: Susan Dugas, Joyce Wagler, Glenna Tapscott, Jillian Goddard, Tisa Zabarylo, Anna Morrone, Julie Hornby, Barbara White and Catherine Flannery.

I would also like to thank senior editor Jackie Kaiser of Penguin Canada, who held my hand for the better part of a year while this effort was being developed, as well as copy editor Liba Berry. Lawyer Tilda Roll and her assistant, Cameron, provided legal expertise throughout.

A woman named Marilyn also contributed.

# Introduction

When my daughter, Eleanor, attended elementary school, one of her teachers surveyed the classroom, asking each pupil, "What does your father do?" The teacher was taken aback by her response, "He's in the murder business." It's been 25 years since I began writing about what, for me, is the most fascinating subject in the world, true crime. Sometimes my occupation has found me benignly poring over a trial transcript in the archives of a law library. On other occasions it has placed me in far more precarious situations. I once sat across a table from a man just released from prison after a 17-year incarceration. A tense moment occurred when he nonchalantly said to my colleague, Mark Bonokowski (now editor of *The Ottawa Sun*), "If you keep taking down notes, it will be necessary to pass a knife through you." We both put away our notebooks.

I have also had the experience of meeting people who are proud of "their" murderers; like the postal clerk in East Auckland, England, whose chest swelled with pride when I inquired about Mary Ann Cotton, a serial killer who lived in her town a century ago.

Over the years I have visited death rows in Texas and Arkansas. In Texas, the three killers I interviewed were all executed within six months of my visit. Among the most interesting prisons I visited was the penitentiary at Marion, Illinois, the facility with the highest-rated security status in the United States. It is not the Holiday Inn.

Inside these pages you will meet the likes of Marie Witte, who solved the age-old mother-in-law problem by having the dear lady murdered. Marie insisted on boiling her mother-in-law's assorted parts and keeping them stored in her freezer.

Not to be outdone by Marie, another vile purveyor of mayhem, Elmer Lord, saw fit to lug his victim around Washington, D.C. in a trunk.

Keeping unwelcome bodies on the move seems to be a passion with some killers. Richard Ivens moved his victim's body so often that even he lost track of its exact location.

Not all killers attempt to dispose of the evidence of their crimes. Some just blast away and leave corpses where they fall. That's what Erik and Lyle Menendez did when they shot their parents to death in the recreation room of their palatial home. Kitty and Jose Menendez were doing nothing more threatening than eating ice cream and strawberries when their nasty sons took their lives.

I invite you to come along with me and share the lives of a select group of individuals who have committed some of the strangest crimes in history.

# CONTENTS

# MURDERS STRANGE
# BUT TRUE

# Ursula Adomeit
# VILLAGE VICE

Georg Richer, 19, made a big play for the most attractive girl in the village. Thirteen-year-old Ursula was one of those blond, blue-eyed German girls who caused pulses to race and heads to turn. The little village of Emslage-Ruehlerfeld, located near the German-Holland border, was home to other pretty girls, but Ursula was different. She looked 21 and had the figure of a silicone-enhanced movie star.

Once Georg was successful in seducing Ursula, she took to sex like Moll Flanders took to haymows. Soon Ursula found herself checking and rechecking her calendar. There was no doubt about it—she was more than somewhat pregnant.

Little Anja came into the world only a few months after her parents married. Within the next four years, three more daughters blessed the union. Anja was followed by Kathi, Alexandra and Petra.

The expanding family did not come about by accident, nor was Georg the instigator. No, Ursula was the aggressive love-making partner of the pair. In fact, Georg was tired most of the time. The poor man hardly got any sleep.

While having a schnapps in a bar one night, Georg met 19-year-old Kurt Adomeit. We will never know exactly what Georg had in mind when he invited Kurt, a truck driver, to move into the Richer home. Now, I would be remiss not to point out that Kurt had the looks of a Greek god, complete with muscles and, we can only assume, the necessary auxiliary equipment.

Georg may have invited his new roomer into his home for financial reasons, but there was some suspicion that he

1

welcomed what he suspected would inevitably happen. Sure as God made little green apples, Ursula and Kurt commenced doing it at every opportunity. Tongues wagged in the village.

You can just imagine the gossip when, on June 6, 1972, Ursula travelled to Meppen, the closest town, and reported her loving husband missing. The local police didn't have to be staffed with a Hercule Poirot to come to a couple of conclusions: Ursula and Kurt were lovers; and Georg Richer loved his four daughters and would never desert them. Once the little grey cells started percolating, police felt that it was quite possible that murder most foul had taken place, but, darn it all, they had no proof that any crime had been committed.

Two days after the missing persons report was filed, Meppen police received word that a vehicle belonging to Georg Richer had been found submerged in a pond in the village of Neuringe right on the Dutch border. Was it possible that he was alive and had attempted to get rid of his car before crossing the border into Holland? On the other hand, had his killer planted the car to make it appear that Georg had fled the country? The vehicle was returned to Meppen, but the only information garnered from the auto was that Georg hadn't been submerged with it.

Months passed. Police explored every avenue which could connect Ursula and Kurt to the missing Georg Richer. Despite their strong suspicions, however, authorities could find nothing concrete to connect the pair to the missing man. A year passed before Ursula filed for divorce on the grounds of desertion. The divorce was granted without delay.

Police made a habit of keeping tabs on the two suspects. The lovers were discreet in public. And it was rumoured that Ursula's four young daughters had accepted Kurt as their father. A year after the divorce and two years after Georg's disappearance, Kurt and Ursula officially tied the knot. The four Richer children, now ranging in age from four to nine years, were bridesmaids.

Another year passed. Rumours reached police that Ursula was stepping out at night when her truck-driver husband was out of town. While on one of his trips, Kurt was arrested in Osnabrück for peddling drugs. He confessed to selling the drugs in several judicial districts and was brought back to Meppen where he was jailed.

Detectives, who well remembered the disappearance of Georg Richer, decided to take advantage of Kurt's one weakness. Unlike husband number one, Kurt was extremely jealous of his overactive wife. Police decided to place a detective, posing as a drunk, in Kurt's cell. He would attempt to elicit incriminating information from the suspect. It didn't take long. The undercover detective bragged that he had met one of the sexiest women in the country in the village of Emslage-Ruehlerfeld at a bar called the Black Lamb. Kurt asked about the woman's name. The detective said he didn't know her last name, but was sure her first name was Ursula. Kurt saw red. He became violent and had to be restrained by guards. Then he blurted out the entire story of his unfaithful wife. He claimed that he shouldn't have expected anything better, because Ursula had cheated on her first husband so that she could bed down with him.

The time was ripe. His interrogators told Kurt that they knew that he and Ursula had killed Georg and buried his body, and urged him to unburden his guilty conscience. Kurt turned pale. He didn't realize that the police had nothing on him; all he had to do was keep quiet and Georg's murder would remain unsolved forever. Kurt slumped into a chair and exclaimed, "I'll show you where the body is buried."

On July 1, 1975, Kurt led police to the skeletal remains of Georg Richer. He told investigators that Georg had not been a jealous man and had probably known that his roomer and Ursula were having a prolonged affair.

Kurt told police that Ursula had put sleeping tablets in Georg's tea. The pills, however, didn't even make the victim sleepy. Frustrated, Ursula put a whole jar of tablets in Georg's tea. Strangely, they had absolutely no effect. Undaunted, Ursula purchased rat poison. She put large quantities of poison in Georg's food, only to be told that her cooking was greatly improved.

Kurt claimed that he told Ursula to give up. Georg was proving to be too difficult to kill. Besides, he thought she should attempt to obtain a divorce, but Ursula was adamant—Georg had to go.

On May 13, 1972, Kurt had returned home at around 10 p.m. The girls were already in bed. Ursula had used adhesive tape to wrap a hatchet. She gave the hatchet to Kurt with the pointed suggestion, "Now is the time to do it. He's asleep." Kurt did as he was told. He struck the sleeping man with all his might. "His head sort of exploded," Kurt said.

Ursula cleaned the blood from the bedclothes and the floor of the bedroom. Together they drove the body into the forest and buried poor Georg. Kurt admitted he had driven Georg's car to the Dutch border and into a pond to lead police to believe that Georg had left the country. He had then caught a bus back to Meppen.

Ursula was advised of Kurt's confession. Initially she denied any involvement, but soon broke down and told all. She added that lust and sin had not been the motive behind the crime and was able to prove that Georg had often beaten her severely.

The evidence of wife beating had some effect on the German court. Ursula and Kurt Adomeit were both found guilty and were each sentenced to the relatively light term of 10 years in prison.

# Charles Albanese
# CUNNING CHARLES ON DEATH ROW

I have always believed that poisoners are the most reprehensible type of killer. Certainly this story's vile dispenser of deadly white powder had little to recommend him. But let's start at the beginning.

Mary Lambert was an 89-year-old live wire who lived with her 69-year-old daughter, Marion Mueller, in the retirement community of Leisure Village located about 50 miles outside Chicago. Both women were healthy and took part in most of the physical activities the village offered.

Marion's daughter Virginia and her husband, Charles Albanese, visited the two women every week. Virginia was extremely devoted to her mother and grandmother and regularly brought them for visits to her home in nearby Spring Grove.

On August 3, 1980, Virginia and Charles had the two women over for Sunday dinner. That very evening, Mary Lambert commenced retching and vomiting. She was rushed to hospital, where she died three days later. The death was sudden, but since Mary was 89 years old, no one thought her demise that unusual. Officially her death was attributed to cardiac arrest.

Twelve days later, Mary's daughter, Marion, died after suffering from much the same symptoms. While no one suspected foul play, the residents of Leisure Village thought it most unusual for two healthy women to die within 12 days of each other. They urged officials to check local restaurants for botulism. The retirement community's water supply was tested. Charles Albanese requested that authorities investigate

5

further. After all, his wife had just lost her mother and grand-mother within a two-week span. Charles, who with his father and brother headed his family's large trophy-manufacturing firm, eventually was satisfied that the deaths were the result of a horrible coincidence.

Nine months passed before the subject of the strange deaths again came to the attention of officials. This time the local coroner was informed that a doctor had found traces of arsenic in blood serum taken from one of his patients who had died suddenly. The patient was Mike Albanese Sr., the father of Charles Albanese. Mike was 69 years old at the time of his death. Not only had he died suddenly, but another son, Mike Jr., had also fallen seriously ill, but did not die. Doctors reported to the coroner that traces of arsenic had also been found in the younger Mike's blood.

Initially, authorities felt there was a possibility that the two men had come in contact with arsenic used for industrial pur-poses. The Albanese family owned the Allied Die Casting Co. Mike Sr. had founded the company and, together with his two sons, Mike Jr. and Charles, ran the prosperous business. However, arsenic wasn't used in the manufacturing process. Hair and fingernail samples were taken from Mike's body before burial and tested for arsenic. Both tested positive. It was as if some evil force had descended upon Charles's in-laws and now his own father and brother.

Although no concrete connection was found between the deaths, the circumstances were under investigation by law enforcement authorities. Virginia and Charles were ques-tioned. Now that his father was dead and his brother confined to a wheelchair, Charles was running the family business. The police received permission from Virginia to exhume the bodies of her mother and grandmother. Both bodies contained large quantities of arsenic; in fact, 370 times the normal level.

The investigation shifted gears. Nurses and doctors who had attended Mary Lambert and Marion Mueller in hospital were questioned. Several nurses remembered that Virginia and Charles had visited the two women on a regular basis. They

6

also recalled that they often brought them cookies and doughnuts.

Detectives delved into Charles Albanese's background. They learned that Charles was a family man who devoted much of his time to his wife and children. Their home was a large sprawling one, complete with swimming pool. Charles had been married three times. His two previous marriages had ended in divorce. He and Virginia had been married since 1972. Although Charles had never committed a violent act, he did have a police record. In 1965, while working as an automobile salesman in Chicago, he was arrested for armed robbery. He had stolen $160 from a suburban home. Since entering the family business, his fortunes had changed for the better. He drew a large salary from Allied Die, owned his own home and drove a Cadillac. In addition, he split the firm's profits with his mother, Clara, and his brother, Mike Jr.

Detectives learned that Charles had been extremely attentive to his in-laws. He had been so successful in ingratiating himself with Mrs. Lambert that he had convinced her to change her will, leaving everything to her daughter, Marion, bypassing a son, Francis. To the elderly lady, this advice seemed reasonable. Her daughter, Marion, lived with her and was a great comfort to her in her declining years. When both women died within a period of 12 days, the entire estate passed to Mrs. Lambert's grandaughter Virginia Albanese. In this way, Charles came to control around $150,000 in cash, as well as a home valued at $95,000. He quickly sold the house for cash.

Nine months later, down at Allied Die, cunning Charles began taking his coffee break with his father and brother. He often brought cookies and doughnuts from home. After one of these coffee klatches, both Mike Sr. and Mike Jr. became violently ill and were hospitalized. Mike Sr. recovered and was released, but each time he nibbled something with Charles, he ended up back in hospital. On May 16, 1981, he died. Mike Jr. remained in hospital, unable to walk.

Police learned that Mike Sr. had left a personal estate of over half a million dollars to his wife. If Mike Jr. had died, and in due course, Charles's mother, Charles would have wiped out his entire family. Not only would he have inherited all their personal fortunes, he would also have full control of the lucrative family business. It is one thing to have suspicions, however, and quite another to develop proof. Police went about uncovering the evidence they needed. All suppliers and customers of Allied Die were canvassed in an attempt to learn if arsenic, in any shape or form, had found its way into the company's hands. They learned that Allied Die sold scrap zinc to a metal-plating firm in Elkhorn, Wisconsin. The manager of the firm, Joe Reichel, told police that he had had a conversation with Charles concerning arsenic. Charles had told Reichel that he was having trouble with insects around his home and wanted advice on how to get rid of them. Joe suggested arsenic and gave Charles two pounds of the poison, which he used in his own manufacturing process.

Police were forced to move quickly. They found out that Charles was planning a trip to Jamaica with his wife and mother. Investigators were convinced that he intended to murder his mother. Charles was apprehended and charged with three counts of murder and one charge of attempted murder.

On May 5, 1982, the accused man stood trial for the murder of his father and his wife's grandmother. He was found guilty on both charges and sentenced to death. Six months later, he was found guilty of his mother-in-law's murder and again sentenced to death. Between trials, Virginia obtained a divorce.

Today, Charles Albanese resides on death row in Illinois's Menard correctional facility. Gone are the loving wife, prosperous business, caring family, large home, Cadillac and swimming pool. Greed has taken it all away. In May 1989, the U.S. Supreme Court refused to hear Charles's last appeal.

Inmate number N22283 has no future other than his pending date with a lethal injection.

# William Archerd
# ANGEL OF DEATH

William Dale Archerd was born in Arkansas. He left his father's ranch at the age of 15 to wander the Midwest, taking odd jobs to keep body and soul together. By the time he was 17, he had gravitated to hospital work, obtaining employment as a hospital attendant. At that early age, he married the first of his seven wives. The marriage lasted four years. His second marriage was even less successful and was terminated after two years.

While employed in Oakland, California, in the 1940s, Archerd met another young lady, who quickly became wife number three. Unfortunately, he and his new bride encountered some difficulty when they were apprehended with heroin in their possession. This little caper resulted in Archerd spending three years in San Quentin after his good wife testified against him.

Upon his release from prison, Archerd drifted from job to job. It is believed that for the next 20 years this tall, handsome man with the shock of thick white hair became a killing machine. His implements of death were insulin and a hypodermic needle. Archerd had become something of an expert on the effects of insulin while working as a hospital attendant.

In 1947, Archerd was employed at the Kaiser Hospital in Fontana, California, when a friend of his, 34-year-old William Jones, was rushed to hospital in a coma. Ten hours later, Jones died of insulin shock, although insulin had not been prescribed for him. At the time, the death was considered puzzling, but no official action was taken. It would be 20 years before authorities would delve into Jones's death and discover that Archerd had profited by $10,000 from his friend's demise.

On May 14, 1956, Archerd's marriage to wife number three

was annulled. The very next day he married Zella Winders. Within a week he was looting his new wife's bank account. It took only a few days for the well to run dry. Archerd called police and told them a fantastic story. He claimed that two robbers had entered his home and injected him and Zella with some mysterious substance, after which they took off with about $500 in cash.

Police investigated but could find no evidence that intruders had been in the home. Archerd insisted that he and his wife had been bound and injected with a hypodermic needle. Next day Zella went into a coma and died before she could be removed to hospital. Official cause of death was listed as pneumonia. Archerd collected $619 in life insurance. The marriage had lasted only 12 days. Zella had more than $10,000 in the bank the day she married. The day she died, her account was down to a few hundred dollars.

Soon after, Archerd married again. If you are keeping track, we are now up to wife number five. It would be a brief liaison. Juanita Plum had recently divorced. Under the terms of her divorce, she came into possession of property that included a $40,000 home. In addition, she received $500 a month in alimony payments. No question about it; Juanita was a fine catch. On March 10, 1958, the happy pair were married in Las Vegas. Two days later, Juanita fell into a coma and died. Her death was attributed to cardiac arrest.

One can only imagine Archerd's surprise—and chagrin— when Juanita's will was read. She left her lady-killing husband exactly one dollar. The balance of her estate was bequeathed to members of her family.

Wife number six was something of a novelty since she survived and lived to testify at her former husband's trial. Not all of Archerd's wives were as fortunate.

In 1960, Archerd and a friend, Frank Stewart, flew to Las Vegas. Just before boarding, Frank took out an insurance policy for $80,000. It covered any accident which might occur on the plane or in the two airports involved. Once in Las Vegas, Frank supposedly fell in the men's room and struck his head. He was rushed to Southern Nevada Hospital, but doctors there could find no physical evidence that a fall had taken place. Next day, Frank's buddy, William Dale Archerd, visited him in hospital. That night, Frank died.

Archerd attempted to collect the insurance money, but the insurance boys balked, and with good reason. They produced a young lady who had visited Frank in hospital and had witnessed Archerd open a parcel containing a hypodermic needle and insulin. Archerd had told the girl he was going to inject Frank with the insulin so he would display the symptoms of a bad fall. Archerd had assured her that, other than rendering Frank unconscious for a short while, there would be no lasting effects from the injection. Archerd didn't collect the insurance and although he was questioned by the police, no charges were laid against the suave charmer.

The year 1960 proved to be a busy one for the angel of death. His divorced brother, Everett, was killed in an industrial accident. Archerd was granted custody of Everett's 15-year-old son, Burney. As official guardian, he was issued a workman's compensation insurance cheque in the amount of $7,000, to be held in trust until Burney reached the age of majority. That cheque was tantamount to a death sentence for the boy. On the day Archerd cashed the cheque, his nephew was admitted to Long Beach Memorial Hospital. The boy had supposedly been struck by a hit-and-run driver. Three hours later, after a visit from Uncle William, Burney's left eye dilated. He lapsed into a coma and was taken to an operating room. The dilated eye indicated pressure on the brain or intercranial bleeding. Doctors drilled burr holes into the skull to relieve the pressure. They were surprised to see no evidence of bleeding or damage of any kind. Thirteen days after being admitted to hospital, Burney Archerd died. Death was listed as terminal bronchopneumonia.

In February 1965, Archerd met 60-year-old Mary Brinker Post. Miss Post was assistant director of publicity for Claremont College and author of the best-selling novel *Annie Jordan*. Two months later, on April 18, they were married. It took our boy 18

11

months to spend the $21,000 his wife had brought to the marriage, as well as $14,000 she didn't have. On October 15, 1996, Mrs. Archerd the seventh filed for bankruptcy.

On October 28, Mrs. Archerd was involved in a minor traffic accident as she drove to the college from her home. Archerd was in San Francisco at the time, but returned to Los Angeles as soon as he received the news. On the day after the accident, he had photos taken of the vehicle and his wife's minor injuries. He put in a claim that same day to the college's insurance company.

On October 30, two days after the accident, Archerd knocked on a neighbour's door to say that his wife wouldn't wake up. An ambulance was summoned and the stricken woman was taken to Pomona Valley Hospital. The next afternoon she died without regaining consciousness. Although no insulin had been prescribed, an autopsy indicated she had died from bronchopneumonia secondary to hypoglycemia.

Seven was not a lucky number for Archerd. Maybe it was because of the prominence of his victim or because the death was so obviously the result of an insulin injection that authorities decided to put William Dale Archerd's life under a microscope. It didn't take long for detectives to uncover Archerd's past, including the fact that not only had he worked as a hospital attendant, he had been employed in an insulin-shock ward for over a year.

A team of eight detectives dug and sifted through the killer's life for the previous 20 years. It is believed that he murdered two friends, a nephew and three wives. Authorities decided to prosecute on the three strongest cases, those of Zella Winders, Burley Archerd and Mary Archerd.

William Archerd was tried and found guilty of murdering all three. It was the first time anyone in the United States was convicted of using insulin as a murder weapon.

On March 6, 1968, Supreme Court Judge Adolph Alexander sentenced Archerd to death in California's gas chamber. For nine years he resided on death row at San Quentin, but in the end he cheated the gas chamber. William Dale Archerd died of natural causes while still in prison.

# Norma Armistead
# ROBBING THE CRADLE

There was a degree of inevitability drawing Mary Childs into the life and obsessions of Norma Jean Armistead. You see, Mary was having a baby and Norma, an obstetric nurse, desperately wanted one.

Mary was a 26-year-old grocery-store employee in Los Angeles, California. Her pregnancy had been routine in every way. On September 20, 1974, she entered the Kaiser Foundation Hospital in Hollywood to have her baby. Mary's doctor estimated the baby would weigh about eight pounds. In the hospital, Mary met Norma Armistead and instantly liked the friendly, outgoing 47-year-old nurse.

That night, Norma administered several drugs to her patient before Mary dozed off. When she woke up in the wee hours of the morning, Mary felt that something was drastically wrong. She had no control over her limbs and was unable to get her mind to focus. She peered at her stomach and was shocked to see that she wasn't big anymore. Was this some kind of fantastic dream? No, there were doctors and Nurse Armistead at her bedside. They were all so serious. Mary tried to concentrate and listen as Norma spoke to the doctors. She told them she had visited the ward minutes earlier to find Mary unconscious with a stillborn baby between her legs. When Mary came to fully, she screamed and kicked until Norma managed to calm her down.

In the next few hours, doctors told Mary that blood tests indicated that her body contained large quantities of narcotics, none of which had been prescribed. Mary was stunned. She had never taken any drugs on her own and informed the doctors of this fact. The medics didn't answer. After all, it was quite customary for women to deny they had anything to do with the death of their own baby.

The stillborn child weighed slightly more than three pounds and had been dead for a week. Something was strangely amiss. The admitting doctor had told Mary that her baby had a strong heartbeat and she could expect a healthy baby. There followed more denials. The consulting doctors didn't bother to check with the admitting physician what they felt were this woman's obvious falsehoods. They suggested she go home and try to forget the whole unpleasant experience. Heartbroken and depressed, Mary did as she was told.

In the following months, Norma Armistead became the very dear friend of Kathryn Viramontes. What a coincidence. Kathryn, who already had three children, was once again pregnant and Norma was an obstetric nurse. The father of Kathryn's unborn child had left her during her pregnancy and she needed a friend. Norma more than fit the bill. She was kind, gentle and caring. She also took a great interest in Kathryn's health, insisting she see her doctor on a regular basis. Kathryn assured her friend that her doctor had told her throughout her term that her pregnancy was normal. She could expect a healthy baby. In mid-May, on her last visit to her doctor, Kathryn was told to expect the birth of her child during the first week in June.

Four days later, Kathryn's nine-year-old son, Richie, ran to a neighbour's house crying that something was wrong with his mother. The neighbour found Kathryn's body on the bedroom floor in a pool of blood under a mattress. Bedsheets and clothing were strewn about the room. The neighbour called an ambulance.

Across town, Norma walked into Kaiser Foundation Hospital carrying a newborn baby. Norma told a physician that she had given birth to the baby on the way to the hospital. The doctor was mystified. This woman, whom he had never seen before, seemed to be past childbearing age. After seeing to it that the baby was cared for, he proceeded to examine Norma.

His suspicions turned to amazement when he discovered his patient had no cervix or uterus. The doctor realized Norma had had a hysterectomy.

Authorities were notified. The strange-but-true tale soon unfolded. Norma, who was living common law with Charlie Armistead, felt she was losing him because of her inability to have a baby. As an obstetric nurse, she had the opportunity to steal a live baby and replace it with a foetus available to her from the hospital morgue. She had given massive doses of drugs to Mary Childs to induce labour and render her helpless. At the time, Mary's doctors had believed their obstetric nurse rather than the confused patient. If they had taken the time to check out Mary's story, the evil that was Norma Jean Armistead would have been stopped then and there. As matters turned out, Norma had walked to another hospital with Mary's baby to try to obtain a birth certificate, telling the nurses she had given birth on the way to the institution. She had refused medical help and left the hospital with the baby. She later procured a birth certificate in the name of Carrie Armistead.

Shortly after, Norma ingratiated herself into the life of Kathryn Viramontes. At the same time, she gained weight in order to appear pregnant. All the while she posed as a caring, concerned friend, more than willing to assist Kathryn through her pregnancy.

On May 16, 1975, while visiting Kathryn, the obstetric nurse injected her friend with various drugs, rendering Kathryn unconscious. To make sure there would be no outcry, Norma placed tape over her victim's mouth and slit her throat, killing her immediately. It is not necessary to go into detail here. Suffice it to say, Norma performed a Caesarean section on the dead woman.

Within 24 hours, the relationship between Norma and Kathryn was known to police. Norma confessed her terrible crimes and gave her reasons. Her common-law husband, she told police, had threatened to return to his wife and children. Norma was convinced that only by producing babies could she prevent Charlie from leaving her.

15

Despite Norma's strange behaviour, psychiatrists found she knew the difference between right and wrong and had acted with full knowledge of the consequences of her actions. In March 1976, she was found guilty of murder and sentenced to life imprisonment.

A postscript to this strange case was provided when Mary Childs's eight-month-old baby, who had been living with Norma and Charlie, was returned to her. Mary sued the hospital and the attending physicians for $24 million. She was awarded $375,000, a large portion of which went to pay legal fees.

# Ronald Bennell
# NOTE PROVED TO BE HIS DOWNFALL

Linda Stewart found herself in the wrong place at the wrong time.

Attractive, 22-year-old Linda lived at 285 Kingsway in Manchester, England, with her mother, grandmother, a married brother, his wife and baby daughter. Linda had her problems. A rather shy, quiet girl, she had never dated much, but was keeping company with one steady boyfriend. The two young people saw each other several times a week.

In 1970, when Linda became pregnant, it was a foregone conclusion that the couple would marry. Unfortunately, the engineering firm where Linda's boyfriend was employed was being liquidated. When the young man found out that he would shortly be unemployed, he informed Linda that they would be unable to wed. Understandably, Linda didn't take the news well, but the two lovers continued to date regularly.

When Linda wasn't out with her boyfriend, she usually spent her evenings with her best friend, Jennifer Earl, who lived about a half mile from her home. On Friday, November 27, 1970, Linda called Jennifer at about 8:30 p.m. She suggested a walk and perhaps a drink at a local pub. Jennifer called for Linda and the two friends walked for a while. Shortly after 10 p.m. they dropped into the Princess Hotel. They consumed two beers each before leaving at around 11 p.m. for the walk home. Linda and Jennifer chatted for a while at the junction of Mauldeth Road and Kingsway before separating to walk the remaining distance to their respective homes.

Just before they parted company, Jennifer noticed a man peering into a store window nearby. Slightly apprehensive, she asked Linda if she wanted her to walk with her. Linda laughed at the suggestion and walked off alone.

Next morning, 72-year-old Gwen Hughes woke up, put the kettle on and took some trash to the dustbin. She remembered to be careful because the path leading to the garden area of her Kingsway duplex had been paved the previous day. As she walked to the edge of the property, Gwen sighted a bundle of clothing on the path. Drawing closer, she saw long red hair flowing from the clothing. Gwen and a neighbour called police.

The body of the young girl bore bite marks on both breasts and the impression of boot marks across her chest. She had been raped and beaten to death. Although the girl's body had been found on the newly paved path, there was evidence of a struggle in an adjoining flower bed. The earth in the flower bed was disturbed and there was a wide opening in a hedge beside the path. Apparently the victim had been accosted on the other side of the hedge and had been dragged through the flower bed and hedge to where the body was found.

Gwen Hughes stated that she had been awakened the night before by a thumping noise. She had gotten out of bed and peered out a window. Although the noise continued, she hadn't seen anything unusual. When the noise stopped, she went back to bed. Other neighbours reported that they had heard the piercing scream of a woman around 11:30 the previous night, but because they often heard strange noises from the busy Kingsway, they had not taken any action.

The area around the body was closely examined. Boot prints taken from the flower bed matched those on the victim's chest. A man's crude metal ring was found in one of the flower beds. Near the path, detectives found a half-eaten meat pie. Investigators initially felt that the meat pie and the ring could have been dropped there days earlier and might have nothing whatever to do with the murder. But these two items took on new significance when Gwen Hughes's handyman told police that on the day of the murder he had cleaned the flower beds and swore that he had left the earth smooth and clean. He took great pride in the hedge and he insisted that there was no opening in it when he finished his work.

When Linda's family reported her missing, the identity of the body on the footpath was quickly established. Detectives went about tracing Linda's movements on the previous night. Linda's friend, Jennifer Earl, related their visit to the pub on the night of the murder. Linda's boyfriend was questioned extensively. He told police that he was supposed to go out with Linda that night, but had called off the date. He and a group of his colleagues from the engineering plant had gone pub crawling to bury their sorrow at joining the ranks of the unemployed. They had been very intoxicated and were remembered at each pub they visited. Police carefully checked the group's movements and were convinced that Linda's boyfriend could not have been the killer.

With the elimination of the most logical suspect, police fanned out, questioning known sex offenders, customers who had been at the Princess Hotel on the night of the murder and anyone who had been near the scene of the crime. One thing puzzled them. The killer had taken away Linda's shoes and purse. Many sex offenders rob their victims but none of the officers involved in this investigation could remember a rapist who carried away his victim's shoes.

Detectives were convinced that the killer lived within a mile of the murder scene. They decided to search all the garbage within a square mile of the tragedy. The city of Manchester cooperated by delaying garbage pickup for a full week so that police could search individual garbage bags. The distasteful task bore immediate results. On Tuesday morning, a pair of ladies' shoes were found in a garbage bag. In the same bag, police found letters addressed to Linda as well as her photograph. Linda's family identified the shoes. A hundred yards down the road, in another bag, investigators found the contents of Linda's purse. It was apparent that the killer had disposed of Linda's belongings in nearby garbage bags as he fled the scene of the crime.

The ring found in the flower bed was sent to the

Metallurgy Department of Manchester University. A report came back stating that the ring was made of stainless steel and had been manufactured at an engineering plant by an amateur who had most probably used a piece of scrap metal to fashion the crude ring. Police then systematically canvassed engineering firms that used such metal. The description of the ring and the description of the man seen by Jennifer Earl were widely publicized.

Detectives knocked on doors and asked the following four questions: Are you acquainted with a man in his early twenties with long blond hair who wears a tan car coat? Do you know a man who hasn't been to work since last Saturday? Have you seen a man with blood or tar on his clothing? Do you know a man missing from home since last Saturday?

Authorities hoped that if their theory was correct, the killer would succumb to the pressure and act in an erratic manner. Their ploy worked. While interviewing employees at the Renold Engineering Works, police were interrupted by one of the company's officers, who gave them a note that had been slipped under a locker door by an employee. It read: "Andy, I want you to tell the firm to send my wages home to my parents, I think I killed that girl, but I'm not sure, but it's my ring they found, so it must be me, tell the cops not to look for me because I will kill myself." The note was signed "Ron."

The writer of the note was well known. His name was Ronald Bennell, an 18-year-old apprentice who lived with his parents and four brothers and sisters close to the plant. Police located Ron at his girlfriend's apartment in Benchill, a suburb of Manchester.

The suspect was taken to the police station, where he related how he had spent the night of the murder. He claimed he had gone to a dance with his girlfriend, had had too much to drink and had become belligerent. After he dropped off his girlfriend, he had picked up a meat pie and chips, which he started to eat as he walked along the Kingsway. He saw Linda walking by and said, "Hello, love." She replied, "Get lost."

Ron had grabbed the unwary girl and pushed her through

the hedge. Linda had screamed as he put his hand around her neck. It was then his ring must have slipped off, he told authorities. He felt the girl go limp, so he dragged her to the path and had sexual intercourse with her while she was unconscious. As she regained consciousness, he'd struck her over the head again and again. Ron claimed that as he ran from the scene, he stepped on the body with his tar-stained boots. On the other side of the hedge, he picked up Linda's shoes and purse. He could give no reason for having picked up these items. He disposed of them in nearby garbage bags.

Bite marks on the body matched plaster casts taken of Ron's teeth. Even the meat pie tossed away at the scene bore the impression of Ron's teeth. His boots had made the prints found on the body. He told police that the coverage given the case by the press had caused him to lose his nerve and write the note which proved to be his downfall.

On March 1, 1971, Ronald Bennell pleaded guilty to murder and was sentenced to life imprisonment.

# Antonio Bento and Maria Neubauer
# PLAYBOY OF BRAZIL

The year was 1941, and while the rest of the world was busy shooting at one another, life was pleasant enough in Brazil, particularly if you were the son of one of the richest men in the country.

Antonio Bento, at the age of 21, had it made. His daddy was loaded, and Tonio lived the charmed life of a playboy. He drank the finest wines, ran around with the most beautiful women and is purported to have sung riotous songs. Life was one party after another.

One night in February, Tonio was carousing in the neighbouring town of Niteroi when he took a fancy to a singer in an exclusive nightclub. Irene Romero had whatever it is you are supposed to have in all the right places. She was cute as a button, with large eyes and long black hair. Tonio, no novice when it came to the opposite sex, fell hard for Irene. The pair talked that night for two hours at a secluded corner table and struck up a deal.

Fast worker that he was, Tonio offered Irene a rent-free apartment in Santa Teresa, one of the classiest sections of Rio de Janeiro. Before you could say "coffee beans," Irene accepted the offer, and one week later was ensconced as Tonio's mistress in a luxury apartment.

Darn it all, Tonio should have stopped right there: for a lad of 21 he had the world by the tail. Unfortunately, he spoiled everything by actually falling in love with Irene. They got along so well together that in the next two years Irene gave birth to two sons, Marco and Isaias. Tonio even gave up the life of a playboy. His daddy bought him a rundown hardware store to get his feet wet in the world of business. He started getting up at seven-thirty in the morning, going to work and returning late in the evening. He kept mentioning things such as maturity, fulfillment and the like, to Irene.

Well, this was ridiculous. Irene became furious. It was unheard of for the son of one of the richest men in Brazil to be working like a dog—too tired to have parties. Irene started to nag Tonio; the nagging soon turned to fighting. One day she went too far, accusing Tonio of being unfaithful to her. Tonio, who had been a good partner to Irene, couldn't forgive her for the insult. He stormed out of the apartment and headed for a bar he knew in Niteroi.

As the night wore on and Tonio proceeded to tie one on, a 32-year-old lady named Maria Neubauer took on the part of consoling, sympathetic listener. She was good company, and Tonio poured out his story of his crushed home life and his love for his two sons.

The couple spent the night together and became close friends. In fact, they became so close that next morning Tonio would have been happy enough to spend the rest of his days with the experienced Maria, but he truly loved his sons and in order to see them he had to call on Irene. Now his life became a topsy-turvy round of going to work, then to Irene's and then to Maria's. It was enough to wear out a man; something had to give.

Well, Maria had the perfect solution. She told Tonio to kill Irene, poison her, simple and neat. He would then have his Marco and Isaias, and above all, he would have Maria. At first, Tonio thought the idea preposterous, but with Maria working on him he started to change his mind. Finally he decided to go through with it.

One night, when Tonio knew his two sons were away visiting relatives, he called on Irene. While they were drinking a bottle of beer, he slipped a vial of poison into her glass. Not waiting for the poison to take effect, Tonio left the apartment and rushed to Maria.

When Maria heard his story she was far from pleased. She

pointed out to Tonio that he had forgotten to clean up the glasses. Tonio killed a half bottle of whiskey to get up enough nerve to go back to Irene's apartment. When he opened the door he found Irene sprawled across her bed, unconscious. He washed the incriminating glasses and the beer bottle.

Poor Tonio was not an experienced killer. In fact, exhausted from the tension and the liquor, he sat down in a soft armchair and fell asleep. In the meantime, Irene started vomiting in the bedroom. She brought up the entire contents of her stomach and then fell asleep, exhausted. When she woke up in the morning, she felt terrible. She staggered into the kitchen and found two washed glasses and a washed beer bottle. (Tonio may have made history by becoming the only person outside of a brewery to wash out a beer bottle.) Irene then discovered Tonio asleep in the chair. She put two and two together and came up with poison.

Irene saw red. She started clawing at Tonio before he was awake. Like a madwoman, she was now screaming at the still-drowsy Tonio. "You will never see the children again. Instead, you will go to prison, and your father will disinherit you for dragging his name into the mud."

In one outburst Irene had vividly described the destruction of Tonio's life. Tonio retreated to the kitchen, grabbed a rolling pin and swung viciously at Irene's head. The first blow knocked her down and Tonio kept swinging until there was very little left of her head. Both he and the kitchen were covered with blood.

Back Tonio went to Maria. When Maria heard this latest development, she put Tonio to bed for a few hours' rest. While he was asleep, she burned his bloodstained clothing. Then she woke Tonio up and explained to him that they couldn't leave Irene's body in the apartment. He would be sure to be suspected. They both went back to Irene's apartment, Tonio for the third time.

Maria took one look at the condition of the kitchen and sent Tonio out to purchase a large wooden crate. While Tonio was out picking up the crate, Maria realized that she had missed her breakfast. She prepared a substantial meal, getting the necessary ingredients from the refrigerator. Each time she went to the refrigerator, she had to step over Irene's battered body.

When Tonio, who was by now a walking zombie, returned with the crate, Maria informed him that they would have to dismember Irene's body. Tonio felt things had gone far enough. He just couldn't do it. Maria said that she would do the nasty job herself.

It seems she had thought of everything, having brought along a saw just for the purpose at hand. Hard-working Maria managed to sever Irene's arms, legs and head. The crate was too small for all the body parts, so Tonio ran out and purchased a suitcase, solving that particular problem. Then the industrious Maria scrubbed the kitchen until it was spotless.

Maria and Tonio had a heart-to-heart talk. She told him that she had a sister, Virginia, who lived in Niteroi, and whom she could trust with their peculiar luggage. Her sister lived with a boyfriend, Waldema, and an 18-year-old son, Eurico, both of whom could also be trusted. The "luggage" was duly stored at Virginia's house.

Now, completely under the domination of Maria, Tonio told neighbours and friends that Irene had fallen ill and was at a sanitorium for an indefinite stay. He moved out of the apartment and placed his two children with relatives.

Irene effectively had disappeared off the face of the earth. Seven months went by, and to all intents and purposes Tonio and Maria had managed to commit the perfect murder.

Well, not quite. Back at Virginia's home, Irene's body had been buried in a tiny courtyard. Virginia was haunted by the fear that as the body decomposed it would create an odour that would lead to its discovery. Each night she sprinkled chloride of lime over the courtyard. But the solution itself started to give off an odour, and neighbours complained.

Finally someone called the police, and the jig was up. Soon the whole entangled web of intrigue was unravelled and Virginia, her lover and son, as well as Maria and Tonio, were taken into custody. Because of the wealth and prominence of his father, Tonio's involvement caused a national sensation.

When the series of trials that followed the arrests were concluded, the three who had disposed of Irene's body each received 18 months in prison. As they had spent more time than that in jail awaiting trial, they were released.

Maria Neubauer was sentenced to nine and a half years' imprisonment. Tonio, the millionaire's son who a few short years before had had everything a man could want, was sentenced to 21 long years in prison.

# Maggie Boo
# LOVE HANDLES

Margaret Crump felt life was passing her by. There she was, decidedly plump, with ever so tiny crow's feet making their unattractive appearance beside her eyes, which in recent months had developed an involuntary squint.

One day, Margaret, who had seen four decades come and go, looked across the breakfast table at her husband of 14 years. Wasn't he a prize? she thought. David spent most of his time collecting money for worthy causes in and around Folkestone, England. When he wasn't complaining about the state of the Commonwealth, he was moaning about his ulcerated leg. Among David's more disagreeable traits, Margaret felt his bouts of depression ranked right up there as the most annoying. Sometimes David was so low he threatened to commit suicide. No one, least of all Margaret, took his threats seriously. It was a loveless marriage that had produced no children.

Year after dreary year, David collected funds for charity, while Margaret pursued her hobby of citizens' band radio. Each evening, after David took his sleeping pills and she could hear him snoring, she would plug in her equipment. Her CB handle was Maggie Boo. Her hobby was her one escape from her boring, loveless marriage.

One fog-enshrouded night in 1986, Maggie Boo received a response from Hawaiian Cruiser. It was like no other response she had ever received. Hawaiian Cruiser had a melodious sexy voice. He flattered Maggie Boo. What's more, he was suggestive. Maggie Boo said nothing to discourage the naughty boy. Each night she would wait to hear David snoring so she could exchange sweet sly insinuations with her Hawaiian Cruiser.

It was agreed. The pair had to meet. Margaret hid those crow's feet as best she could and pulled out the few invading gray hairs. She and Hawaiian Cruiser met in a restaurant. The sexy voice belonged to 20-year-old David Belsham, a skinny young man with a severe case of acne. If you can imagine Ichabod Crane, you pretty well have the picture.

Despite their physical deficiencies and the discrepancy in their ages, Maggie Boo and Hawaiian Cruiser got along famously. They met often and soon became lovers. Juices dormant these many years once again flowed freely within Margaret Crump. Life was worth living, after all. Belsham was attentive, polite and, above all, terrific in bed.

In time, Margaret introduced Belsham to her husband. Crump never suspected for a moment that this young lad was anything more than a fellow citizens' band enthusiast. Eventually Margaret met two of Belsham's friends, Stephen Farthing and Paul Thompson. When Belsham requested that the two men, who had recently been asked to leave their rooming house, move in with the Crumps, Margaret agreed it would be a good idea. Even her husband liked the arrangement. They could do odd jobs around the place, allowing him more time for his charity work.

For a while, all went well. Farthing and Thompson had a roof over their heads, Crump had two built-in handymen, Belsham had done a favour for two friends and, of course, we all know what Margaret was receiving in quantities she had once only fantasized about.

In the deception business, one must realize that things can't go on forever. In 1987, David's ulcerated leg so bothered him that he had to be hospitalized. Belsham moved into the Crump house to keep Margaret company.

Playing house appealed to Belsham. There is good evidence he had fallen in love with Margaret and dreaded the fast-approaching day when her husband would be released from hospital. He and Margaret discussed their predicament. They would do the honourable thing. They would tell her husband of their love for each other. No doubt, he would be civilized and drop out of the picture. After the divorce, they would marry and live happily ever after.

Well, folks, David did come home from the hospital. Margaret and Belsham told him their intentions. Rather than take the news calmly, David said he would rather die than grant his wife a divorce. In addition, loud and clear, he ordered Belsham and his two buddies out of the house.

No one left the Crump residence. In the next few days, you could cut the tension with a knife. Each evening, Crump went to his room, took his sleeping pills and went to sleep alone. Downstairs, Belsham, Margaret, Farthing and Thompson plotted his demise. They would make the murder appear to be a suicide. After all, David had suffered from depression for years and had often mentioned suicide to anyone who would listen.

On July 16, 1987, David went to his room, extracted several sleeping pills from a bottle on his night table and took them with a glass of water, as was his custom. Margaret, realizing that he would take his usual large quantity of sleeping pills as he read his Bible in bed, brought him a cup of coffee. She had solicitously dissolved several sleeping pills in the coffee before taking it upstairs. David grumbled a thanks and drank his coffee.

Next morning, Stephen Farthing found David dead in bed. He called an ambulance. The ambulance attendants noted the empty medicine bottle, observed the room was otherwise neat and tidy and concluded that David had committed suicide by means of an overdose.

Nothing would have been done about the open-and-shut case had a relative of David's not called the Folkestone Police Station the day following his death with the information that David had written to her two weeks before, informing her that he believed the four conspirators living in his house planned to kill him. He had also told her of his wife's ongoing affair with Belsham. Evidently, Crump had sneaked downstairs one night and had overheard the entire plot. Although he was alarmed, he couldn't bring himself to believe that his wife and her friends would actually kill him. David was wrong.

An autopsy was performed. The results indicated that David had taken a large quantity of barbiturates, about 12 pills, several of which had not been absorbed into the bloodstream by the time death occurred. The attending pathologist also discovered cotton fibres in David's nose, mouth and lungs, indicating that the victim could have been suffocated with a pillow.

The investigation might have bogged down at this point had David Belsham kept his mouth shut. However, like so many killers before him, he had an irresistible urge to tell someone that he had committed the perfect murder. Belsham chose a buddy in a pub. He related in detail how Margaret had laced the coffee with sleeping pills. They had waited awhile before climbing the stairs and finishing the job with a pillow. Belsham's drinking buddy scampered down to the Folkestone police station to tell what he had heard.

All four conspirators were arrested, tried and found guilty of David Crump's murder. Because of his youth, Paul Thompson received an indefinite prison term, while Stephen Farthing, Maggie Boo and Hawaiian Cruiser were sentenced to life imprisonment.

# Tyrone Borglund and Eric Peever
# THE AXE MASSACRE

The murders were atrocious, cold-blooded acts committed by boys not old enough to vote.

In January 1988, seven individuals lived in the three-bedroom bungalow on Fourteenth Avenue in Mission, B.C. The residents of the house had experienced diverse upheavals en route to the small town located about 65 kilometres east of Vancouver.

Karsten Madsen met Leny van Rikxoort in 1977 in Vancouver. Karsten, at 27 years of age, had been married, divorced and deeply involved with another woman before meeting Leny. His marriage to Sharon Peever had brought two children into the world, Eric and Michael, who remained with their mother after the divorce. When he met Leny, he was also the father of Jason, a bouncing eight-month-old, the result of his last involvement.

Leny and Karsten married in 1978. Their daughter, Michelle, was born that same year. Little Jason was also a part of their family. The Madsens relocated often in the following seven years, eventually settling in Mission. Like many Canadian families with young children, they required two incomes to keep a roof over their heads. Karsten made a precarious living as a drywall installer. Despite the ever-present need for more money, the Madsens appeared to be happy. They were outgoing and well liked. The family consisted of four individuals living in the bungalow on Fourteenth Avenue. They would all become victims.

In 1985, the Madsens applied to become foster parents. Their motives have come under close scrutiny. Certainly the $500 they would receive monthly from the B.C. Ministry of

Social Services was a factor. There is some evidence that the money enabled them to purchase a new car. Whatever the motivation, 14-year-old Tyrone Borglund moved into the Madsen home. The addition of Tyrone to the household brought the number of residents in the bungalow on Fourteenth Avenue to five.

Initially, things went well, but it wasn't long before Tyrone became disruptive around the house. From time to time, Leny reported his behaviour to the ministry. On more than one occasion, Tyrone was removed and placed in another foster home, but was taken back by the Madsens when he promised to mend his ways.

As the years passed, Eric and Michael, who were living with their mother, Sharon Peever, grew to be teenagers. Eric, the older of the two, was thrown out of his home by his mother's common-law husband when he was caught stealing from the house. Eric contacted Karsten, his biological father, and moved in with the Madsens in Mission. Eric and Tyrone seemed to get along well. They were approximately the same age and soon became close friends.

The sixth player in the tragedy that would follow was on stage. One more player was required to complete the cast. Eric's younger brother, Michael, contacted Karsten and moved into the bungalow in Mission. The full complement of seven individuals was now gathered in the house on Fourteenth Avenue.

Karsten and Leny knew they had problems. Michelle and Jason behaved like normal youngsters, but the three older boys were a handful. On more than one occasion, the police contacted Leny. The boys had become petty thieves. They even stole from their own home. Karsten had to keep a careful eye on his liquor. Small items often went missing. Leny gave the boys severe tongue-lashings, which seemed to sink in at the time, but which had little lasting effect.

Tyrone and Michael shared sleeping quarters in the basement and it was there that the three boys planned the murder of the other four members of the family. Karsten, Leny, Michelle and Jason would all be murdered. The boys would take money from the master bedroom, steal Leny's Toyota and take off for Fort Saint John.

On the night of January 17, 1988, the stage was set. Tyrone suggested the axes. They were weapons of opportunity, just lying there in the house. The boys practised swinging the axes down there in the basement. Upstairs, the house was quiet. Everyone was asleep. Eric sneaked upstairs and returned with some wine and pear brandy. The boys took long swigs from the bottles. Tyrone and Eric, equipped with the axes, slowly climbed the stairs. Michael carried a maul. He would later testify that when the reality of what they were about to do came to him, he couldn't go through with the plan. He left his fellow conspirators and returned to the basement.

Tyrone and Eric continued to the master bedroom. Karsten and Leny were sleeping soundly. The moves had been well planned. Tyrone would kill Karsten while Eric took care of Leny. Tyrone lifted the large axe above his head and brought it down with all his might on the sleeping man's skull. The force of the blow split open Karsten's head. Leny awoke with a start. She screamed, her hands instinctively shielding her head, but there was no escape. Eric brought the axe down. Her arms may have deflected the initial blow so that the first swing didn't render her unconscious. We will never know how many times Eric swung that axe, but at some time in the midst of the blood and the passion, he dropped the weapon and ran to the refuge of the basement. Tyrone finished the gruesome task in the bedroom.

Eleven-year-old Jason was awakened by the noise. Rubbing sleep from his eyes, he strolled into the master bedroom. Only half-awake, he couldn't quite absorb the scene he was witnessing. He said, "What are you doing to my mum?" Three vicious swings from Tyrone's axe and the little boy lay dead on the bedroom floor.

The next to wake up was nine-year-old Michelle. She too was drawn to the source of the noise. Tyrone intercepted her at the doorway. She met the same fate as Jason. There was no more noise from upstairs in the house on Fourteenth Avenue in Mission, B.C.

Down in the basement, there was plenty of excitement. They had actually done it. True, Tyrone was the ringleader, but they had all been involved in one way or another. Now that it was over, Eric felt he owed Tyrone an explanation. After all, he had retreated during the height of the attack. Tyrone assured him there were no hard feelings. In the end they had accomplished what they had set out to do.

The three boys entered the room of carnage. Their plan was working. In minutes they removed all the bills from Karsten's wallet and Leny's purse. The keys to the Toyota were there in her purse just as they had expected. It didn't take long for them to get out of the house, leaving behind four bodies hacked to death in the bedroom. The teenagers wheeled the Toyota out of the driveway and headed toward Fort Saint John, 790 kilometres to the northeast. Good times lay ahead. Only then did Tyrone and Eric notice that their clothing was spattered with blood.

Once in Fort Saint John, the boys purchased booze, called friends and partied. Two days after the killing spree, Tyrone was picked up for drunk driving. The Toyota was soon traced to Mission, B.C., the bodies discovered and the bloody multiple murders exposed.

What had triggered the vicious attack that had taken four lives? According to Tyrone, they were angry at Leny because she had given them another one of her patented tongue-lashings and had forbidden them to watch TV. All charges against 15-year-old Michael Peever were dropped in exchange for his testimony. After the murder trial, in which he appeared as the Crown's star witness, he was placed anonymously in a group home somewhere in British Columbia.

Tyrone and Eric stood trial for murder in adult court. Their claim that they had taken the axes into the Madsens' bedroom solely to frighten them was not believed by the jury. It took only three hours' deliberation to find both boys guilty of murder.

Tyrone Borglund, 16, and Eric Peever, 17, were sentenced to life imprisonment with no possibility of parole for 25 years. They are presently serving their sentences.

# Ernie Brown
# GROOMED TO KILL

Since time immemorial, certain married women have scorned their legal mates for butlers, chauffeurs, gardeners, cooks and other assorted gentlemen in the employ of their well-heeled hubbies. You would think busy husbands would be wary of the hired help, especially if they are what is commonly called hunks.

Ernest Brown was a hunk. He stood a tad over six feet and had a chiselled countenance complete with two attractive dimples, which served to light up his face when he smiled that seductive smile of his. And as for Ernie's muscles, they had muscles of their own.

In 1929, Ernie hired on as a groom-gardener with Cattle Factors Ltd. of Saxton Grange, Yorkshire. The isolated farm was a thriving business operated by Fred Morton. Now, Fred wasn't a bad guy. It was just that he was terribly busy and had precious little time for his wife and two-year-old daughter.

Let me tell you about Dorothy Morton. There is no other way to put it—Dorothy was stacked. She was a gorgeous woman with an outstanding figure. When she went into Sherburn-in-Elmet to shop, heads turned to gaze upon what many considered to be the most beautiful woman in all of Yorkshire.

It was Dorothy's love of horses that placed her constantly in the company of groom Ernie Brown. Fred Morton was often away on business. And Ernie had monkey business in mind. Initially, Dorothy didn't fall into Ernie's arms. No sir, he had to work for her affection, but eventually nature took its course. The two handsome young people bedded down at every opportunity and thus formed two angles of a very dangerous triangle.

Dorothy attempted to break off the affair but Ernie wouldn't hear of it. When she forced the issue, he threatened her. Poor Dorothy. What had once been a thrilling experience had become a vulgar, risky game. She wanted out. She even thought of telling her husband about the entire sordid affair, but she was too afraid.

In June 1933, Ernie threw a snit when Fred asked him to perform some menial task around the farm. He quit his job and left. Dorothy drew a sigh of relief. After four years of threats and intrigue, it was over. Her relief was short-lived. Ernie either changed his mind or found that jobs were not that easy to come by. He also may have missed the sex he had grown accustomed to for the past four years. Whatever the reason, Ernie showed up back on the farm one day when Fred was away on business. He threatened to tell all unless Dorothy phoned her husband and succeeded in having Ernie rehired. Dorothy did as she was told. Fred took Ernie back into the fold as an odd-job man. Resenting his new lowly status, Ernie became a surly lurking presence, forever bad-mouthing Fred Morton.

On September 5, Ernie went over the brink. Knowing that Fred was away on business, he entered the farmhouse and struck Dorothy in front of Ann Houseman, her daughter's nurse. Ernie picked up a shotgun and ordered Ann out of the house. Although terrified, the nurse refused to leave. Ernie calmly sat down and cleaned the weapon in front of the two frightened women.

At 11:30 p.m., Ann and Dorothy were relieved to hear Fred's car chugging into the farmyard. Ernie left the house, apparently to get out before the boss arrived. He took a kitchen knife with him. The women were shocked when Ernie re-entered the house a few minutes later, exclaiming, "The boss has been here and gone out again."

Desperately, Ann and Dorothy engaged Ernie in conversation. Around 2 a.m., Ernie left the house once more. A few minutes later, the women heard a strange crackling sound. Dorothy peered outside. The garage was a blazing inferno. She attempted to use the telephone but found that it was out of order. No doubt Ernie had cut the wires. Hurriedly, the women dressed Dorothy's daughter and rushed outside. Fearful of being sighted by Ernie, they hid in a ditch, spending the rest of the early-morning hours huddled there. When they saw Ernie leave in a wagon, they made their way to Towton, about a half mile away, and told authorities about their terror-filled night.

The local fire brigade arrived, closely followed by Ernie Brown. The fire was extinguished and the Mortons' gutted Chrysler was examined. In the front passenger seat were the charred remains of what had once been a human being. The head, arms and legs had been burned into cinders, but keys and a diamond ring left no doubt that the body was that of Fred Morton.

The ensuing investigation revealed that the farm's telephone wires had been cut with a knife and that Fred had been shot to death before the car and garage had been set on fire. Shotgun pellets had entered Fred's heart. Apparently the weapon had been held directly against his stomach. It was quite amazing that although all of Fred's upper body had been consumed by the fire, investigators found a few square inches of flesh that miraculously had not been burned. Shotgun pellets and gun wadding were found in this small portion of flesh.

Ernie Brown was taken into custody and charged with Fred Morton's murder. His trial fascinated England, not because of the rascal himself, but because of Dorothy Morton, who was the Crown's star witness. The 30-year-old Dorothy, as beautiful as any movie star, took the witness box and revealed all the juicy details of her affair with the family groom. She even admitted that, on one occasion only, she had been intimate with another chap while carrying on with nasty Ernie and living with her husband. For shame! Such things just didn't happen in Yorkshire.

The prosecution proved that Fred Morton's shotgun,

which Ernie had taken from the farmhouse on the night of the murder, was the murder weapon. They also proved that the kitchen knife found in Ernie's possession had been used to cut the telephone wires.

It was all too much. The Yorkshire jury found Ernie guilty of murder. He listened unmoved when the presiding judge sentenced him to death by hanging. As he was led from the courtroom, he took one fleeting glance at Dorothy. An angry crowd of 1,000 hurled insults at Dorothy as she walked to a waiting vehicle.

On February 6, 1934, Ernie Brown was hanged at Armley Prison, Leeds.

# Eugene Chantrelle
# HE WASN'T GRANTED HIS LAST REQUEST

Elizabeth Dyer fell hard for her schoolteacher. While this is not an uncommon phenomenon, Lizzie took her infatuation far too seriously. Then, again, who can blame her; she was only 15. Her teacher, Eugene Chantrelle, who should have known better, was a mature 34.

Chantrelle had been educated in Strasbourg and Paris. He claimed that he had attended medical school, but for reasons of his own had not bothered to obtain his medical degree.

In 1867, we find suave, aristocratic Eugene teaching Greek, French and Latin in Edinburgh, Scotland. The handsome teacher stood straight as an arrow and sported a shock of wavy brown hair.

Lizzie pursued Chantrelle with dogged determination, using all her wiles, which even at 15 were appreciable, to land her teacher. She succeeded to such an extent that certain expected lunar regularities became uncharacteristically absent and Lizzie found herself pregnant. This rather embarrassing state of affairs was made more difficult by the fact that her mother despised Chantrelle with a passion.

When Lizzie's parents heard of their daughter's delicate condition, they agreed that a marriage was an absolute necessity. In August, the pupil and her teacher tied the knot.

The marriage was not a happy one. In the following years, Chantrelle displayed a vile temper, which erupted at the least provocation. In 1876, the couple had three children, Jack, Louis and a newborn baby. They lived in a double flat on George Street, which consisted of a kitchen, parlour and a classroom on the lower floor, and three bedrooms on the top attic level.

By 1877, Chantrelle was guzzling a bottle of whiskey every day at home. Every afternoon he could be found at his favourite watering hole, the Hanover Hotel. Just to complete the picture, the suave teacher of foreign languages liked to frequent the local house of ill repute only a block away on Clyde Street. Let's face it, Chantrelle was not what you would call a good family man.

The Chantrelles retained a servant, Mary Byrne. It is from her that we learn that the master of the house belittled his wife in front of the children, often referring to her as "that bitch." Sometimes he struck her. On those occasions, Lizzie retreated to her mother's home, but she always returned, determined to make a success of her marriage.

Life went on in its turbulent way. Once Lizzie went as far as to have her husband jailed for striking her, but when it came time to press charges, she relented. The family managed to have an almost peaceful Christmas in 1877, despite the head of the household being sloshed to the gills most of the time.

Chantrelle's drinking and carousing had caught up to him in a financial way. Although at one time he had given private language lessons, he found his pupils dropping off one by one until the classroom in the flat was a quiet, deserted place. A loan from the bank kept the wolf from the door for a while, but as time passed the bank began pressing Chantrelle to pay back the loan.

In desperation, the teacher attempted to supplement his income by working as a part-time insurance agent for the Star Accidental Assurance Co. He sold only one policy to a personal friend, but while employed as an agent, he inquired extensively as to what legally constituted an accidental death which would be paid off by an insurance company.

Instead of continuing with Star Accidental, Chantrelle called as a customer on the Accidental Assurance Association of Scotland. Here he purchased three policies. He insured maid Mary Byrne's life for £100 pounds. He also insured his own life and Lizzie's in the event of death by accident for £1,000 each.

Lizzie, who was well aware of the insurance policies, told her mother, "My life is insured now. Momma, you will see that my life will go soon." Although Mrs. Dyer was alarmed at hearing her daughter utter such ominous words, she assured Lizzie that she had nothing to worry about. Momma was dead wrong.

On New Year's Eve, 1877, the family had a pleasant evening meal, after which the children were put to bed. Lizzie and Eugene sat in the parlour for the rest of evening until midnight, when the sound of the bands playing at Edinburgh Castle swept over the city. Mary was invited into the parlour to enjoy the music through the open window. Shortly after midnight everyone went to bed.

Next day, the family woke up and proceeded with their usual routine. At eleven o'clock, Mary was given the rest of the day off. She spent the day at the home of a friend, returning at 9:45 that night. Chantrelle greeted Mary, informing her that Lizzie wasn't feeling well and had gone to bed. Mary went directly to her mistress's bedroom and chatted with Lizzie, who assured her that she was feeling better than she had earlier in the day. Lizzie asked Mary to peel an orange for her. Mary did so and gave her mistress one wedge, leaving the balance of the orange on a plate. She then retired for the night.

According to Chantrelle, he had polished off a bottle of whiskey in the parlour before looking in on Lizzie at about midnight. He also claimed that he and his wife had made love, but considering Lizzie's illness, most believe the claim to be a fabrication. Chantrelle then retired for the night.

Next morning, while Mary was busy heating water in the kitchen for tea, she heard a loud moan from the bedroom. She ran to Lizzie's side and found her very pale, lying in bed as if unconscious. She also noticed stains on the pillow and bedclothes which she assumed was vomit.

Mary ran from the room, woke Chantrelle and told him to call a doctor immediately. He entered his wife's room, followed in a few moments by Mary. Chantrelle asked Mary if she smelled gas. She told him she didn't think so, but after a little while detected an odour she took to be gas.

Chantrelle left the house in search of medical assistance. Dr. James Carmichael, who knew Chantrelle, accompanied him back to the house. The doctor smelled gas immediately and had Lizzie moved to another bedroom. He sent for Dr. Henry Littlejohn, who arrived in minutes. Dr. Littlejohn came to the conclusion that Lizzie was near death and would not recover. He too decided that gas was responsible for her condition. He ordered that the patient be removed to the Royal Infirmary and that the gas company be called to inspect the house.

Lizzie's mother was informed of her daughter's serious illness. She showed up with her family physician, Dr. Gordon. The doctor checked Lizzie's symptoms and came to the conclusion that her condition had not been caused by escaping gas. He believed that her illness was the result of narcotic poisoning. Dr. Douglas MacLagan at the hospital also figured Lizzie was suffering from opium or morphia poisoning.

When Chantrelle arrived at the hospital, he became furious on learning that doctors thought Lizzie had been poisoned with a narcotic. He stormed out of the hospital in a rage. When he cooled off and returned to see his wife, he was informed that Lizzie was dead. Throughout the excitement and the tragedy, Chantrelle stayed well oiled.

The doctors were on the horns of a dilemma. They believed Lizzie had been poisoned by opium because of the symptoms she had displayed. However, many of those same symptoms were consistent with gas poisoning. The gas company found that a gas pipe had been purposely loosened. A gas company employee stated that the pipe could have been wrenched loose in the matter of a second or two.

Police investigating Lizzie's death concluded that someone had poisoned her with opium. They felt that when Chantrelle was summoned by Mary and entered the bedroom, he instantly decided, in a drunken sort of way, that his wife's death would not be considered accidental and he would therefore not be able to collect the £1,000 insurance. To make certain that her death appeared accidental, he loosened the gas pipe, figuring a leaking gas pipe would be accepted as a bona fide accident.

It was also believed that Chantrelle had fed Lizzie opium so that she would be totally out of it when he turned on the gas. But why did he go to the trouble of loosening a pipe rather than just turning on the gas? Detectives felt that Chantrelle, despite his hateful ways towards his wife, was attached to his children. He didn't want to harm them or himself. Still tipsy from his previous night's drinking, he was awakened suddenly by Mary and knew he had to fake gas poisoning to collect that insurance. A quick pull of the pipe while Mary was out of the room solved all his problems.

An autopsy did little to clear up the situation in that it failed to establish the cause of death. The presence of opium could not be proven as it disappears rapidly in the system. However, traces of opium were found in the vomit stains recovered from Lizzie's pillow and bedclothes. One must remember that Chantrelle had medical training. He maintained what amounted to a small apothecary on the premises, which contained a large supply of opium.

Eugene Chantrelle was taken into custody and tried for the murder of his wife. He was found guilty and sentenced to death.

On May 30, 1878, Chantrelle made his mark in criminal history. When asked if he had a last wish, he replied, "Send in three bottles of champagne and a whore." Next morning he was hanged as a chaplain recited the Lord's Prayer. Eugene Chantrelle went to his death without being granted his last request.

# Styllou Christofi
# ONE MEAN MUMMY

It is my opinion that sons should treat their mothers with respect, no matter what the circumstances. This is especially true if you happen to have a mean mummy who doesn't like your wife. Sound like the beginning of a Greek tragedy? Well, that's exactly how it turned out. Mrs. Styllou Christofi was a mean mummy extraordinaire.

Mrs. Christofi hailed from Cyprus. The 53-year-old peasant woman had been born to poverty and remained illiterate all her life. She had never left her home village until she travelled to London, England, to visit her son, Stavros.

Rather than being proud of her son's accomplishments, Mrs. Christofi was furious that he had abandoned the way of life she cherished back in Cyprus. The truth of the matter was that Stavros had carved out a new and comfortable life since emigrating to England in 1937. He was a wine waiter in a fashionable restaurant in London's West End. Along the way he had married Hella, a pretty German girl whom he loved dearly. The Christofis had three young children and a comfortable home. All in all, the ambitious Greek boy had done very well for himself and his family.

Stavros's mother simply didn't see it that way. She watched with steely eyes, hatred oozing out of every pore. How dare this interloper Hella poison her son's mind so that he had become more English than Greek? Each evening he went off to his soft job, a far cry from the sun-drenched days in the fields back home. And the children? Were they to grow up in this prosperous society, never understanding the work ethic which was such an important part of their heritage? Mrs.

Christofi was further frustrated by not being able to speak English. She was effectively cut off from conversing with her daughter-in-law and her grandchildren.

On July 29, 1954, at precisely 8 p.m., Stavros left his home for work as he did every evening. His mother had been living with him now for the better part of a year. It just hadn't worked out. On three different occasions, she had moved out, and three times she returned. The incessant insinuations about casting aside his roots had started all over again.

Mrs. Christofi blamed Hella for all the discord in the family. The venomous feeling directed towards Hella didn't go unnoticed. Hella, who couldn't converse with her mother-in-law, often became depressed because of the obvious animosity displayed by the older woman. Finally, it was unofficially agreed that Hella would take the children and visit her family in Germany. When she returned, Mrs. Christofi would leave for Cyprus. In Mrs. Christofi's mind, she was being tossed out of her own son's home. What's more, the expulsion was tantamount to being removed from his life.

This night would be different. Stavros kissed Hella goodbye, unaware that he would never see his wife again. Once he was out of the house, Hella put the children to bed. The two women busied themselves cleaning the kitchen. Without warning, Mrs. Christofi picked up a heavy metal plate used to collect ashes from the stove and struck Hella on the back of the head. The unconscious woman fell to the floor. Mrs. Christofi proceeded to strangle Hella with a scarf belonging to one of the children.

The house was deathly quiet. For the next few hours, Mrs. Christofi was a busy mummy, but her deeds were performed with a singleness of purpose.

At 11:30 p.m., John Young, the Christofis' next-door neighbour, took his dog for a run in the backyard. He noticed a bonfire in the adjoining yard. John shouted but received no response. He peered over the brick wall separating the two properties and observed what he thought was a mannikin burning in the fire. As he turned to go back into his home, he

45

saw someone leave the Christofi house and walk towards the fire. Young later stated, "I left when I saw someone I recognized. I thought all was in order." John Young was wrong. Mummy dearest had just come out to stoke the fire. She was burning her daughter-in-law.

About 1 a.m., Mr. and Mrs. Burstoff were driving to their home in Hampstead when they were hailed by Mrs. Christofi. In broken English, she said over and over, "Fire. Burning. Children sleeping." The Burstoffs accompanied Mrs. Christofi to her home and discovered the badly burned body in the backyard. They called police. While they waited, Mrs. Christofi told the Burstoffs, "My son marry Germany girl he like. Plenty clothes, plenty shoes."

Police were quickly on the scene. They found bloodstains on the kitchen floor which had been partially cleaned. Beside Hella's body they found paper which had been soaked in paraffin. Hella's wedding ring was not on her finger, but was recovered from Mrs. Christofi's room. In a dustbin were three portions of a child's scarf. The scarf had been cut into pieces in order to remove it from Hella's neck.

Police questioned Mrs. Christofi. She told them, "I wake up, smell burning, go downstairs. Hella burning. Throw water, touch her face. Not move. Run out, get help." Through an interpreter, Mrs. Christofi claimed that she and her daughter-in-law had been on perfect terms. She had gone to bed that night, leaving Hella in a good mood doing household chores.

In due course, Mrs. Christofi was arrested and charged with Hella's murder. Her trial was unique in that every word was translated into Greek. The English jury took only a matter of hours to find Mrs. Christofi guilty of murder. She was sentenced to death. All appeals failed. The execution was to proceed as scheduled.

On the day before the execution, it was revealed, via the British press, that the chief medical officer at Holloway Prison had filed a report before the trial, stating, "The clinical picture is that of a nonsystemized disillusional mental disorder." The doctor had insinuated that Mrs. Christofi was incapable of realizing that what she had done was wrong.

This caused quite a disturbance, and great efforts were made to commute the condemned woman's sentence at the last minute. All these efforts were doomed to failure and Mrs. Christofi was hanged as scheduled.

Only after her execution was it revealed that Mrs. Christofi was no amateur in the not-so-gentle art of murder. Back in 1925, in Cyprus, she had killed her mother-in-law by ramming a burning torch down her throat. The crime had been one of hate and jealousy involving her husband and his mother. Inexplicably, on that occasion, she had been acquitted. As I said, Mrs. Christofi was one mean mummy.

# Gordon Frederick Cummins
# WARTIME RIPPER

The winter of 1942 was one of fear and chaos in war-torn London, England. Thousands of allied servicemen stationed there worked hard and played hard, while each night Hitler's Luftwaffe rained bombs on the streets of the city.

Normal criminal activity took a back seat to the larger task of protecting the country from a common enemy. It required an extraordinary series of events to capture the population's interest in anything other than war news. Such a series of events began on the night of February 9, 1942.

Evelyn Hamilton was a respectable 42-year-old pharmacist who had recently moved to London from Hornchurch, Essex. An electrician found her body lying on the floor of an air-raid shelter in Montagu Place, Marylebone. Evelyn's silk scarf was wrapped around her mouth and nose. Her clothing was in disarray and her open handbag was found beside her body. It had been rifled and some of the contents had spilled out on the floor. Police also found a flashlight nearby. No fingerprints other than those of the victim were found on any of the items. Evelyn had been manually strangled to death. From the bruise marks on her neck, police believed that the killer was left-handed.

While murder can never be said to go unnoticed, Evelyn Hamilton's murder would not have received the notoriety it did in war-ravaged London but for one fact. She was the first victim of a maniac who was to become known as the Wartime Ripper.

The very next morning, the body of Evelyn Oatley was found in her flat on Wardour Street, Soho. Evelyn was a prostitute who often had clients visit her in her flat. She was found naked on her bed. Her killer had strangled her with his bare hands. Once again, the open purse was found close by the body. The killer had dumped out most of the contents of the purse and, as had been evident in the Hamilton murder, had taken whatever money the purse contained.

Evelyn Oatley's body had been horribly mutilated around the lower stomach with a can opener, which the killer had thrown onto a couch. Because some of the mutilations resembled those inflicted by the infamous Jack the Ripper before the turn of the century, the British press dubbed the killings the work of the Wartime Ripper.

Police noted the similarities between the two murders committed a day apart. Both women had been strangled; both had been robbed; and both appeared to have been killed by a left-handed person. In the Oatley case, the murderer had left fingerprints on the can opener, but a check with Scotland Yard failed to match the prints with any on file. Apparently the Wartime Ripper had never been arrested.

Three days later, neighbours grew concerned when Margaret Florence Lowe failed to follow her usual routine. Police were called to her one-room apartment on Gosfield Street off Tottenham Court Road. They forced the door open. Inside, on the bed, lay Margaret's nude body under a quilt. A scarf was wrapped around her neck and the lower portion of her stomach had been mutilated. The killer had left several clear fingerprints in the room. These were checked against those lifted from Evelyn Oatley's can opener. They matched. The Wartime Ripper had struck again.

While Scotland Yard was actively investigating this latest murder, they received another urgent call. Unbelievably, the Wartime Ripper had struck for the fourth time in four days. The body of Doris Jouannet, 32, the wife of a hotel owner, was found in her two-room flat in Paddington approximately one hour after she was strangled to death. A silk scarf was wrapped around her neck and she had been mutilated in the same manner as the other victims.

The killings had taken place with such rapidity that Scotland Yard was having difficulty correlating all the information garnered from the four crime scenes. They knew they were dealing with a sex maniac who robbed, strangled and mutilated his victims. There was little doubt in anyone's mind that he would continue to kill until he was either apprehended or dead. Authorities didn't have long to wait.

On the same night as the Jouannet murder, another woman was attacked. Greta Heywood was different from the previous victims of the Wartime Ripper. She survived. Greta was in a Piccadilly bar when a good-looking young airman joined her. He seemed friendly enough and proved to be a pleasant, charming companion. When he suggested that they drop into another bar located nearby, she agreed but pointed out that she had to return to the original bar to keep a prior date for dinner.

Everything was totally in order until they stepped out onto the streets of blacked-out London. Without warning, the airman pulled Greta into the doorway of an air-raid shelter. No words were spoken. He clamped his hands around Greta's neck and proceeded to strangle her. Greta grappled with her attacker and dropped her flashlight. It fell to the sidewalk, attracting the attention of a passerby. Greta's assailant heard the man approaching and immediately ran away. In his haste he dropped his service gas mask. The moment that gas mask fell to the sidewalk, the Wartime Ripper's brief but horrific career came to an abrupt end.

The young man who heard Greta's flashlight fall to the sidewalk picked up the gas mask and turned it over to police. Inside was the service number of its owner—525987. A check of RAF records identified the owner of the gas mask as Gordon Fredericks Cummins. Before Cummins could be located, he struck again. Minutes after his attack on Greta Heywood, he picked up Catherine Mulcahy, who drove with him in a taxi to her apartment. Once inside, he immediately attempted to strangle her. Catherine screamed and desperately fought for her life until finally Cummins fled.

Within hours, the wanted man was located and arrested.

Initially, Scotland Yard was stunned to learn that Cummins had apparently been in his dormitory asleep when two of the murders had taken place. The billet passbook indicated that he had been in the barracks at the time two of the women had been strangled. Several roommates said they had seen him go to bed and get up in the morning. This mystery was solved when police questioned two fellow airmen who had witnessed Cummins sneaking out of his quarters after he thought everyone was asleep. They even located one man who had sneaked out with Cummins.

Cummins's fingerprints matched those found at the scene of the crime. To further solidify the Crown's case, a fountain pen and cigarette case belonging to two of the victims were found among Cummins's personal effects.

Strangely, the accused man denied killing anyone. Adjudged sane, Cummins stood trial in the Old Bailey. His wife appeared in court every day. She believed completely in her husband's innocence. No one else did. The English jury took less than an hour to find him guilty of Evelyn Oakley's murder.

On June 25, 1942, Gordon Frederick Cummins walked unwaveringly to the gallows. No one will ever know why this man, who had never been in trouble in his life, turned into a maniac for four days in February 1942.

# George Cvek
# HITCHHIKER FROM HELL

It didn't take long for the police of several states to realize that they had a diabolical sneak thief, rapist and killer on their hands.

In November 1940, a Bronx couple picked up a hitchhiker on the Pulaski Skyway in New Jersey. The young man, who introduced himself as John Mitchell, was polite and charming. He told the couple that he had spent some time in Boys Town, Nebraska, and was hitchhiking to Maine to visit his sister. Boys Town, the home for troubled boys founded by Father Edward Flanagan, was well known, depicted in many movies and magazine articles. When Mitchell related how he had lost all his money and his suitcase in a lavatory, the Bronx couple offered him a small amount of money to tide him over. Initially, John refused the offer, but gradually let the money be forced into his hands. He insisted on getting the young couple's name and address so that he could repay their kindness.

Five days later, John Mitchell showed up at his benefactors' Bronx apartment. The woman of the house was alone, but when she recognized John, she immediately let him in. He explained that he had been successful in obtaining employment, but needed a few dollars to tide him over until pay day. The woman had no cash in the house and told him that her husband would be home in a few hours. She prepared a sandwich for John, who complained of having a headache.

While she was placing a bottle of aspirin on the kitchen table, John sneaked up behind her, grasped her neck in a headlock and dragged her into the bedroom. He tied the woman's hands with one of her husband's neckties and thrust a handkerchief into her mouth. After raping her, John stripped the apartment of valuables.

Three months later, the thief struck again. This time he introduced himself as Joe Mitchell of Boys Town. He told a woman that he had met her husband while hitchhiking and would wait until he returned home from work. He stayed for two hours before requesting aspirin. Using the same method as he had employed in the first attack, he tied his victim, shoved a handkerchief into her mouth and looted the apartment of valuables. Fortunately, the woman was not raped.

On February 4, 1941, John Pappas, a wealthy importer, returned to his third-floor apartment on Grand Concourse in the Bronx to find his wife lying dead on her bed. She had been strangled.

John had been married a year earlier in Alexandria, Egypt. His wife was a rare beauty, but was extremely shy in her new surroundings. He told police that she never left the apartment alone. Groceries were delivered once a week by one of his friends. His wife had no relatives or friends living in the U.S.

John was amazed that the crime scene indicated that his wife was acquainted with her killer. Two partially filled wine-glasses and two empty coffee cups were on a table. Beside them was a tray of cookies and a water goblet. Nearby, on another table, was a bottle of aspirin. A lamp was overturned on the floor. Mrs. Pappas's rings had been torn from her fingers and other jewellery was missing from the apartment.

The killer had stuffed a handkerchief into his victim's mouth and had used his own necktie to tie her hands. He had knotted a towel around her throat. She had not been raped.

A wedding photograph, normally kept in the bedroom, was found in the living room. Mrs. Pappas had used her very best china to serve her guest. Her husband told detectives that she only took out her good china for special guests. He could offer no explanation as to why his extremely shy wife had obviously played hostess to her killer.

Fingerprints lifted from the water goblet didn't match those of anyone who had normal access to the Pappas apartment, nor did the FBI have any records of these prints.

Detectives were sure that the reported rapist and thief had graduated to murder. There were simply too many similarities in the three cases under investigation—the aspirin bottles, the handkerchiefs and the neckties. Because one victim had been raped and the others spared, it was theorized that the prime motive for all three crimes was theft. The rape had been an afterthought. Mrs. Pappas may have been killed because she didn't comply with the intruder's demands. The day after her murder, investigators learned that a man had attempted to gain entrance to three other apartments in the neighbourhood, but had been turned away.

Father Flanagan of Boys Town was contacted concerning anyone named Joe or John Mitchell who had been a resident of his well-known home for boys. The beloved priest replied that their man was an impostor. He added that several individuals had written him about a boy named Gerry Mitchell who claimed to be from Boys Town. It was obvious that someone was using the good name of the home to obtain money from unwary strangers.

Father Flanagan enclosed a postcard sent by the impostor to Boys Town. No doubt the card had been written to impress a potential victim. It read, "Dear Father Flannigan, Just a few lines to let you know that I am well and hope you and the rest of the boys are the same. Please don't worry about me, because I am being taken care of by the nicest people I ever met. Am writing the details in a letter which will follow this. So long." The card was signed "Gerry." Father Flanagan, anxious to have the impostor out of circulation, pointed out that his name had been misspelled and that each time the letter "r" had been written, it had appeared as an inverted "v."

Eight days after Mrs. Pappas's murder, the man with the convincing hard-luck story struck again with tragic consequences. An unwary motorist picked him up hitchhiking between Newark and Trenton. He told the man he was John Mitchell from Boys Town. Mitchell later showed up at the man's house in Philadelphia when only his pregnant wife was at home. Once inside, he raped her, stole anything of value he could carry and left. As a result of the violent rape, the woman lost her baby.

On March 3, 1941, Mrs. Elizabeth Jensen, 34, was found dead in her Bronx apartment. She had been tied with a necktie and a handkerchief had been forced into her mouth.

Because the two cases where murder had been committed were located not more than a mile apart, detectives began canvassing hotels and rooming houses in New York, looking for every name used by the Boys Town impostor.

It was a mammoth task, but it paid dividends immediately. The very day officers began canvassing the area, they discovered that a man fitting the killer's description had often stayed at the Mills Hotel on Seventh Avenue. The hotel was staked out on the chance that the suspect might show up. Sure enough, he walked into the lobby and checked into a room using the name G. Kolosky of Harrisburg, Pennsylvania. When detectives checked the registry, there were the telltale inverted "v"s in the word "Harrisburg." Police knew they had their man.

Kolosky was taken to a police station and searched. An ID card was found on his person, revealing his real identity to be George Joseph Cvek. He admitted his identity, but denied all knowledge of any crimes. When he was informed that his fingerprints matched those found on the water goblet in the Pappas apartment, he broke down and confessed to the Pappas murder. Mr. Pappas remembered that he had once picked up Cvek, who was hitchhiking into New York City.

Cvek refused to discuss the Jensen murder or any of his other crimes, although he agreed that he was the culprit in all these cases.

In May 1941, Cvek was tried and convicted of the murder of Mrs. Pappas. The following year he was executed in Sing Sing's electric chair.

# John Dietz
# OUTLAW COUNTRY

Little disputes sometimes lead to big disputes and on occasion big disputes lead to bloody murder. That's what happened in the backwoods of Wisconsin at the turn of the century.

Our tale of woe began in 1904 when John Dietz left his watchman's job at Price Dam and, together with his wife, Hattie, purchased a section of land along the Thornapple River. One end of another dam, known as Cameron Dam, rested on Dietz's land. Both dams were owned by the Chippewa Lumber and Boom Co.

John left his job at Price Dam on the Brunnette River under bitter circumstances. He claimed he was still owed wages, while the company insisted that he had been paid in full. The matter became an obsession with John. He truly felt he had been cheated by the company and that there was very little he could do about it.

John and his two robust sons, Leslie and Clarence, built a substantial house and barn. He watched as millions of feet of logs roared down the river through Cameron Dam. In time, he got a bright idea. He posted a sign forbidding trespassers from setting foot on his land. This effectively shut down Cameron Dam, which meant that no head of water could be established to allow the flow of logs to the waiting sawmills downriver. In addition, John let it be known that the dam would remain inoperable until he was paid the sum of $8,000 for the 80 million feet of logs that he estimated had already gone downriver since he purchased his land. When John took this bold and, at the time, unheard-of move, there were six million feet of logs behind the dam.

The company obtained an injunction forbidding John from interfering with the transportation of their logs. John chose to ignore the injunction. As a result of this latest development, a warrant was issued for John's arrest. Two armed deputies were dispatched the 60 miles from the county seat at Hayward to John's backwoods home to make the arrest. Three company men joined the two deputies.

The horse-drawn wagon carrying the five men made its arduous way to John's enclave. As they approached Cameron Dam, they were greeted by John's not too friendly welcome, "Hands up, you sons of bitches!" he shouted. He then commenced to shoot. So did a friend and neighbour Valentine Weisenbach, who was hidden from view. One deputy fell off the wagon as the horses, startled by the gunfire, reared and galloped away. Just for fun, John and his friends took shots at the deputy as he ran for his life. The man had no way of knowing that John and Val had no intention of killing him. They were just having a little sport, backwoods style. In due course, Val Weisenbach was arrested and charged with attempted murder. He was found guilty and received a term in the penitentiary. No one dared bother big bad John Dietz.

Friends pleaded with John to give up his battle with the lumber company, as well as with the county and the state. They felt he couldn't win. John thought otherwise. His family, including his beautiful wife, Hattie, and two eldest sons, Leslie and Clarence, were totally loyal. So were his two daughters, Myra and Helen. For five years, this remarkable family didn't allow a trespasser on their property. All attempts to operate the dam failed.

From time to time, authorities attempted to arrest John, but each time they tried they were met with a barrage of bullets. On one occasion Clarence was wounded by a lawman's bullet. A deputy was also wounded in one of the mêlées.

In order to end the feud, the company paid John's claim for back wages. The amount was $1,717, a veritable fortune in those days. John refused to be pacified. He insisted they pay him that $8,000 before everything could be settled.

In isolated areas of Wisconsin, it was customary for teachers to live in their students' homes. The teacher would be paid by the parents, who would later collect their outlay from the local school board, which in this case was the Winter School Board located some 10 miles from the Dietz home. John, who believed strongly in education, hired a tutor for his children.

On September 6, 1910, John and son Clarence drove into Winter. He not only wanted the money he had paid the tutor, he also wanted reimbursement for rent and heat. The school board balked and a fist fight broke out. John pulled out a pistol and fired at a clerk of the school board, Bert Horel. Horel was wounded, but survived. For the umpteenth time, a warrant was issued for the arrest of John Dietz.

Sheriff Mike Madden, relatively new to the area, had heard all the stories of the Dietz family and had made it his mission to bring John to justice. The sheriff deputized two local men. They made their way to a point in the woods where they could keep the Dietz home under surveillance. When they observed members of the family hitching up a wagon, they correctly figured their quarry was preparing for a trip into town. The sheriff and his deputies placed themselves in an advantageous position to intercept the Dietz wagon.

Unknown to the the sheriff and his men, only Clarence, Leslie and Myra were in the wagon. Instead of meekly surrendering, they started shooting in typical Dietz fashion. Clarence took a bullet in his left arm. Myra suffered a flesh wound in the back. Leslie got away through the thick woods. The sheriff and his party drove the wounded Dietz offspring to the hospital in Winter, where both quickly recovered.

The story of young people being ambushed by lawmen in the backwoods of Wisconsin made the big-city newspapers. There was tremendous sympathy for the youngsters, who were depicted as babes in the woods rather than the stubbornly loyal offspring of the growing legend that was John Dietz. Major newspapers sent reporters to Wisconsin to cover the ongoing story of obstinate John and his family.

The governor of Wisconsin, J.O. Davidson, realizing that

a bloodbath could take place in his state, decided to personally intervene. He sent an envoy to the Dietz home. Waving white handkerchiefs, the governor's party carried written documents from the governor, guaranteeing that all criminal charges against John and his brood, except for the wounding of Bert Horel, would be dropped. Once again, John said thanks but no thanks. He wanted the Horel charges dropped and full payment for all the logs that had gone through Cameron Dam. The governor couldn't acquiesce to John's requests. The official party told John that both sides were now at an impasse and that he would be well advised to have his family leave while the going was good. John's wife and children wouldn't hear of such a thing. They would stay to the bitter end. As the governor's party left the Dietz home, John raised the American flag and prepared to do battle.

That fall, an official posse of 60 armed men surrounded the Dietz property. The entire episode had captured the imagination of the public. Forty newspaper reporters were on hand, as were 1,000 hearty individuals from nearby towns. It didn't take long for the deputies to fire at anything that moved in John's house or barn. The Dietzes responded in kind.

One of the deputies, Oscar Harp, was shot in the head and died on the spot. The shooting continued all day. The house was a shambles, literally destroyed by gunfire. John was badly wounded in the left hand and bled profusely. Late in the afternoon Helen, barely a teenager, realized that her entire family would sooner or later be annihilated. She came out of the house waving a white flag. Helen wanted a doctor for her father, who she felt might bleed to death. She returned to the house accompanied by a doctor and a priest. At the urging of his wife, John was talked into surrendering. The battle was over. It has been estimated that over 2,000 shots were fired by the opposing sides. The entire family was taken to Winter, where John revealed that he had given in because Hattie was pregnant.

A year later, John stood trial for the murder of Oscar Harp. He defended himself and received commendations from lawyers and judges on the manner in which he conducted his defence. Despite his eloquence, he was found guilty and sentenced to life imprisonment. Ten years later he was pardoned by the governor of Wisconsin.

John Dietz died of natural causes in 1924 in a Milwaukee hospital. At his side when he breathed his last were his wife, Hattie, and his six children.

# Diane Downey and Linda Prudden
# LESBIAN KILLERS

It has been said that no one is aware of what goes on in the privacy of other people's homes. Certainly the outside world had no idea of the turbulent life being led by Robert and Diane Downey of Piscataway, New Jersey.

Robert was a mild-mannered, pleasant man who worked at two jobs to support Diane and their three young children, ages 7, 5 and 3. She was forever after Robert to spend more time at home with her and the children. This minor bone of contention was overshadowed by a car accident involving Diane which took place in March 1980. Diane recovered from her severe injuries, but was unable to take part in normal sexual activity from then on. Robert was understanding and supportive. He loved his wife and declared that he would allow no physical injury to come between them. Diane felt that now, more than ever, she required her husband's companionship. Robert tried to be home more often, but the pressure of his two jobs didn't allow him that much time away from his places of employment.

It was while convalescing from her injuries that Diane met Linda Prudden, a married woman in her thirties who was herself the mother of two boys. The women became close friends. They saw each other every day and, on many occasions, Diane and her children slept over at Linda's house.

In time, Diane and the kids were spending more time at the Pruddens' than at their own home. By November 1981, Diane was, to all intents and purposes, living full-time at Linda's. Robert was understandably miffed. He had been a good and faithful husband and father. Why was his Diane behaving this way? With Christmas just around the corner, he wanted his wife and children to return home. That's when Diane informed Robert of her little secret. She and Linda were lesbian lovers. Well, you could have knocked Robert over with a feather but, after giving the matter some thought, he accepted a situation he could do little about. He told Diane that he still loved her and pleaded with her at least to bring the children home for Christmas. Diane promised to do so.

Two days before Christmas, a neighbour was working in his garage when Diane Downey ran across the street and told him her husband had received a terrible beating. He was lying on the kitchen floor. The man summoned police, who rushed to the scene. They met Diane and Linda sitting in a car parked in the driveway of the Downey home.

The officers were surprised at the sight that greeted them inside the house. It looked as if someone had literally spattered blood over the entire floor and walls of the kitchen. The living room and kitchen were in total disarray, with furniture overturned and drawers pulled open. In the middle of the blood-spattered kitchen lay Robert Downey. He had obviously put up a terrific struggle for his life. Later, an autopsy would reveal 48 stab wounds all over his body.

The two women were questioned. Diane told detectives that she had last spoken to her husband the previous night. That morning, she, along with her three-year-old daughter and her friend Linda, was delivering Christmas presents to Robert. Upon entering the house, they discovered Robert's body. When asked where the three-year-old had been when they had gone inside with the presents, they both said they had left the youngster in the car. They couldn't give any reason why the little girl hadn't accompanied them into the house.

Detectives firmly believed they were investigating a murder that had taken place during the course of a robbery. They were gentle and respectful to Mrs. Downey, assuming she had just suffered a great loss.

One of the investigators noticed that Diane had several Band-Aids on her hands. He idly inquired how she had hurt herself. Diane replied that when she had first sighted her husband's body, she had clutched a glass off the kitchen counter. She had dropped the glass, breaking it on the counter. To steady herself, she had placed her hand on the counter and had cut herself.

The detective recalled having seen the broken glass, but the kitchen counter was at the far end of the room, away from the doorway. Surely Diane would have seen her husband on the floor long before making her way across the room to the counter. Now aware that there might be more to this murder than originally met the eye, the detective inquired where the Band-Aid packaging had been discarded. Diane told him that she had gone to the car to fetch and apply the bandages, but couldn't recall what she had done with the packaging.

The door of the Downey home was examined. It had been jimmied to appear as if an intruder had gained entrance. However, it was an amateurish job and had obviously been forced open from the inside.

Within the next 24 hours, a team of detectives learned that Diane had been seen the night before in her distinctive white station wagon in front of her home at around the time the murder had taken place. A thorough search of the Prudden home uncovered a hunting knife. Laboratory tests indicated that this knife matched wounds on Robert Downey's body and fit rips and tears in his clothing.

Both women were arrested and charged with Robert's murder. The details of their lesbian relationship came out at their trial. Each claimed that the other had wielded the hunting knife. They admitted to their deep love for each other and stated that Robert, who refused to give up his wife, had to be put out of the way. While he'd appeared to condone his wife's actions, he was forever pleading with her to return home. The lovers had decided to kill him and in the eyes of the law were equally responsible for his death.

Diane Downey and Linda Prudden were found guilty of the murder of Robert Downey. In 1983, both were sentenced to life imprisonment.

# Laura Fair
# SHE WASN'T LUCKY IN LOVE

You would have to say that Laura Fair was not lucky in love. At the tender age of 16, Laura married William Stone, a liquor salesman from New Orleans. A year later, he died of cholera.

Laura, a blond, blue-eyed Southern beauty, returned to school, but soon gave up her quest for a higher education in favour of marriage to one Thomas Grayson. Where Stone had been preoccupied with selling the demon rum, Grayson was intent on drinking Louisiana dry.

When sloshed, which was most of the time, Grayson had the distressing habit of joining Laura in bed with a pair of six-shooters, which he would fire at the most inopportune times. Laura fled to California, where she obtained a divorce.

Never one to let the grass grow under her feet, Laura strolled down the aisle for the third time in 1859. Lawyer William Fair stayed married to Laura for two years, during which time Laura gave birth to a bouncing baby girl, Lilliam. Unfortunately, William blew his brains out in a doctor's office in San Francisco, which had the effect of terminating not only his marriage, but his life, as well.

William left his wife and daughter with little in the way of worldly goods. Laura had one asset—a diamond ring given to her by her late husband during happier times.

In 1863, Laura took her daughter and moved to Virginia City, Nevada, to seek her fortune. She raised some cash on her ring and managed to rent a large rooming house called Tahoe House. The 50-room establishment was a success from the very beginning.

One day, lawyer Alexander Crittenden took a room at the

Tahoe House. The lives of Laura and Alex would never be the same again. Alex was no ordinary legal beagle. He was a blue blood from Kentucky whose family was on a first-name basis with generals and senators.

Alex fell hard for Laura. The old rascal should have known better. There he was, well into his fifties, with a wife, Clara, and seven children. When he met Laura, he had already celebrated his silver wedding anniversary. But love does not always take age or circumstances into account. Laura and Alex met clandestinely for about a year before they grew careless, or simply didn't give a damn. It matters little. The results were the same.

Clara, who still lived in San Francisco, came to Virginia City to visit one of her daughters. She quickly learned of her husband's prolonged romantic entanglement. Stories of the love affair between the influential lawyer and the successful businesswoman had been making the rounds for a full year. The pressure was too much for even randy Alex. He and Laura took a trip to San Francisco, where he did the unthinkable. He arranged a dinner date with his wife and his mistress.

Laura found Clara a real charmer, if a little on the plump side. In fact, the two women got along famously, considering their respective relationships to the man sitting between them. Clara gingerly suggested that Laura drop out of their lives. Laura replied that she would never give up Alex. So much for the pleasant dinner party.

For the next few years the affair between Laura and Alex continued unabated. They often talked of Alex divorcing his wife, but the wily lawyer always hedged. Like many a middle-aged Casanova, he wasn't quite willing to leave the mother of his seven children. Of course, he didn't want to give up the thrills and spills of his lovemaking with Laura either. It took a long while, but eventually it got through to Laura that Alex would never leave his wife. She became extremely jealous of her rival.

There were scenes. On one occasion, Laura lost her cool and marched into the Crittenden home in the middle of the night, demanding to talk to her lover. Alex showed up at the top of the stairs and shouted down, "I am utterly disgusted with you." Laura left in a huff, but received some measure of satisfaction when, a few months later, Alex forced his way into her room with the same general demands. Things were heating up.

During this tense and turbulent period, Laura met and married Jesse Snyder. Jesse was well aware of the relationship between Laura and Alex. At the time, a rumour circulated that Laura had paid Jesse $10,000 to go through with the marriage. She may have felt that once married she would be more desirable to her true love, Alex. Her plan didn't work. Alex informed her that nothing much had changed. Instead of requiring one divorce, they now needed two. Clever as a fox, Alex told Laura to get her divorce first. Just as Jesse had agreed to marry Laura, he now quickly consented to divorce her. Some said that Alex paid him $10,000. If this was the case, Jesse was no fool. He'd managed to make $20,000 for a few months of not-unpleasant employment.

Laura pointed out to Alex that it was his turn to divorce. Instead, Alex said that his wife was taking one of her many trips to Virginia City and it would be in poor taste for him not to meet her. (Clara was in San Francisco.) Laura was livid. It finally dawned on her that her lover never intended to leave his wife. Laura learned that Alex was to meet his wife aboard the ferry *El Capitain*, at the Oakland dock. Unknown to her lover, Laura planned to be aboard that ferry. On a cool fall day in November, Alex and Clara were united aboard the *El Capitain*. Laura found them on the crowded deck, sitting arm in arm. Their eldest son, Parker, stood nearby. Laura pulled out a chrome-plated pistol and fired at her lover. Alex slumped to the deck. Laura disappeared among the passengers on the crowded ferry. Parker and a harbour police officer searched the ferry and soon located the desperate woman. Parker turned to the police officer and said, "This is the woman who murdered my father." Parker was wrong. Laura wouldn't become a murderer until two days later, when Alex expired. Laura replied, "I do not deny it. He ruined me and my child."

On March 27, 1871, Laura Fair stood trial for murdering her lover. The proceedings lasted a month, with the outcome never in doubt. Laura had planned the murder down to the last detail. She had purchased the murder weapon and had followed Alex onto the ferry. She had even visited the boat the day before the murder to study the layout. To these accusations, Laura's counsel could only plead that she had purchased the pistol for protection and had been insane at the time of the shooting. To establish that Laura was madder than a March hare, her lawyers claimed that she had told them God had married her to Alex and that she was really his wife, not that interloper Clara. This line of defence didn't work. The jury took only 45 minutes to find her guilty.

All was not lost, however. In February 1872, the Supreme Court of California reversed Laura's conviction on two technicalities which had absolutely nothing to do with her innocence or guilt. In September of the same year, Laura stood trial for the second time. This time the jury retired for three days before returning the surprising verdict of not guilty.

Laura then embarked on a lecture tour and for a while was something of a celebrity. After all, it isn't every day that a woman kills her lover in front of his son and wife, admits it and then walks out of the courtroom a free woman. But Laura's prosperity was short-lived. Her lawyers sued her for large legal fees and collected.

In 1913, Laura's only daughter, Lilliam, was found dead in an empty room in New York City. She had starved to death. Laura Fair lived until 1919, when she too died in poverty in San Francisco. She rests today in that city's Woodlawn Cemetery.

# John Fiorenza
# THREE GRAVE MISTAKES

Killers, for reasons known only to themselves, seem to have an affinity for bathtubs. Many infamous murderers down through the checkered history of crime have positioned their victims in tubs. Canada's Terrence Milligan killed his wife in her bath. England's George Smith placed so many of his wives in the tub that he will forever be known as Brides-in-the-Bath Smith.

On April 10, 1936, two upholsterers, Theodore Kruger and his assistant, John Fiorenza, attempted to deliver a love seat which had been re-covered to the apartment of Mr. and Mrs. Lewis Titterton at 22 Beekman Place in New York City. The two men arrived at 4:30 p.m. to find the door to the Titterton apartment ajar. Receiving no response to their knocking, they walked in. They found Mrs. Titterton quite dead in the bathroom, lying in a half-filled tub of water. She was wearing only a pink pyjama top, which was fastened around her neck and had been used to strangle her.

Detectives were soon on the scene. From the condition of the interior of the apartment, they ascertained that Mrs. Titterton had been raped and murdered in her bedroom, after which the killer had placed her body in the bathtub. They ruled out robbery as a motive since there was no sign of a search and nothing had been taken from the apartment.

Mrs. Titterton's wrists bore signs that they had been bound with cord, which was verified when police found a 13-inch piece of five-ply cord under her body. The killer had obviously cut away a much longer cord and removed it, inadvertently leaving behind the smaller piece of cord found in the tub. The cord was examined closely. It appeared to be of a type used in

Venetian blinds. The Titterton apartment had Venetian blinds, but none had been cut away. Apparently the killer had brought the cord with him, which led detectives to believe that the rape had been premeditated. The bed upon which the rape had taken place was dismantled and carted away for laboratory analysis.

It was established that the murder had occurred between 10:30 and 11:30 a.m. on the day the body was discovered. Mrs. Titterton had talked to a friend on the phone at 10:30 a.m. At eleven-thirty, a boy delivering dry cleaning had received no answer when he knocked on the door. He had heard the phone ringing inside the apartment, and when no one responded, he figured there was no one at home and left.

Mrs. Titterton was an attractive, 33-year-old woman, who was happily married to an executive of the National Broadcasting Company. Lewis Titterton initially came under some suspicion. Although he had been at work in the NBC building all day, he had left the building on several occasions, which would have enabled him to travel to his apartment, kill his wife and return to work. When questioned, he pointed out that husbands usually don't rape their wives before murdering them. His interrogators tended to agree with him.

During the one-hour interval when the murder had taken place, W. A. DeWitt, a writer, was in his study overlooking the roof of the Tittertons' building. He watched as a fat man in blue overalls walked slowly across the roof of 22 Beekman Place. The mystery man turned out to be Dudley Mings, the janitor of the building. Mings explained that he had gone to the roof to repair a door. The door had been repaired, but it was impossible to verify when Mings had performed the job. He, like Lewis Titterton, remained a possible suspect.

Meanwhile, the boys down at the lab had tested the bedspread taken from Mrs. Titterton's bed. They came up with a length of gray horsehair and a dab of orange paint. Hot to trot, they went about extracting samples of horsehair from the padding of every suspect's clothing. The single strand of hair didn't match samples taken from the clothing of Lewis

Titterton, Dudley Mings, the boy who claimed he had attempted to deliver dry cleaning on the day of the murder, or other tradespeople who had called at the building.

The orange paint matched paint recently applied to the Tittertons' fire escape. The painters turned out to be real characters. They admitted that one of the perks of their chosen profession was the opportunity to gaze at assorted women in various stages of undress. Several stated that Mrs. Titterton often strolled around her apartment scantily clad. They had looked, but swore they had never touched. The painters were eliminated as suspects when detectives learned that the bedspread had been placed on the fire escape to be aired.

In desperation, police sent samples of the cord found under the body to cord manufacturers and samples of the horsehair to companies using horsehair in the manufacture of their products. They struck pay dirt. The cord that police thought was Venetian-blind cord turned out to be the kind used in the upholstery business to bind padding. They also learned that horsehair was used in the upholstery trade.

A light went on. Weren't those guys who found the body in the first place delivering a recently upholstered love seat to the Titterton apartment?

Theodore Kruger, the owner of the upholstery shop, had a clean record, but such was not the case for his assistant, John Fiorenza. John had served time for stealing automobiles and was currently on parole. Kruger, who knew of his employee's criminal status, recalled that on the day of the murder John had phoned in advising him that he had to report to his parole officer that morning. He had arrived for work at the upholstery shop around 12 noon.

John was taken into custody, although police knew they scarcely had enough evidence to gain a conviction. They were counting on a confession and they got it. Cunning rascals that they were, the New York cops obtained a sample of John's semen. They told him they were comparing it to semen found on Mrs. Titterton's bedspread. John had no way of knowing that no identifiable semen had been found. When detectives informed him they had a match, John panicked and told all.

Some months earlier, John had called on Mrs. Titterton to perform some repair work on her furniture. She had been scantily clad and the thought of having her preyed on John's mind. It got so that she was all he could think about.

On the night before the murder, John thought up the excuse to tell his boss. He made his way to Mrs. Titterton's apartment, knowing full well that her husband would be at work. He had no trouble gaining entry as Mrs. Titterton recognized and trusted him. He tied her up with cord he had taken from the upholstery shop, then raped and killed the defenceless woman before placing her in the bathtub in a crude attempt to simulate suicide.

John made three grave mistakes: he dropped that incriminating piece of cord; forgot to remove the pyjama top from around his victim's neck; and shed a piece of horsehair from his clothing onto Mrs. Titterton's bed.

John Fiorenza pleaded guilty to murder and was sentenced to life imprisonment.

# Lawrence Foye
# HOTEL HORROR

Lenore Gilbey had once been married to Anthony Gilbey, heir to the Gilbey gin fortune. In those days, she had travelled the world, attending the premier social events of the various countries she visited. In the early 1980s, the middle-aged mother of three devoted her time to charitable causes, both in Europe and the United States.

Through no fault of her own, Lenore was to cross paths with Lawrence Foye. While Lenore was at home in the fine salons of Europe, Lawrence hailed from that section of the Bronx known as Fort Apache, one of the toughest areas in the entire U.S.

On August 5, 1983, Lenore was registered at the Gorham Hotel in New York City. The Gorham is a small, well-appointed establishment located close to the downtown Manhattan action. On this particular night Lenore was alone in her suite on the sixteenth floor, unaware of the various events going on in the hotel which would affect her life.

Nothing was heard from Suite 1603 until the next day when, a little after 4 p.m., a maid discovered Lenore Gilbey's body. She had apparently been suffocated with a pillow. Her bedroom was in total disarray. Lenore's clothing and personal effects were strewn around the room, but it was impossible to tell what, if anything, was missing. The suite yielded Lenore's fingerprints, but no others, which indicated a clever or extremely fortunate killer.

Detectives examining the suite were attracted to the balcony. They noted that drapes from the penthouse suite above hung down the side of the building to within several feet of the balcony. It was conceivable that the killer had gained entrance to Lenore's suite via the balcony. He would have had to have been an agile and daring man to have climbed down the outside of the building holding on to drapes which could give way at any time.

Investigators questioned hotel staff for any strange or unusual events which may have taken place in the hotel on August 5 or 6. A desk clerk told them that two female guests reported that they had been frightened out of their wits when they had walked smack-dab into a nude black man in the hall outside their rooms. The man had said nothing and had hastily walked away. The women had checked out of the hotel but were easily located. They felt that they could identify the man if they saw him again. Police learned that one of the two women had told a porter that she had seen a man in drag leaving the hotel sometime on the morning of August 6. She described the man as black and wearing a pair of women's blue shorts, a red blouse and slippers. To top off his strange appearance, the weird-looking individual was wearing a shower cap. The woman felt that this man and the nude man she had encountered in the hall were one and the same.

Detectives canvassed all the occupants of the hotel. One man who claimed that he possibly had useful knowledge agreed to tell all in exchange for anonymity. On the afternoon of August 5, this guest—a businessman—met a black man, Lawrence Smith, in a downtown bar. The two men drank all day and ended up in his suite. At one point he and Smith had an argument, which culminated with him throwing Smith out of the suite into the hall. There was one thing—Smith had been stark naked. Convinced that Smith must be the man who had startled the two women in the hall, detectives felt that he was also the man who had so conspicuously left the hotel in drag the following day. Could he be Lenore Gilbey's killer?

The embarrassed businessman turned over everything Smith had left in his suite. This consisted of a sweatsuit, a book, a pair of football tickets and some photographs, but no identification. The businessman stated that Smith had told him that he worked in a downtown print shop not far from the hotel. The two women involved identified the photographs as the man they had seen in the hall.

The hunt was on for Lawrence Smith, although investigators were certain that their suspect had used a false name. The crime was reconstructed. Smith had accepted an invitation to take part in a homosexual encounter with the visiting businessman. They had argued. Smith had been thrown out of the ninth-floor suite into the hall, stark naked, where he had encountered the two women. He had hastily made his way to the stairway exit and had walked up to the roof, looking for a way out of his dilemma. Finally, at the front of the hotel, he had seen the exposed drapes leading partway down to the sixteenth floor and Lenore's balcony. He had climbed down the drapes and had jumped the remaining distance to the balcony, never knowing or caring who occupied the suite.

Smith's initial intent was to obtain clothing and any money he happened to come across. Suddenly he was face-to-face with Lenore Gilbey. How horrified this woman must have been. Here she was, 16 storeys up, yet there lurking in front of her as if he had flown in the window, was a desperate nude man. Smith's idea of obtaining clothing took a back seat to the sexual assault which followed. Then, in order to conceal his crime, he placed a pillow over Lenore's face until she died of suffocation. There is some evidence that he slept with the body. Next morning, Smith found some clothing he could get into and left the apartment. It was then that he was seen leaving the hotel.

Police canvassed print shops located near the hotel, asking employees if they recognized Smith's photograph. It wasn't long before they located their man. His real name was Lawrence Foye, a bad actor who was convinced that he had gotten away with murder. At first he denied having had anything to do with the killing, but when faced with his own photographs, he admitted to the homosexual liaison with the businessman. After he was told that he had been identified as the man who had been seen wearing Lenore Gilbey's clothing on the day after the murder, he confessed.

It had all happened just as the police had theorized. He hadn't entered Lenore's suite with the intention of assaulting and killing her, but simply to get something to wear. Things had gotten out of hand. In addition to the items the police already knew were taken from the murder sceen, Foye confessed to having taken a cosmetics case which he had later thrown away. This case was located in an alley described by Foye.

The accused man was tried for the murder of Lenore Gilbey. His attorneys came up with a rather unusual defence. They claimed that their client had been subjected to a homosexual attack which had caused him to run out of the businessman's room. A psychiatrist testified that the attack, coupled with the alcohol Foye had consumed, had rendered him temporarily emotionally disturbed and not responsible for his actions.

The New York jury didn't buy Foye's story. He was found guilty of felony murder, robbery and burglary. The presiding judge, Sybil Hart Kooper, described his crime as one of the most vicious cases ever placed before her. She sentenced Lawrence Foye to 25 years to life with no possibility of parole.

# August Franssen
# DETECTIVE'S AD STRUCK PAY DIRT

Before the turn of the century it was not unusual for small towns to enlist the assistance of private-detective agencies to solve major crimes. Let's face it, local sheriffs often did little more than shove the town drunk into the hoosegow every Saturday night. They were ill equipped to deal with murder most foul.

It was only natural for the good folks of the tiny village of Edgeville, just outside New York City, to elicit the aid of the famed Pinkerton Detective Agency when one fine morning they woke up to find an almost nude male body in their midst.

The local coroner carted away the body and soon related his findings. The victim was a stranger to the village. He had been struck a vicious blow to the back of the head with a barrel stave, which had been found beside the body. The single blow had killed the man, but the killer had made sure that he was dead by stabbing him with a penknife just below the heart. The body had been stripped of all clothing with the exception of socks, a shirt and underwear.

Nothing like this had ever happened in Edgeville before. The townsfolk were incensed. They called on the Pinkertons to solve the case and bring the culprit to justice.

Detective George Bangs took over the investigation. He viewed the body and, in the style of that other great private eye, Sherlock Holmes, came to several conclusions. Facial features indicated to Bangs that the victim was of Teutonic extraction. His fingers were long and uncalloused, with well-trimmed nails. Bangs guessed that the man may have been an artist. His socks were knit from very fine wool often favoured by German manufacturers. The man's shirt had tiny holes in the chest area. Bangs surmised that a monogram had been ripped from the shirt in order to conceal the victim's identity. When Bangs connected the little holes, he came up with the letters A.B.

The clever detective knew he was in on a tough one. He decided to try a long shot by inserting the following advertisement in the *New York World:* "Information wanted about German artist, aged about twenty-eight, initials A.B., who came to this country within the past few months and who has for more than a week been missing from usual haunts."

The ad struck pay dirt. Bangs was contacted by Jacob Kuenzle, who claimed that he not only knew the man described in the ad, but roomed with him in the German district of New York. Bangs called on Kuenzle immediately. In the room the two men shared, he found several shirts monogrammed with the initials A.B Jacob told Bangs that his roommate's name was Adolph Bohner. In return, Bangs informed Jacob that his buddy was most probably a murder victim.

Adolph Bohner turned out to be an artist just as Bangs had suspected. His work wasn't being well received and he was always short of funds. He had left his fiancée, Rosa, back in Strasbourg. It was she who had embroidered his initials on his shirts.

Bangs contacted the Pinkerton Agency in Germany and told them to check out the Bohner family, as well as Adolph's fiancée, Rosa. He soon had a report back that Adolph came from a well-respected family. Rosa was playing the field in her fiancé's absence. In particular, she was seeing one August Franssen, the son of a shoemaker. Shortly after Adolph left for New York, August was suspected of stealing money from his father and had disappeared.

Bangs procured a photograph of Franssen and showed it to Jacob. A few male friends had visited Adolph in their room, but Jacob was uncertain whether Franssen was one of them or not. The only outstanding thing Jacob could remember about one of the visitors was a distinctive leathery smell about his person.

Bangs knew that Franssen had followed his father's profession of shoemaker in Europe and was now certain that his man was in New York working in the shoe trade. His theory received a setback when Rosa was questioned further and revealed that Franssen was in Alsace and visited her often.

The Pinkertons descended like bloodhounds in and around Edgeville seeking out shoemakers or anyone who worked in leather. They located a shoemaker named Heinkel who had hired an Arthur Frances, whose description fit that of August Franssen. The man no longer worked for Heinkel.

Bangs was in a quandary. He was firmly convinced that Arthur Frances was August Franssen, but his theory didn't hold water if Rosa was to be believed. An agent was sent to question Rosa for the third time. She now admitted that she had lied earlier. In fact, she felt certain that Franssen had skipped to the United States.

Although the Pinkertons had identified a major suspect, they still had not located him. It was decided to place one of their agents, German-speaking Wilhelm Mendelsohn, in the German area of New York City. The Pinkertons believed that this would be the most logical location for the fugitive to settle.

Mendelsohn canvassed shoe manufacturers, ostensibly looking for employment. He didn't locate Franssen, but he did find a factory where his quarry had previously been employed. A co-worker of Franssen's gave the detective the name of a bar where Franssen often spent his evenings. Mendelsohn became a regular at that bar. Sure enough, one fine evening, Franssen strolled through the swinging doors.

Detective Bangs knew they had their man, but realized he didn't have enough evidence to gain a conviction. He was positive that Franssen had been in love with Rosa and had followed Bohner to New York to kill him and eliminate him as a rival for Rosa's affection.

The Pinkertons decided to play out the string. Influence was used to secure a position for Mendelsohn in the shoe factory where Franssen was employed. The two men became bosom buddies. In the following weeks, Franssen received small loans from Mendelsohn. The two men met every day at the saloon.

Gradually, Franssen confided in the detective. He was an artist who hated his job in the shoe factory. He simply had to get away from New York, but didn't have the money to move to California. Maybe his friend Mendelsohn could help him out. He really didn't want a loan. He would sell some of his belongings. He had a suit in hock which he would sell to Mendelsohn really cheap. Mendelsohn said he would purchase the suit if it fit him. Franssen handed over the pawnshop ticket.

Accompanied by Detective Bangs, Mendelsohn retrieved the suit and showed it to Jacob Kuenzle, who positively identified it as belonging to his former roommate, Adolph Bohner.

That did it. Franssen was picked up and charged with murder. All the evidence against him was circumstantial, but it was extremely strong evidence. Franssen was found guilty and sentenced to death. His lawyers won him a second trial on a technicality and this time succeeded in securing a guilty verdict with a recommendation for mercy.

August Franssen had come within an ace of getting away with murder. Only dogged detective work by an independent agency proved his undoing. He was sentenced to life imprisonment.

# Richard Fredericks
# BODY DOUBLE

It's rather distressing to all concerned when a supposed murder victim walks into a police station. It doesn't happen every day.

A Mexican rancher discovered the body one day in 1953 as he walked through one of his fields. It wasn't a pleasant sight. The woman had been beaten about the head so severely that her features were beyond recognition. Most horrific of all was the absence of the victim's hands.

Mexican police were soon at the crime scene. A cursory examination of the clothing worn by the dead woman indicated that she was American. Because the body was found near Ensenada, about 50 miles south of the California-Mexican border, the Los Angeles police were notified. An American detective was dispatched to assist in the investigation.

There was precious little to help the officers identify the dead woman. She had been dead for weeks and the body had been ravished by the elements. Obviously her killer had cut off her hands and had picked the isolated area to dump the body in order to make identification difficult, if not impossible.

A description of the murder victim was widely distributed in California and Mexico. She was five feet six inches tall and weighed 115 pounds. She had a mole on the right side of her neck. When found, she was wearing a red blouse and jeans.

The publicity soon brought practical results. A distraught woman drove down from San Diego, deeply concerned that the murdered woman could be her daughter. She viewed the body and burst into tears. "It is Olga," was all she could say between sobs. After giving the woman time to compose herself, detectives asked her how she could be sure, considering the condition of the victim's face. They were assured by the victim's mother that Olga had worn an identical red blouse and jeans. The mole on the corpse's neck was further proof, the woman told them.

During this discussion, a police doctor informed the woman that the victim had three gold teeth and indicated their position in her mouth. Sadly, the woman nodded. Now she was absolutely positive. Her Olga had three gold teeth in exactly the same positions.

Next day, the same newspapers that had solicited information to help identify the handless body in the field revealed that the victim's name was Mrs. Olga Carrino, a San Diego mother of two young sons, aged five years and nine months.

Four days passed before an attractive young woman walked into a San Diego police station. She told the officer in charge, "I am Olga Carrino and I am not dead. What's more, I have my two hands." With that declaration the woman pushed her hands forward to make sure the startled officer saw what she was talking about.

Olga had quite a story to tell. Her husband, Fernando, was employed on a tuna clipper fishing in the Pacific. Because he would be away for some time, she and her two young sons had moved in with her in-laws. The arrangement hadn't worked out. They had fought and she had stormed out of the house and had gone to live with a girlfriend.

Olga had heard of her "death" only about an hour before walking into the police station. Her girlfriend had shown her details of her demise in a four-day-old newspaper. Olga had immediately informed her family that she was alive and well and then had gone directly to the police station. Yes, she wore an identical red blouse and jeans as the dead woman. Yes, she had a mole in exactly the same location on her neck as the murder victim. Most amazing of all, Olga had three gold teeth in the same places as the handless body. She opened her mouth and showed the detectives her teeth. There was no question about it: whoever had been murdered and dropped into that Mexican field was not Olga Carrino.

81

Detective Charles F. Stewart of the Los Angeles Police Department was studying missing persons reports in a routine manner when information on one of the documents rang a bell. He had recently read the facts and figures about a woman's body found in Mexico that were startlingly similar to the missing persons report he was scanning.

The missing woman was Ruth Fredericks. She had been reported missing by two friends who hadn't seen her for more than a month. The women had made a date with Ruth to go to the movies. The three had made arrangements to obtain a babysitter for their children. Ruth simply hadn't shown up.

The two friends had inquired as to her whereabouts from her husband, Richard. He didn't volunteer any information and seemed extremely cavalier about the whole thing, which is why they took it upon themselves to report her missing. They felt that Ruth would never voluntarily leave her three children. Ruth was five feet six inches tall, weighed 115 pounds, had a mole on her neck and often wore a red blouse and jeans. She also had three gold teeth.

Stewart believed the handless body found in Mexico was Ruth Fredericks. He interviewed the two women who had reported Ruth missing and got an earful. They had known Ruth for two years. During that time, her husband, Richard, was a holy terror. He continually screamed at his wife. Often Ruth would show up with a black eye or a bruised arm. When Ruth disappeared, they figured she must be dead, because there was no way she would leave her five-year-old son and the two younger children.

They informed Detective Stewart that the five-year-old had stopped attending school. Upon learning this, one of the women had gone to the Fredericks' home and found it vacant. She checked with the Fredericks' immediate neighbour and was told that Richard had sold his car, packed his belongings and had flown to New Jersey with the three children. Richard had worked in New Jersey before moving to California.

Detective Stewart called on the insurance company where Richard had been employed. He learned that his man had been transferred from New Jersey and for a while had been a friendly valued employee. In the past year, he had undergone a remarkable change in personality. He consistently harped about his wife being unfaithful, although, as far as anyone at the insurance company knew, Ruth Fredericks was a faithful wife and loving mother.

When an employee found a gun in Richard's locker, he had informed Ruth of his discovery. Ruth had told her husband's colleague that Richard's behaviour was so bad she was considering having him confined.

Evidently, Ruth was able to talk Richard into entering a psychiatric hospital for observation. He stayed only a week before signing himself out. After his short spell in hospital he became moodier than ever and hardly communicated with fellow employees at the insurance company. Finally, Richard confided to a co-worker that his wife was a tramp and had run away with a sailor. He said he wasn't sorry and that he was better off without her.

After tracing Richard to Maplewood, New Jersey, Detective Stewart flew there for a face-to-face confrontation with his suspect. Stewart knocked on the front door of the man who he believed had brutally killed his wife and chopped off her hands. He introduced himself and was graciously invited into the house by Richard. Stewart gingerly inquired, "Your wife's name is Ruth, isn't it?"

Homicide investigators claim to have heard it all, but it is doubtful if Detective Stewart was prepared for Richard's reply. "Her name's Ruth and I killed her."

Richard went on to explain that on the previous January 6, he and Ruth were in the backyard of their Van Nuys residence. He had accused her of being unfaithful. She became furious, screaming that he was wrong and that he must be crazy. When he retreated to the garage, she followed. He saw red, picked up a mallet and struck her on the head. He couldn't stop swinging until his wife's face was nothing more than a mass of flesh. He carried her body to his workbench, where he chopped off her hands with a hatchet. He then buried the hands in the backyard and placed Ruth's body in the trunk of his car. In an effort to dispose of the body, he drove to Mexico, crossing the international border at Tijuana. No one searched the interior of his vehicle or asked him to open his trunk. Relieved, he drove to Ensenada and dumped his wife's body in an isolated field.

Richard told Stewart that he thought he was home free when he read that the dead woman had been identified as Olga Carrino. When he learned that the error had been discovered, he panicked and fled to New Jersey.

Stewart had Los Angeles detectives dig in Richard's backyard. Sure enough, right where Richard said he had buried them, they discovered the hands of Ruth Fredericks.

Richard Fredericks waived extradition and was returned to California to stand trial. He was found guilty of murder in the second degree and received the strangely lenient sentence of one to 10 years' imprisonment.

# Pat and William Gil
# KILLER WITH A PENCHANT FOR TRAVEL

Certain murderers firmly believe that their victims' bodies should be transported great distances in order to avoid detection. Who can forget Winnie Ruth Judd who shipped one of her victims halfway across the United States? Considerate Winnie accompanied the body on the train. Canadians tend to send unwanted bodies to Newfoundland, for reasons known only to themselves.

In this story, the killer with a penchant for travel is Patricia Gil, a fine cut of a woman, who stood a lofty five foot two inches tall and weighed in at a pudgy 220 pounds. Pat lived with Jose Ramos for nine years. The pair had two children before calling it quits. Shortly after the breakup, Pat married William Gil and moved into a home on Chicago's West 47th Street. The house had once been Saint Christopher's Rectory.

A year later, Jose learned of the marriage and was furious. After all, the substantial Pat was the mother of his two children. It didn't matter to Jose one little bit that for six of the nine years he had lived with Pat, he himself had been legally married to a woman named Juanita.

On the evening of May 25, 1980, William Gil and 17-year-old Danny Anderson, a boyfriend of Pat's younger sister, were listening to the car radio in the Gils' backyard, while Pat, inside the house, was on the phone with a furious Jose. Jose told her he was coming over to give her a piece of his mind. She said, "No way, Jose," but Jose wasn't deterred. Scared sick of her former lover, she went out to the backyard and asked William for moral support and the use of his .38-calibre pistol. William fetched his weapon from the glove compartment of his vehicle and passed it over to his wife.

Jose arrived and told Pat in no uncertain terms that he thought it downright inconsiderate of her to have married William behind his back. To illustrate his displeasure, he'd brought along a baseball bat, which he swung with reckless abandon against a door. Certain that her head was about to be Jose's next target, Pat pulled the trigger of the .38, propelling a bullet directly through Jose's neck. This latter move by Pat definitely discouraged Jose from inflicting further abuse. He slumped to the floor, deader than a mackerel.

William and Danny ran into the house. Danny's first reaction was to call police, but William made him put down the phone. He counselled his distraught wife. Well, "counselling" may be too strong a word. Actually, he said, "Get the hell out of here." Pat gathered up her children and took them to her mother's. When she returned to the former rectory, she found that Jose's blood no longer soiled the kitchen floor. What's more, his body was nowhere to be seen.

While gazing at the sanitary condition of her kitchen, Pat was interrupted in her reverie by police officers who were responding to a neighbour's complaint that they had heard a shot. Pat swore that there had been no gunfire. Someone was obviously mistaken or playing a prank on the police. Satisfied that that was the case, the police left the Gil residence.

William confided his little secret to Pat. He had deposited Jose in the trunk of the dead man's own car, a 1973 Chevrolet. It remained there for four days. On May 29, William, with Jose in the trunk, headed south. Pat and Danny Anderson followed in Pat's car. They drove and drove until Jose's old heap broke down in Ashland, Kentucky. The conspirators hired a tow truck and had the vehicle hauled into the West Virginia hills. Once there, they temporarily abandoned the Chevy and spent a few hours visiting Pat's uncle and aunt, Lucy and Herbert Dancy, in Coal City. After leaving her relatives, Pat and the two men purchased a large can of gasoline. They returned to the abandoned Chevy and doused it with gas. A match did the rest. The West Virginia sky lit up like a home run at SkyDome.

Pat, William and Danny jumped into Pat's brown Plymouth and headed back to the friendly confines of Chicago.

On June 10, the odour emanating from the abandoned car came to the attention of the police. They pried open the trunk. Voilà, there was what was left of Jose.

The state medical examiner prepared a dental chart of the man in the trunk. He was able to tell authorities that the hands of the victim had been bound with a leather belt. The man had been dead for two to three weeks. Although the body was badly decomposed, the victim had kept one hand firmly closed, enabling authorities to obtain fingerprints.

Meanwhile, the Chevy was undergoing forensic examination. The car's licence plates had been removed, but police were able to obtain the vehicle's serial number. The ownership was traced to one Jose Ramos of Chicago.

Chicago detectives were contacted. They quickly located Juanita Ramos, who informed them that her husband had left home on May 25 and hadn't been seen or heard from since. She added that Jose drove a 1973 Chevy and gave the investigators the name of her husband's dentist. The dental chart from West Virginia was forwarded to Jose's dentist, who positively identified the victim as his patient, Jose Ramos.

Now that the body in the trunk had been identified, police were left with the taxing problem of who in the world would take the trouble to transport a dead man into the hills of West Virginia. Juanita could give no logical explanation as to why her husband's body had been carted over 500 miles from their home in Chicago. Several individuals had seen the wreck being towed to the spot where it was found. No one thought it that unusual. Evidently, cars are often abandoned in the hills of West Virginia.

Detectives interviewed Jose's friends and relatives. They learned about his relationship with Pat Gil. Pat was contacted and admitted that she had lived with Jose, but swore up and down that she had had nothing do to with his murder. During their investigation, detectives learned of Pat's relatives in West Virginia, Lucy and Herbert Dancy. They lived in Coal City, only a couple of miles from the abandoned Chevy. The Dancys were located and, without hesitation, told police about Pat's sudden visit. Herbert remembered the day—May 29. In fact, Herbert remembered quite a bit. He told detectives he had received a phone call from his niece, Pat, advising him that her car had broken down in Pemberton and that they were travelling in two vehicles.

Herbert had driven to meet her, after she had made her way to Coal City in a Plymouth. Pat was accompanied by two men, her husband, William, and her sister's boyfriend, Danny Anderson. All three followed him back to his place in the Plymouth. They had a short but pleasant visit. Pat said they had to leave to attend to the broken-down vehicle. That's the last Herbert saw of the Chicago branch of the family.

In due course, the tow-truck operator was located. He well remembered towing the car into the hills. How could he forget? That car gave off the most peculiar odour.

As they say in the murder business, enough is enough. Chicago detectives paid one last visit to Pat. She sensed the jig was up. Pat told the officers about the funereal trip to West Virginia. She maintained that Jose would have killed her with the baseball bat had she not plugged him in the neck.

In November 1982, Pat and William Gil were convicted of voluntary manslaughter. Both were sentenced to 18 years' imprisonment. Danny Anderson received a suspended sentence.

Ironically, when the state of Illinois overhauled its crowded prisons in 1987, two of the prisoners who received early releases were Pat and William Gil. Both were released after serving less than five years behind bars.

# Ed Grammer
# A BURR UNDER HIS SADDLE

Ed Grammer was office manager of the Climax Molybdenum Co. in New York City. He had a good job, a loving wife, Dorothy, three children and a nice home in the Bronx. There was one burr under Ed's saddle and that was his penchant for playing the field. I'm not talking horses here.

Her name was Mathilda Mizibrocky, a winsome lass who worked for the United Nations. She met Ed at a bowling alley and soon found herself engaged in a more horizontal activity, which many categorize as not only pleasant, but athletic as well. Mathilda had no idea that her Ed was already married. She often mentioned that he should make an honest woman of her. Ed came up with excuse after excuse, but finally hung his hat on their different faiths. He was Protestant; she was Roman Catholic. But who knows, if they stayed in bed long enough, the rules might change.

When Ed's father-in-law died, Dorothy dashed off to Baltimore to care for her mother. Ed was delighted. Dutiful husband that he was, he wrote Dorothy to stay as long as she liked. She stayed several months. Ed took the opportunity to spend a pleasant two weeks with Mathilda in Chicago during his wife's absence. Ed was so obsessed with Mathilda that he neglected to write to his wife in Baltimore.

Dorothy was concerned. She phoned Ed's office and spoke to Jean Bilelo, his girl Friday. Like all good secretaries, Jean was cool. She wired her boss to get in touch with his wife. Ed phoned Dorothy and assured her that his letters must have gone astray. Despite his protestations, the seed of suspicion had been planted in Dorothy's mind.

Meanwhile, Mathilda continued to apply marriage pressure. Ed continued to hide behind their religious differences, but was having an increasingly hard time keeping Mathilda at bay. Then there was Dorothy with her snide insinuations. She was even threatening to leave her still-grieving, ill mother and return to hubby's ever-loving arms. It was enough to make any self-respecting adulterer cringe.

Ed took a trip to Baltimore to placate Dorothy. He may also have taken the trip to murder her. The results were exactly the same for Dorothy. She ended up dead.

On August 19, 1952, Ed spent the day with Dorothy. That evening they stopped for drinks on the way to the train station, where Ed would catch the train to New York. He later claimed that he had had five or six slugs of Scotch and water. Dorothy had nursed one.

It was after midnight when two policemen, Officer Paul Hardesty and Sergeant John Eurite, stood in amazement as a blue driverless Chrysler sped down the street, caromed off a telephone pole and drove out of control up an incline, finally coming to a standstill as it rolled on its side. The two men were no more than 10 metres from the vehicle when it came to a full stop. Inside was the body of Dorothy Grammer.

The officers noted that the car's engine was still running. They extracted a pebble from under the front of the accelerator pedal, which had kept the accelerator pressed down and had enabled the car to run without the aid of a foot on the pedal.

Dorothy had been bludgeoned about the head. The officers didn't have to be Einsteins to come to the conclusion that she couldn't have sustained her injuries in the car crash. The vehicle's interior wasn't damaged in any way. The dead woman's purse and eyeglasses were missing. It appeared that the person who stuck the pebble under the accelerator pedal believed that the vehicle would plunge over an embankment on the other side of the street, burst into fire and obliterate the evidence of murder.

Next day, Dorothy was identified and her husband was

advised of the tragedy. He returned immediately to Baltimore. As soon as it was learned that Ed had been with Dorothy about an hour before the murder, he was taken into custody and questioned.

After several hours of questioning, Ed confessed, but gave no reason for killing his wife. He told officers that he had been high on the Scotch he had consumed and had stopped the car on the way to the station. He had stepped out of the vehicle, picked up a small pipe conveniently lying at his feet and had beaten his wife to death. Ed claimed he couldn't remember anything after that. He stated that he didn't even know if he had started up the car of if he had put the pebble under the accelerator. He had staggered down the road and caught the train to New York. Ed signed his confession and that should have been that, but it wasn't.

Ed had remembered to take the train and remembered to take from the murder vehicle documents pertaining to his work and turn them in to his office upon his arrival in New York. He remembered to have his suit dry-cleaned the first thing next morning. In fact, Ed had a selective memory. He remembered to leave Mathilda out of his confession, thereby denying authorities an obvious motive.

When Ed retained the services of a competent lawyer, things changed appreciably. He maintained that he had not killed his wife. He said he would have confessed to anything in order to get some sleep.

Ed pleaded not guilty. Other than the revealing confession he'd given earlier, the prosecution had precious little concrete proof to connect Ed directly to his wife's death. The murder weapon was never found and no one had seen Ed commit the foul deed. The prosecution traced Mathilda, who told of her undying love for Ed and his reluctance to marry her because of their religious differences. Of course, Mathilda now knew that Ed, the snake in the grass, had been married all the time.

Defence attorneys pointed out that if Ed had actually taken his wife's life, he had done it on the spur of the moment. After all, he could have obtained a divorce in order to marry

Mathilda. Then there was Mathilda's statement that she had asked Ed to marry her; he had never proposed to her. Had he divorced his wife, she would have married him in spite of the fact that her religion forbade her to marry a divorced man.

Did Ed have a real motive to plan the death of his wife? Did that pebble lodge under the accelerator by accident, as Ed claimed? Did he kill Dorothy during a domestic dispute while under the influence of alcohol as he had originally claimed in his confession? Conviction of premeditated murder meant a mandatory death sentence. Murder in the second degree was punishable by life imprisonment.

Ed had elected to be tried by a judge only. His decision predicated whether Ed would live or die. The presiding judge found him guilty of first-degree murder. The Court of Appeals unanimously rejected Ed's appeal in the fall of 1953. On June 11, 1954, Ed Grammer was hanged for the murder of his wife, Dorothy.

# Charlie and Lionetti Haynes
# A TALE OF HORROR

The nature of the crime that follows might not be for those with weak stomachs. They should consider reading these pages well after breakfast. Forewarned is forearmed.

On February 24, 1978, two derelicts were searching for anything of value in a dumpster in Eugene, Oregon. They opened a garbage bag and found more than they bargained for —a female thigh and breast. Police were called, the area was secured and the body parts were removed for analysis. Forensic scientists were able to ascertain that the body parts had belonged to a woman between 20 and 30 years old, weighing approximately 140 to 160 pounds. The body had been dissected with a knife, and the breast bore several teeth marks.

Detectives scanned reports of missing women and came up with Pamela Bruno, 24, who fit the description. Pamela had been reported missing by her husband on February 22, two days before the gruesome discovery in the dumpster.

The Brunos lived in a rundown apartment building in nearby Springfield. Johnny Bruno claimed that his wife had disappeared on February 17. He had awoken to find her gone, but hadn't notified police until February 22 because Pamela had often disappeared for a few days at a time. She was a heavy drinker, frequented local bars and, to put it kindly, was extremely promiscuous. Bruno admitted that he himself was not a candidate for canonization. He had been convicted in Washington State, together with Pamela, for contributing to the delinquency of a minor. Both had taken part in lewd sex acts with 15-year-old girls. They were not the salt of the earth.

Police felt that the victim was Pamela Bruno when they had her blood type checked from records in Washington. It matched the type taken from the body parts found in the dumpster. Johnny was advised that his wife might have been a murder victim. He didn't act surprised. A search of the Bruno apartment failed to uncover any trace of blood. If Pamela Bruno had been butchered, it had not been done in the Bruno apartment.

Johnny was taken to police headquarters for further questioning. When it was suggested that others might have been involved in Pamela's murder, Johnny opened up. He implicated Charles Haynes, 31, a colleague of his at a tree-planting company, and Haynes's wife, Lionetti.

Johnny told an unbelievable tale of horror. The murder had taken place at the Haynes residence on West Fifth Avenue in Eugene. On February 21, the Brunos had visited the Hayneses for a day of drinking and smoking pot. Everyone agreed that a session of group sex would nicely break up the day. At the last moment, Pamela decided not to participate. The two men tied her up and that's when things got out of hand. Johnny told detectives that Lionetti had inflicted the initial stab wound, after which Charles had stabbed Pamela several times. Johnny claimed he had stabbed his wife only once.

The three participants suddenly realized that Pamela was dead. Charlie blurted out, "We got to do something about this now. We're going to have to cut her up." His suggestion was met with unanimous approval. Pamela's body was lugged to the bathtub. Johnny Bruno told detectives in graphic terms not necessary to repeat here how he helped to drain the blood from his wife's body and to butcher her. The body parts were placed in plastic bags and deposited in various dumpsters around Eugene. The only portions ever found were the thigh and breast discovered by the two derelicts.

Charlie and Lionetti Haynes were located at their home and taken into custody. On May 23, 1978, Johnny Bruno stood trial for his wife's murder. His statement given to police detailing the horrible crime had been taped and was now played back to the jury. Understandably, it had a devastating effect. In addition, medical experts testified that the severed breast had been mutilated extensively by human teeth. They also confirmed that the body parts contained minuscule amounts of blood, lending credence to Bruno's testimony that the body had been strung up and drained of blood for some time before it was dissected. These facts pointed to a deliberate murder and cover-up to avoid detection rather than a wild sex orgy that had gotten out of hand. Defence lawyers paraded an array of experts who attempted to cast doubt on Johnny's sanity. They had a difficult time overcoming the defendant's own statement that he definitely knew right from wrong.

The jury also heard that Johnny had been so drunk at the time of the murder that he could hardly remember what had transpired. His lawyers insinuated that he was afraid of Charlie Haynes and would do whatever his dominant colleague suggested. The jury didn't buy the defence arguments. They deliberated only three hours before finding Johnny guilty of felonious murder. He appealed the verdict but his conviction was upheld. Johnny Bruno was sentenced to life imprisonment, a sentence he is presently serving. He will be eligible for parole on March 13, 1998.

Charlie Haynes chose a rather complicated move called a "trial by stipulated facts," which is the next thing to pleading guilty. It differs in that it enables the accused to appeal the verdict. Charlie was sentenced to life imprisonment. He appealed on a technicality, but his appeal failed and his sentence stood. His lawyers took his case all the way to the Oregon Supreme Court and won their client a new trial, but it was all for naught. In May 1981, Charlie stood trial for Pamela Bruno's murder. He was found guilty and again sentenced to life imprisonment. He too is presently serving his sentence in the Oregon State Penitentiary. Haynes was paroled in January 1997.

After almost two years of delays and postponements, Lionetti Haynes was tried and convicted of first-degree manslaughter. Throughout her trial, she maintained that she was innocent of the charge. Despite her protests, she was found guilty and sentenced to 20 years' imprisonment, with the two years already spent in jail to be applied against her sentence. Lionetti Haynes was paroled from the Oregon Women's Correctional Center on March 11, 1985.

# George Hlady
# TRAGIC END TO A NEW LIFE IN A NEW LAND

It was just another working day for Eino De Witt and Wally Sempke on the McIntyre River. The two men were perspiring under the hot August sun that day in 1952 when Eino spotted a strange-looking object in the water near the south side of the McIntyre. The men lowered a skiff off their big derrick scow and rowed across the river to investigate.

The strange-looking object was the body of a man floating face down. A half-inch rope was looped tightly around the man's neck with one strand wrapped across his mouth like a gag. In addition, there was a two-inch gash on the right side of the victim's head. Two heavy steel plates were tied to the dead man's neck and feet with wire. These plates were risers used under railway tracks at switching points. They could be found stacked anywhere along the rail line and, in fact, these two plates were stamped as being the property of the Canadian Pacific Railway.

Back in 1952, the twin cities of Fort William and Port Arthur were separate entities, which were eventually united to form what we now know as Thunder Bay. At the time of the murder, railway officials had become concerned about the high incidence of grain thefts from CNR and CPR railway cars. Thieves were breaking boxcar seals and carting away bushels of grain. Others were even more brazen, drilling through the boxcars and letting the grain run directly into bags outside the cars. Because of the proximity of the parked railway cars to the point where the body was taken out of the water, officials believed that the murder could, in some way, be connected to the theft of grain.

An autopsy indicated that the unidentified man had already been dead when he was submerged in the McIntyre. In addition to the blow on the head, he had been manually strangled. His clothing proved to be untraceable and there was no documentation found on the body to assist in identification. Callouses on the victim's hands indicated that he worked at physical labour, but decomposition made fingerprinting impossible. He wore a ring engraved with the initials W.H.

Dr. A.E. Allin, chief pathologist for the attorney-general's department, informed police that the dead man had a long scar along the back of his body. The scar was the result of a lung operation in which a rib had been removed. Once seen, it is doubtful anyone would forget that livid scar.

Police received a hot lead when Ignace Hyriciuk reported that a tenant of his, Josef Panok, had been missing for some weeks. Ignace explained that his tenant had recently immigrated from Europe with his wife and young daughter. They had rented a tiny house on dilapidated Simpson Street in Fort William. Ignace went on to tell investigators that the Panoks' friend, George Hlady, lived with them. Ignace was taken to the morgue to view the body but couldn't say with any degree of certainty that the dead man was his tenant.

Detectives drove to the tiny house on Simpson Street. Once there, they learned that the Panoks didn't rent the entire house, but occupied two cramped rooms on the second floor. Mrs. Panok, an attractive brunette, couldn't speak English. The officers' questions were translated by well-built blond George Hlady. George explained that he and Panok were friends from the Ukraine.

With George translating, Mrs. Panok told the officers that she wasn't worried about her husband. He was in Winnipeg visiting a family named Kummel, who lived on Bannerman Street. Police suggested that she and George view the body in the morgue to assist them in their identification attempts. Mrs. Panok readily agreed.

When she looked down at the horrible sight of the decomposed corpse, Mrs. Panok cried out, but after settling down she stated that the dead man was definitely not her husband. George Hlady agreed. Both swore they had never seen the initialled ring before.

Investigators, under the direction of Port Arthur police chief Tom Conner, learned of a missing man, a lumberjack, whose initials were W.H. Several individuals identified the ring as belonging to the missing man. After viewing the body, they all agreed that the dead man was not the elusive W.H.

This minor mystery was solved when W.H. showed up. A giant of a man, he had been on a drunken spree to end all sprees, and had found himself in Copper Cliff with a monumental hangover and no money. He had not heard of the murder until he returned to Port Arthur. W.H. stated that the ring had belonged to him and that he had given it to a man named Panok as a reward for helping him out once when he was in a fight in a beer parlour.

W.H. accompanied police to the morgue and positively identified the dead man as Josef Panok. He recognized the long scar, explaining that he had worked with Panok many times under the hot sun when both men had been stripped to the waist. But how could this be? Panok's wife and best friend had already viewed the body and had sworn they didn't know the identity of the dead man.

Police, now wary of Mrs. Panok, checked out the Kummel family who supposedly lived on Bannerman Street in Winnipeg. There was no such family. When Chief Connor called on Mrs. Panok this time, he brought along his own translator. He asked his suspect, "Why didn't you identify your dead husband at the morgue?" Mrs. Panok replied, "Hlady told me not to. He threatened to kill me if I did. He and Josef went out to steal wheat and only George came back."

Mrs. Panok went on to tell the officers that her husband and George had known each other in Germany, where they dabbled in the black market. When their illicit business dried up, George made his way to Canada, promising to arrange for the Panok family to follow him. True to his word, he made arrangements for the Panoks to emigrate and was successful in getting Josef employment on a CPR work gang.

Living conditions were primitive. She, her husband and George all slept in the same bed. Daughter Karen slept alone in the only other room, the kitchen. According to Mrs. Panok, George had asked her to leave her husband and go to Toronto with him. She had refused his offer and the tension had become unbearable in the enclosed living space.

George was picked up at his place of employment on the railway. When presented with Mrs. Panok's statement, he agreed to it all, but he swore he had not killed Josef Panok. Lodged in jail, George made another statement to police. He said that he and Josef had gone out on the night of the tragedy to steal wheat from the boxcars. Just as George was about to break the seal and open the boxcar, Josef sneaked up behind him and put a rope around his neck. George said he grabbed at the rope with one hand and swung around with the other, striking Josef a blow to the head, which sent him reeling against the side of the boxcar. He then related that he had tied the rope and the steel risers to the body and tossed it into the McIntyre River.

Mrs. Panok filled in the rest of the evening by telling investigators that George had returned to the house around midnight, pale and shaken. Later, she would testify in court, "I couldn't sleep and I asked him again where Josef was. He told me he had killed my husband and thrown him in the river."

George stood trial for the murder of Josef Panok. He pleaded self-defence, but couldn't account for the tiny broken bones in the victim's neck which indicated manual strangulation. The jury could not dismiss the obvious motive, that of a love triangle. They chose to believe that George had killed Josef in an attempt to possess his wife.

George Hlady was found guilty of the murder of Josef Panok. On April 28, 1953, after all appeals were exhausted, he was hanged at the Port Arthur jail.

Mrs. Panok, accompanied by her five-year-old daughter, returned to Germany shortly after the conclusion of George's trial, her dreams of a fresh start in the new world shattered forever.

# Jack Holmes and Harold Thurmond
# SAN JOSE MOB LYNCHED KIDNAPPERS

We like to believe that lynching has become unfashionable. It is distressing to learn that this unsavoury, if not downright nasty, practice was very much in vogue well into the twentieth century in many areas of the United States.

In 1933, Alex Hart owned one of the largest department stores in San Jose, California. His 22-year-old son, Brooke, had just graduated from Santa Clara University and had been made a junior partner in the prosperous business.

At six o'clock on November 9, 1933, Brooke, his father and sister were the last to leave the store. They locked up and waited while Brooke walked the three blocks to a parking lot to pick up the family's Studebaker.

Alex Hart and his daughter waited for some time before deciding that Brooke must have misunderstood that he was to pick them up. They made their way home, but still there was no sign of Brooke. After calling his friends, they decided to inform police. By ten o'clock that evening, the terrible thought that Brooke could have been kidnapped coursed through the minds of the missing man's family. At ten-thirty, their worst fears were realized. Alex received a phone call: "We have your son. We want $40,000 for him. Keep the police out of this if you want to see him alive."

Alex informed police of the call, but nothing further was heard from the kidnappers for a few days. Quite unexpectedly, a young girl knocked on the Harts' front door with a note she claimed had been given to her by a stranger who had asked her to deliver it to the Harts. On the scrap of paper were the words "We have Brooke and are treating him right."

Another day passed before the Harts' Studebaker was found outside San Jose. The vehicle provided no clues leading to the location of the missing man. The kidnappers kept in touch. They again contacted Alex by phone on November 15, giving detailed instructions as to where to drop off the ransom money. This time Alex was able to keep the kidnapper on the line long enough to have the call traced. Police sped to a San Jose garage and picked up Harold Thurmond.

Now, Harold wasn't your average run-of-the-mill lowlife. He came from a respectable family and had never been in any trouble before he tried his luck at the kidnapping game. When questioned, he told police that he had an accomplice, Jack Holmes, who was also taken into custody.

The two men confessed and told authorities the same story. Both were unemployed and had had time on their hands to hatch their amateurish plot. They had plucked Brooke off the streets of San Jose as he was getting into his Studebaker. Together with their captive, they drove in his car to the San Mateo–Hayward Bridge. Once there, one of them knocked Brooke out with a brick brought along especially for that purpose. Both men had a hand in tying Brooke up with wire and weighing him down with a slab of concrete.

Just as they were about to toss him off the bridge, Brooke regained consciousness and started screaming. It was dark and no cars passed by during the interval it took to complete the job. Brooke, screaming hysterically, was tossed off the bridge. For good measure, Harold took a few potshots at Brooke, but didn't think he hit his target. Brooke quickly disappeared from sight.

It was a heartless, cold-blooded recital of murder of a well-liked, well-respected member of the community; consequently, there was great concern for the safety of the two confessed killers. They were placed in the San Francisco Prison for safekeeping. Inexplicably, six days later, they were removed to the less secure Santa Clara County Jail and lodged in separate cells on different floors.

On Sunday, November 26, 17 days after the abduction,

Brooke's body was found. Two duck hunters came across the partially decomposed body about a mile south of the bridge. The concrete used to weigh down the body had come loose, allowing it to surface.

In San Jose, word of the cold-blooded cruelty displayed by the two men in custody spread throughout the community. The Hart family was respected; Brooke had been well liked. It was as if the city was waiting for an excuse to spring into action. The recovery of Brooke's body confirming the terrible rumours was that excuse.

A crowd, estimated at 15,000, congregated in front of the jail. Many were young men in their twenties, the same age as Brooke and the two men in custody. Some were former school chums of the murdered man. Children were held high in the air so they could get a better view of what was about to take place.

Sheriff Bill Emig was aware of the community's ugly mood. He had prepared for just such an eventuality, having enlisted the assistance of 20 county officers and state highway patrolmen. Equipped with shotguns and tear gas, they covered every window and door. Alex Hart, devastated at the news that his son's body had been recovered that day, still summoned enough strength to make an impassioned plea in front of the jail, imploring the crowd to go home. He was hardly heard over the din of the mob.

Sheriff Emig had set up barricades at the front of three alleys beside the jail. Sixty men charged the barriers and were repulsed by tear gas. On the fourth try, they crashed through. Using planks and pipes from a nearby construction site, they broke down the doors of the jail. Inside there were only three officers between them and the killers. These officers were quickly disarmed.

Deputy John Moore was forced to lead the mob to Jack Holmes's cell. Holmes, frightened out of his wits, begged, "For God's sake, give me a chance." The mob laughed and proceeded to inflict a severe beating on their quarry. On they went, up to Harold Thurmond's cell. It was empty. Terror-stricken,

Harold had managed to find a hiding place among pipes in the ceiling. He was spotted, pulled down, tied with rope and dragged down the stairs headfirst.

The two murderers, now almost unconscious, were taken to Saint James Park. Harold was strung up on a large tree. His execution didn't go well. He choked to death at the end of the rope. Jack was made to look at his friend's body before he too was hanged. Someone in the mob knew how to make a proper hangman's knot, so Jack didn't suffer as much as his companion.

It was over. The mob pressed forward, ripping and tearing at the clothing of the dead men for souvenirs. Citizens boasted that they had taken part in the lynching. For years after, souvenirs of the event could be purchased in and around San Jose.

An inquest was held into the two deaths, but no indictments were issued and no one was ever prosecuted for the lynching. The governor of California expressed the mood of the city when he stated, "I would pardon those fellows if they were charged. I would like to parole all kidnappers in San Quentin and Folsom to the fine patriotic citizens of San Jose."

# Brian Hood and Jennifer Reali
# POSSESSED BY PASSION

Attractive Jennifer Vaughan did all the proper things. She attended the University of Washington, made the varsity rowing team and dated often. They were great, carefree days in the early eighties. Jennifer thought they would last forever. She was sure of it when she met Ben Reali, a career army man. In 1984, they married and were soon the proud parents of two daughters, Tinneke and Natasha.

Despite the appearance of tranquillity, Jennifer was not happy. Although her marriage was stable and her lifestyle secure, she longed for something more. Her existence in Colorado Springs had become routine—housework, the kids, and above all, staid, boring Ben. There was definitely no excitement in Jennifer's life; that is, until Brian Hood came upon the scene.

Brian hailed from Houston, Texas, where his dad was big in the insurance game. After graduating from Angelo State College in 1986, he married Dianne, who had been his steady girlfriend throughout his college years. The young couple moved to Colorado Springs, where Brian, like his father, pursued the insurance business. He also joined the Fellowship Bible Church and became deeply involved in the religious life. Following her husband's advice, Dianne joined the church as well. Both devoted much of their time to ecclesiastical pursuits and led a strict, devout life. They had three children: Jerrod, 7, Leslie, 5, and baby Joshua.

In 1989, Dianne was told she had contracted lupus. Although her form of the disease was not life-threatening, she had to take extremely good care of herself and lead a quiet life. Sexual activity had become a thing of the past. Brian, stout-hearted fellow that he was, told his wife not to worry about their lack of intimacy. His religious beliefs would see him through the crisis and would fill the void left in their sex life.

Wouldn't you just know it—Brian met Jennifer Reali at Bally's U.S. Swim and Fitness Club. He took one look and religion flew out the window. As for Jennifer, she thought she had died and gone to heaven. A hunk had dropped into her lap, so to speak. The pair had lunch. A few days later, Brian called on Jennifer when hubby and kids were absent, ostensibly to discuss her insurance program. We know for a fact they discussed other things, because they had intercourse on top of a convenient washer-dryer in the laundry room.

After this initial exhilarating experience, Brian became a rather demanding lover. He seemed to require sex practically all the time. Jennifer loved every minute of it. She insisted that Brian accommodate her with a variety of methods and positions. It was all great fun, but wouldn't it be wonderful if they could be together all the time without sneaking around the sickly Dianne and boring Ben?

Brian racked his brain and came up with the rationalization that satisfied his morals. He explained to Jennifer that they could kill Dianne, which would be no more of a sin in the eyes of God than if he divorced her. Besides, all things considered, God would forgive them. Jennifer, now totally dominated by her lover, agreed. Dianne had to go.

Brian advised Jennifer that the opportunity to kill Dianne would present itself in two weeks when his wife would be attending a lupus support-group meeting and would be vulnerable as she returned home. According to Brian, the entire adventure would be akin to a religious experience. They would be free to fulfil their every desire. Jennifer heartily agreed.

In preparation for the great event, Jennifer had her husband Ben take her out to a shooting range, where she practised shooting with one of the guns from his collection. While Jennifer was busy practising, Brian and Dianne went away on a three-day marriage-encounter weekend. On the very date the murder was supposed to take place, Brian informed Jennifer that their affair was over. He was returning to his wife and that was that.

Undaunted, and maybe more possessed than ever, on the designated night, Jennifer took her husband's gun, donned a black mask and camouflage fatigues and headed for the Otis Park Community Center. Inside, Dianne was attending her lupus support-group meeting. Jennifer hid in some bushes and waited for her victim. When Dianne emerged from the centre with a friend, Karen Johnson, Jennifer caught up to the pair and attempted to grab Dianne's purse. Dianne threw her purse at her attacker, shouting, "Take it!" Instead, the disguised figure shot Dianne in the back. As Dianne spun away to run back into the centre, she fell to the ground.

Karen watched in terror as the assailant ran to Dianne's side. Then, as the wounded woman begged for mercy, Jennifer shot her through the heart. She then drove home. Karen's screams soon brought assistance, but it was too late for Dianne. She lay dead on the sidewalk.

Investigating officers were not fooled by the attempt to make the attack look like the work of a mugger. Muggers do not usually remain at the crime scene to execute a wounded victim. No, it looked like a deliberate, planned assassination. Brian was informed of his wife's death and was devastated. However, it didn't take detectives long to learn through the army grapevine that Ben Reali's wife, Jennifer, was doing what comes naturally with the husband of the dead woman.

On the day of Dianne's funeral, Brian was arrested and charged with her murder. Two weeks later, Jennifer was charged with first-degree murder and conspiracy. The trials of the accused were sensational. Sexual revelations liberally sprinkled with religious beliefs made for juicy testimony. Jennifer confessed that she had shot Dianne, but claimed that Brian had ordered her to do the job. Captain Ben Reali bowed out of the scenario by filing for divorce and gaining custody of his two daughters.

Brian was the first of the pair to stand trial. His lawyers put all the blame on Jennifer, painting her as a woman who saw her lover returning to his wife. Solution—do away with the wife. The ploy didn't work. Brian was found guilty of conspiracy to commit murder. He was sentenced to 37 years in Colorado State Prison.

In March 1992, Jennifer stood trial. She was found guilty of murder in the first degree, as well as conspiracy to commit murder, and was sentenced to life imprisonment with no possibility of parole. Brian Hood and Jennifer Reali are presently serving their sentences.

# Dr. James Hudson
# SWINGER KILLED WIFE AND DAUGHTER

The first 12 years of James and Kay Hudson's marriage went along famously. Of course, for 10 of those years, Kay had no idea that her dentist husband was a real swinger. Dr. Jimmy was careful. He loved to travel and only dated women when he was out of town.

Jimmy wasn't averse to taking part in group sex. When he approached Kay with the great idea that she join him in fun and games, she was appalled and refused to have anything to do with her husband's jollies. That's when she realized that her marriage was in trouble. Kay felt that adopting a child might be the solution to straightening out her rocky union.

In April 1983, the Hudsons had no trouble adopting a baby girl, Wilma Dale. They were prime adoptive parents. After all, Jimmy was a partner in a prosperous dental practice and Kay had recently attended the University of North Carolina, where she had finished a master's degree. To the outside world, the Hudsons, with their impressive home in Oak Ridge, North Carolina, were a respectable, well-educated couple. Kay knew better.

For a while after the adoption, Jimmy seemed to settle down. He was more attentive to Kay and doted on his new little daughter. His solicitous attitude didn't last. When Wilma Dale became ill, Jimmy dropped her like a hot potato. He complained that Kay paid too much attention to their daughter and neglected him. After Kay found letters from strange women describing specific sex acts they had enjoyed with her husband, she knew the end of her unstable marriage had come. She also realized that her husband had turned into a sexually aggressive man who bore no resemblance to the young man she had married.

In March 1986, Kay wrote a long letter to Jimmy outlining the reasons she was leaving him. She pleaded with him not to attempt to find her and assured him that she and Wilma Dale would make out fine on their own.

Jimmy read the letter left for him by his wife. He called police, but was told there was little they could do. There was no law preventing a mother from leaving her own home with her daughter. A few minutes later, Jimmy had a bright idea. He called police a second time, advising them that he was in hospital after having suffered a heart attack. He begged them to bring Kay to the hospital.

The fake heart-attack ploy worked. Kay was driven to the hospital, where the estranged couple had a meeting. During the course of the conversation, Jimmy wheedled Kay's address out of her. In return, he promised to receive help from a psychiatrist. Kay insisted on living separately from her husband, at least until he renounced his kinky lifestyle.

A few days later, on March 24, a blood-spattered Jimmy drove to a police station and told the first officer he met, "I think I killed my wife and daughter." According to the dentist, his wife had attacked him with a knife. Further than that he couldn't remember. Jimmy was hustled off to hospital to take care of wounds to his chest and hand. They proved to be little more than superficial.

Police entered Kay's apartment and found her body and that of her three-year-old daughter, Wilma Dale. Both had been stabbed repeatedly. Jimmy was arrested and immediately underwent a battery of psychiatric tests to ascertain if he was fit to stand trial. Tests indicated that he was sane, which gave the state the right to impose the death penalty if the accused was found guilty of murder.

Jimmy's trial did not focus on whether he committed the murders, but whether or not he should receive the death penalty. The prosecution revealed that the two victims had been the recipients of vicious beatings before being stabbed to death. The jacket and T-shirt Jimmy was wearing on the night of the murders were introduced as evidence. Both were devoid of slashes and cuts, although Jimmy swore he was wearing them when he received the wounds to his chest as he and Kay struggled for possession of a kitchen butcher knife. The prosecution's implication was clear. Jimmy could have inflicted the superficial wounds to his own chest after he murdered his wife and daughter.

Statements given to the police by Jimmy were read into the record. He confessed to having had several affairs, but always with women from out of town because of his prominence in the community. On the day of the murder, Jimmy had been with Wilma Dale all day. He had dropped off his daughter at Kay's apartment at 6 p.m. and had lingered for some time. Kay had asked him to leave, and that's when the trouble had started. She had become violent and Wilma Dale had started to cry. Kay had slapped his face and had come at him with a butcher knife. That's the last thing Jimmy said he remembered. He had no recollection of the actual stabbings, but did recall washing the blood off his hands and face in the kitchen. He claimed that was when he took off his jacket and T-shirt.

Jimmy admitted that both his marriage and his dental practice had deteriorated because of his unusual sex life. For example, he told of his attempt to make Kay join a nudist colony with him. She would have no part of any of his sexual activities. As the years passed, she more or less consented to his going his own way. The letters she found were the straws that broke the camel's back.

Defence attorneys paraded an array of psychiatrists to the witness stand who stated that Dr. Jimmy was a severely disordered personality. They related that in previous times in his life he had suffered from amnesia and had blanked out distasteful episodes. They claimed that he'd suffered from emotional shock on the night of the murders and truthfully couldn't remember the killings.

The prosecution wasn't through. A fellow prisoner of Jimmy's gave testimony. This man, who was the prison librarian and a three-time killer, had volunteered to give testimony after seeing photographs of Wilma Dale's body. He informed the court that Jimmy told him he had killed his wife and had then waited 20 minutes before stabbing his daughter. This threw some doubt on Jimmy's claim that he had operated in a state of emotional shock and had no knowledge of the crime. Although the defence attempted to discredit the librarian, who had already spent 20 years in prison, it was clear to the jury that he had nothing to gain and had put himself in considerable jeopardy by coming forth to testify.

On April 11, 1987, the North Carolina jury found Jimmy guilty of first-degree murder in the case of his daughter and second-degree murder in the case of his wife.

Dr. James Hudson, the once-prosperous dentist with the attractive wife and ostentatious home, managed to save his life. He was sentenced to life imprisonment for the murder of his daughter and 50 years for the murder of his wife. He is presently serving his sentences.

# Richard Ivens
# KILLER MOVED BODY FROM PLACE TO PLACE

It takes more than your average riot, murder, or stuffed ballot box to gain the attention of the Chicago police. Despite past indiscretions perpetrated by the good citizens of Chicago, the year 1906 started off nastier than most. Three women, Mrs. E.F. Mize, Mrs. Maude Reese and Mrs. A.W. Gentry had been murdered in the last three months of 1905. The city's finest had no idea who had committed these crimes.

Understandably, the police force was under increasing pressure to solve the murders. They were totally demoralized when Fred Quimba walked into a police station and told the desk sergeant in a stage whisper, "There's a dead woman in my front yard."

Fred lived on the corner of Fullerton and Orchard Streets. Within minutes, police officers were speeding to the area to secure the crime scene. The boys back at the station house, now certain that they were dealing with murdered woman number four, were somewhat miffed when they received word that there was no body in Fred's front yard.

Fred couldn't explain the absence of his very own personal corpse. Police looked at him skeptically, thanked him for being such a public-minded citizen and told him to be sure to give them a call if he found any more bodies.

An hour later, the very same desk sergeant who had been both aggravated and amused by Fred Quimba, received a phone call from one J.H. Rush, who exclaimed, "There's a dead body in my yard." Mr. Rush went on to explain that he lived on the corner of Fullerton and Orchard. Once again, police officers were dispatched to the now-familiar area. They located

Rush, but surprise of surprises, for the second time on the same day they failed to find a body.

Mr. Rush and his wife were escorted to the police station. They described the dead woman in detail. There was no doubt in their minds that they had seen the woman and she had definitely been dead. Someone must have removed the body when they left to telephone police. So insistent were the Rushes, the police agreed to return to the scene. The Rushes' credibility escalated when detectives discovered bloodstains on the ground where the couple had allegedly seen the body.

Chicago flatfeet were now convinced that they were investigating the case of a body which, in some mysterious way, had become mobile. Any doubts were dispelled when Frank Hollister walked into a police station. Unlike Fred Quimba and J.H. Rush, Frank's approach was quite different. He said, "I'm Frank Hollister and I want to report the disappearance of my wife."

Frank turned out to be somewhat of a heavyweight. He was the owner of the Hollister Printing Co., one of the largest printing firms in Chicago. According to Frank, his wife had left their home early the previous morning. She had visited a grocery store where she left instructions for her groceries to be delivered. The groceries had arrived at the Hollister residence at 10 a.m. She had then ordered flowers to be delivered to the Methodist Episcopal Church, where she had a 3 p.m. appointment to take part in choir practice. She hadn't shown up.

On January 13, 1906, Edward Ivens walked into a police station to report that his son Richard had found the body of a woman. Edward explained that he owned a carpentry shop on Belvin Avenue and a livery stable next door. He kept horses and wagons at the stable. His son Richard fed the horses and cleaned out the stable every morning at 5 a.m. Richard had found the body in the vicinity of the stable.

This time there really was a body, that of Mrs. Bessie Hollister. She had been beaten about the head and had been strangled to death. A 48-inch length of wire had been wound around her neck. Near her body, police recovered a 12-inch length of green string.

Detectives soon learned that the wire was used by florists and the green string was of a type often used by upscale grocery stores. The Hollisters' maid was questioned. She volunteered that when Mrs. Hollister left the house that morning, she had taken along a beautiful gold clock for repair. The maid had wrapped the clock in white tissue paper and had secured it with green string she had saved from the grocer's.

A thorough search of the crime scene and adjoining areas failed to turn up the clock, but police did find a muff and purse belonging to Mrs. Hollister. The killer had obviously covered these items with leaves which had blown away.

When blood was found on the floor of one of Edward Ivens' wagons, police were convinced that someone had killed Bessie Hollister and had moved her body, for some unknown reason, from place to place, possibly using the horse and wagon in Ivens' stable. Everyone who had reported seeing the body was questioned again and, this time, believed.

Police decided to interrogate the individual who had actually come up with Bessie Hollister's body, namely, Richard Ivens. They knew that Richard's brother owned a florist shop and that Richard had access to the type of wire used to strangle Mrs. Hollister. Armed with this information, they had Richard relate his every move on the day of the murder. Business had been slow and he claimed that he had spent much of the day and night alone. When a search of his premises uncovered a jackknife with a small length of green string adhering to the blade, Richard was arrested and taken into custody.

Richard broke down. He told police, "I've got the clock. I found it beside Mrs. Hollister. I was going to pawn it. But I didn't kill her. I had nothing to do with that." He turned the clock over to police.

After only one day in custody, Richard confessed to Mrs. Hollister's murder. In his own words, he said, "I killed her. I chased her and slugged her. I took her money. She pleaded with me to take her home, said I could keep the money and she wouldn't tell anybody. I hit her again and again and then we came to Fullerton and Orchard. I saw a piece of wire in the gutter and twisted it around her neck and pulled it tight. As I walked away, I saw a man hovering over the body. When he went away, I went back. I thought she was dead and threw her over the fence and into the yard. I went away a couple of blocks and then got to worrying that she wasn't dead. I saw another man running away from the yard and figured he'd found her. I went back. I thought her leg moved and figured I'd better move her. I went back behind the fence and threw the body over my shoulder and carried it to the stable. I hitched up a team to a wagon and drove out, but didn't go far. I returned and dumped the body close to the stable."

Richard stood trial for the murder of Bessie Hollister. He recanted his confession, claiming that he had been beaten by police to extract it from him. Throughout his trial he professed that his only crime was finding the body and stealing the clock. No one believed him.

Richard Ivens was found guilty of first-degree murder and sentenced to death. He was hanged on June 22, 1906. No evidence was ever brought forward implicating him in the murders of the three Chicago women killed in late 1905. These crimes remain unsolved.

# Bahar Kandlbinder and Wolfgang Grunwald
# HUBBY WOLF AND MISTRESS BAHAR

Inge Hermann was only 19 years old when she fell in love with Wolfgang Grunwald. Her mother was fit to be tied. Mrs. Hermann simply didn't understand how an attractive girl like her daughter could fall for a no-goodnik like Wolf. The boy had no job and no prospects. Besides, he had an atrocious complexion. Surely, with all the eligible boys in Munich, Germany, her Inge could do better.

Mrs. Hermann's opinion became academic when Inge, due to an unfortunate miscalculation, found herself definitely pregnant. Quick as a bunny, she and no-goodnik Wolf became husband and wife.

The marriage, born out of necessity, was not a happy one. The responsibilities of married life didn't change Wolf one iota. Two years after he and Inge tied the knot he still had no job and no prospects. When he chose a mistress, Inge felt it prudent to pack up her baby and go home to Mama.

Wolf's mistress, a 32-year-old Turkish woman, was gainfully employed as a masseuse in a shop that featured massages of a specialized nature. Folks, you know what I mean. Living with Bahar Kandlbinder had one positive effect on Wolf. He got a job in a manufacturing plant. When Inge filed for divorce, Wolf didn't oppose the action. In fact, considering that he was the recipient of all those massages on a regular basis, we must assume that he was rather pleased with the way things were working out.

On June 19, 1974, Inge failed to arrive home from her job at a gas station at her regular time of 4 p.m. Her mother immediately reported her missing to police. Inge had always arrived home promptly since she and her baby had moved in with her mother.

Police located Wolf at home watching television with Bahar. He told detectives he had no idea where his estranged wife could be. There where no new developments for two days.

The possibility that Inge might have run away was eliminated when a lock tender on the River Isar in Munich found a woman's purse containing some money and identification papers belonging to Inge Grunwald. The river was dragged but nothing further was uncovered.

The next day, a man, walking in the woods about nine miles from the city, came across Inge's body lying below a steep incline. He ran to the nearest telephone, which was some distance away, and called the police. Inge had been hacked to death with a hatchet. Her scalp was virtually split open. The blows had been struck from behind. She was fully clothed and had not been sexually interfered with in any way. An investigation of the crime scene indicated that Inge had been killed beside a logging trail at the top of a steep incline. Her body had been rolled down the incline to where it was found.

The logging trail was closely examined. Casts were made of tire tracks and footprints leading to the edge of the incline. One set of footprints belonged to the victim. The other two had been made by a man and a woman.

Detectives were able to reconstruct the circumstances of Inge's murder. Accompanied by a male and female, she had walked 25 yards from the car that had made the tire tracks. Here she was struck several times from behind with a hatchet. Inge had fallen, bleeding profusely. She was then dragged the rest of the way to the steep slope and pushed over the edge. The body rolled some distance, finally coming to a stop. A list of clothing worn by the murdered woman when she went missing was given to authorities by her mother. The body was dressed in all the clothing listed, with the exception of a red velvet jacket.

The logical suspects were hubby Wolf and his mistress Bahar. The tires on Wolf's Opel Kadet were checked against the cast made of the tire tracks at the scene of the murder. Much to investigators' surprise, they didn't match. Although the suspects' shoes were the correct sizes, they did not match the prints taken near the logging trail. The suspects' clothing was examined for blood, but none was found.

Munich police had no idea why Inge had been murdered, but they were sure her husband and his mistress were the culprits. They set up investigative procedures, which lack the glamour of the fictional murder investigation, but which more often that not snare the killer in real life. Dry-cleaning establishments were canvassed in an attempt to find out if Wolf or Bahar had deposited any bloodstained clothing. Hardware stores were checked for the purchase of a hatchet before the date of the killing. It was theorized that Wolf may have been cunning enough to purchase new tires immediately after the murder.

Sometimes one connecting clue is uncovered in a massive investigation. On this occasion, everything attempted by the police came up aces. The hardware store where Wolf had purchased a hatchet on June 13 was found only four blocks from his apartment. The clerk who had sold him the hatchet knew him by sight. Police also located the tire shop where Wolf had purchased new tires. Inge's missing red velvet jacket was not located in a dry-cleaning establishment, but the bloodstained jacket was found in a playground near the River Isar.

Wolf was informed of the evidence pointing to his guilt and immediately confessed to his involvement. He vehemently denied that he had killed Inge, claiming that Bahar had struck the fatal blows. According to Wolf, his wife had threatened to commence proceedings to have Bahar confined to a mental institution. Although Inge had no legal right to take such action, Bahar believed it was possible and decided to kill her antagonist. The pair picked Inge up and drove out to the woods, ostensibly to discuss the impending divorce. Wolf had purchased the hatchet at Bahar's instructions. He had waited in the car while Bahar struck the fatal blows. His mistress had then summoned him to help drag the body to the edge of the slope and push it over. Wolf admitted that he should have informed police of the murder, but by the next morning he believed that it was too late. That's when he went out, changed the tires of his Opel Kadet and threw away both his and Bahar's shoes.

Now it was Bahar's turn. She too confessed involvement, but named Wolf as the killer. According to Bahar, the reason for the killing was Inge's threats to inform Wolf's employer that he had stolen goods and money from the plant. To complicate matters, Bahar had attempted to break off her relationship with Wolf. For her trouble, he had beaten her black and blue. After that little episode, Bahar never again mentioned leaving him. She claimed that it was she who had stayed in the car at the time of the murder and Wolf who had inflicted the blows with the hatchet.

Police believed Bahar's story. She was a short, tiny woman. Tests indicated that it would have been impossible for her to have inflicted the fatal blows without standing on something like a box or step stool.

Bahar Kandlbinder was found guilty of being an accessory after the fact of murder. She was sentenced to two and a half years' imprisonment. Wolfgang Grunwald was found guilty of murdering his wife and was sentenced to life imprisonment.

# Ernst Karl
# MURDERED WOMAN'S BODY DISSECTED

On May 10, 1973, a garbage man in Vienna, Austria, took the cover off a trash can outside a retail store and stared directly into the lifeless face of a young woman. Within minutes, a horde of officials were swarming the area. The murdered woman's body had been dissected. Body parts were found in other trash cans close by. It was sheer luck that the contents of all the cans had not been taken away by a garbage truck and disposed of in the city dump.

The body was taken to the morgue where an autopsy revealed the following facts. The victim had been between 18 and 22 years of age, had stood 5 feet two inches tall and had weighed 102 pounds. She had been dissected by someone with no medical skill who had used a common butcher knife and hacksaw. Sexual intercourse had taken place shortly before or at the time of death, which had taken place two days previously in the afternoon or early evening.

It was obvious that other than the girl's body parts, the contents of the trash cans had come from the nearby shops. Police believed that the killer would not have disposed of the body outside his own shop. Questioning of the shop owners in the area proved that this was the case. All were cleared of any involvement in the murder.

Reports of missing girls in Vienna were checked out. None matched the girl found in the garbage can. Photographs of the dead girl were widely distributed and featured in local newspapers. This effort bore fruit. Martin Katz of the Albo Manufacturing Co. called police. He was sure the dead girl was Ilse Morscher, a clerk at Albo. Martin had taken it upon himself to check out the Human Resources Department of his company. He was told that Ilse had simply failed to show up for work one day and had never inquired about salary due to her.

Police were told by Albo's personnel staff that Ilse was 21 years old and lived alone in an apartment. She had no casual or steady male friends and had worked in Vienna for only three months. Ilse was a shy girl, well liked by everyone. A newcomer to the city, she spent most of her spare time taking in the sights that Vienna had to offer. The woman's apartment was searched, but yielded nothing that would lead to the identity of the killer.

Girls at Ilse's office informed detectives that Ilse had told them she planned on visiting the Prater, Vienna's famous amusement park, on the Friday evening she disappeared. As the autopsy had revealed that Ilse's last meal had consisted of sausage and candy, typical amusement-park fare, police surmised that she could have met her killer at the park.

A canvass of sausage sellers at the Prater turned up the vendor who had sold Ilse her last meal. He positively identified her from her photograph and swore that she had been alone. Next, police conducted a door-to-door search for anyone who had seen the young woman leave the park. Several people who lived in the area came forward, informing police that they had seen Ilse walking alone. From that point on, she simply vanished. Detectives believed that somewhere along the route, Ilse had been either dragged or lured inside an apartment by a rapist who killed her and dissected her body. Each apartment building-dweller in the area was questioned. Many were eliminated as suspects. Others had their apartments searched from top to bottom.

It was in this way that Johann Rogatsch became a prime suspect. For starters, Johann had been previously convicted of minor sex offenses. Blood was discovered in his bathroom. The blood was not his type, but was the same type as that of Ilse Morscher. Police dismantled the plumbing in the apartment and discovered bone chips and hair in the drains. Charred bits of women's clothing were found in the basement furnace.

Johann was questioned for hours. Initially he denied any involvement, but eventually he broke down and confessed. According to Johann, he had lured Ilse into his apartment, wanting nothing more than a friendly kiss. When she repulsed his advances, Johann said he panicked and gave the girl a karate chop, a martial art he had only recently taken up. He must have hit her too hard because she crumpled to the floor, dead.

Johann conveniently omitted the rape from his confession, but it did him little good. On January 4, 1974, Johann Rogatsch was found guilty of rape and first-degree murder. He was sentenced to life imprisonment at the federal prison at Stein.

All things being equal, when the cold steel bars of the ominous prison closed behind Johann, that should have been the last heard of the rapist/killer. But such was not to be the case. His path crossed that of prisoner Ernst Karl.

Ernst, an inmate since 1968, wasn't rowing with both oars in the water. He had been a rookie police officer in Vienna in 1968 and had been on the force only four months when he made headlines. In the wee hours of April 4, Patrolman Ernst Karl radioed headquarters that he had just been in a shootout with two gangsters inside a public garage. Fortunately, he had shot the two men dead.

Detectives were at the scene in a matter of minutes. Sure enough, the rookie had plugged the two hoods in the head. They lay on the floor of the garage in pools of blood. Both had weapons clutched in their hands. Next morning, newspapers hailed Ernst as a hero. The public ate up the story. Here was a police officer of whom everyone could be proud. Everyone, that is, except the police.

Police felt that there was nothing of value in the garage. Why were the men there at 1:30 a.m.? Upon checking out the dead men, Walter Poettler and Johann Khisl, police learned that they were small-time hoodlums who pulled off the odd swindle and rolled the occasional drunk; hardly big-time gangsters.

Detectives took another look at their own man, Ernst, who

obviously had a fantastic aim to have shot two armed men in the head before either one could get off a shot. Someone got the bright idea that if the two hoods were blackmailing Ernst, he might have decided to kill them.

A full investigation was conducted into the patrolman's background. It was discovered that he was a homosexual. Ernst was confronted by his superiors and admitted that he was being blackmailed. He was turning over almost all his salary to the blackmailers in return for their silence about his sexual orientation. Finally, he decided to kill them. According to his reasoning, he would rather kill them let them blackmail him into committing crimes in order to provide them with more money. To Ernst's way of thinking, they were criminals who deserved to die.

The Austrian court didn't see Ernst's point of view. He was found guilty of murder and sentenced to 20 years' imprisonment at the federal prison in Stein. Once incarcerated, our Ernst soon gained a reputation as a law-and-order nut. If a prisoner committed the smallest infraction, Ernst held a mock trial and meted out what he felt was appropriate punishment. He soon came to be the most feared man in the institution.

This was the man whom Johann Rogatsch met when he first entered prison to serve his sentence. Johann didn't notice that the other prisoners stayed clear of Ernst. He had only one thing in mind, escape. He approached the former police officer with a scheme. He needed a partner and told Ernst that the best way to escape would be to take one of the warden's children as a hostage. Little did Johann know that he was talking to a man who was a stickler for law and order, a man who punished others for stealing a cigarette; in short, a real fanatic.

One day the two men were alone in the yard when Johann went over his plan with Ernst in detail. That was enough for the one-time cop, who decided that Johann was about to commit a crime and had to be punished. Without warning, Ernst clasped Johann's neck in his huge hands and squeezed the life from the unsuspecting prisoner. Guards ran to the scene of the attack, but it was too late. Johann was dead and Ernst was proud of what he had done.

When he stood trial for murder, Ernst made an impassioned plea for law and order in prison. He told the court he would do everything in his power to see that justice was served efficiently and swiftly.

Ernst Karl was found guilty of murder and given a life sentence. Since his incarceration for the second time at Stein, there has been a marked decrease in crime within the prison.

# Yvonne Kleinfelder
# OPPOSITES ATTRACT

It has been said that opposites attract.

Yvonne Kleinfelder was 39 years old back in 1975 when she met John Comer, who was three years her senior.

Yvonne was born and grew up in Chicago. Never one to aspire to higher education, she dropped out of high school and became a drifter, one of those rootless girls who jump from bar to bar, sometimes serving hooch to eager customers, sometimes performing as a stripper. In the 1960s, she was arrested three times for being an employee of a house of ill repute.

In the early seventies, Yvonne delved into the shady world of witchcraft, gravitating to a group known as the Foundation Faith of God. Sometimes she sold the organization's literature on the street corners of Chicago. Often she toiled in the group's kitchens.

Yvonne, who weighed around 125 pounds and stood only five feet, one inch tall, discovered that she had the extraordinary ability to dominate weaker personalities. Enter John Comer, a six-foot, 180-pound, good ol' southern boy. John had attended the University of Alabama, leaving that institution to work with a large manufacturer of pinball machines in Chicago. In time John was promoted to foreman. From all accounts, he was a regular fellow who got along well with employees and acquaintances.

Not long after the Satan worshipper and the pinball-machine foreman met in 1975, they became lovers. John moved into Yvonne's apartment at 745 West Gordon Terrace. Initially, their relationship might have been normal, but we do know that before many months had passed, John was showing fellow employees strange injuries to his body. One co-worker would later state that when John removed his shirt, he observed welts on his back that resembled ugly streaks left by a lash.

In 1978, John was admitted to hospital on three different occasions, suffering from injuries to his back and face. He was no longer the robust specimen he had been when he had first moved in with Yvonne. He was now 30 pounds lighter and was forever showing up with strange and unaccountable injuries, such as a cut ear or a rope burn around his neck. Toward 1980, John's acquaintances noticed that he was always broke, even though he was earning a good salary.

Friends guessed that John's girlfriend, Yvonne, had a strange hold over him and that it was she who was inflicting the damage to his body. It was difficult to fathom why John didn't simply walk away from his nemesis as his friends suggested, but he never did heed their advice.

At 9:30 a.m. on May 1, 1980, Shemia Brewer, a 24-year-old acquaintance of Yvonne's, was surprised when Yvonne called at her apartment in a rather agitated state. Yvonne told Shemia that her roommate was hurt and asked her to accompany her back to her apartment.

Shemia was astounded when she entered Yvonne's apartment and saw John under a table. His hands were tied to two of the table legs and his body was covered with a blanket. Yvonne told her that John had been burned while trying to extinguish a fire. Because Yvonne didn't have a phone, the pair made their way to a restaurant, where Shemia called police and an ambulance.

While the two women discussed the entire matter, Yvonne related that she had told a little white lie. John hadn't put out a fire at all. She had burned him by throwing boiling water on him. And why had she done such a thing? Yvonne explained that John had talked out loud and in general had misbehaved at a prayer meeting the previous Friday. He simply had to be punished.

Shemia returned to Yvonne's apartment while Yvonne

made a side trip to visit her pastor. In minutes, police and ambulance attendants were undoing the ropes which bound John's hands to the table legs and those which tied his ankles together. Although badly burned, John was alive. As the paramedics carried him away on a stretcher, he was able to say only three words, "Yvonne boiled me."

Police took a statement from Shemia. They couldn't believe that John Comer had been lying on his back in that horrible condition for six days since the previous Friday. Shemia was able to fill in the police with more details which had been related to her by Yvonne. Evidently, beating up on John was an almost daily occurrence. Yvonne had beaten John with a whip and had kicked him about the head. When he attempted to attack her, she had doused him with boiling water. Yvonne had confessed to Shemia that she had planned the fight and had boiled the water expressly to throw at John.

Detectives located Yvonne at the Church of the Good Shepherd (she wanted to cover all the bases), where her pastor, Brother Edward Bartus, turned her over to police. Yvonne was charged with aggravated battery. The day after her arrest, she was questioned by detectives. She had an amazing story to tell.

Yvonne and John had been living together for five years. As the years passed, John showed less and less respect for her. As a result, she gradually inflicted more severe punishment on him. She started off beating John with a belt. He never objected and never fought back. In time, Yvonne bought a whip and often flogged him until he bled. On the night she lost her cool, she waited until John was dressed only in his shorts. She boiled a large pot of water and liberally doused the shocked man with it.

In the midst of the interrogation, two unusual events took place. Yvonne abruptly asked the detectives to hold her hands and pray with her. While thus engaged, they received a message from the hospital that John Comer had died. Yvonne Kleinfelder was charged with his murder.

A post-mortem revealed a major flaw in Yvonne's story. The area of John's wrists that had been protected by rope had not been scalded, indicating that the boiling water had been thrown on him after he had been bound to the legs of the table. When faced with this information, Yvonne confessed that she had broken John's spirit. He would obey her every command. On the night of the tragedy, she had ordered him to take off his clothing. He complied like a child. She kicked and beat him unmercifully before tying him to the table. Just as the postmortem revealed, she doused him with the boiling water after he was tied to the table. John was left there to suffer for six days before Yvonne sought help. During that time she did a lot of praying to the devil.

On December 10, 1980, Yvonne Kleinfelder was found guilty of murdering John Comer. She was sentenced to 25 years' imprisonment. After serving 11 years in Illinois's Dixon Correctional Facility, she was paroled on January 14, 1992.

# Marc Lepine
# MISOGYNISTIC MADMAN

The Ruger Mini-14 semi-automatic .23-calibre rifle is manu-factured in the United States. Each year the Connecticut firm that produces the weapon exports about 2,000 units to Canada. The Ruger has several advantages over other weapons. It weighs only six and a half pounds, is extremely accurate and can hold 50 rounds of ammunition in its magazine. Each one of those 50 rounds contains enough explosive power to hurl a lead slug towards its target at over 3,000 feet per second. The Ruger is an excellent rifle for hunting deer and other game.

On December 6, 1989, Marc Lepine used the rifle to kill fourteen innocent young women in Montreal.

Marc was born Gamil Gharbi to a French-Canadian mother and an Algerian father, Rachid Liass Gharbi. His parents married in 1963, but separated in 1971 when Gamil was seven. There is evidence that the boy was abused by his father, whom he grew to detest. As a teenager he had his name legally changed to Marc Lepine, taking his mother's maiden name. He and his younger sister, Nadia, were raised by their mother.

In school, Marc gained the reputation of being a loner who achieved excellent grades. In reviewing Lepine's history, it appears that he made only half-hearted attempts at carving out a career. He enrolled in a junior college, but didn't complete his studies. He subsequently took a computer course and a course in chemistry, giving up on both these endeavours. He attempted to enlist in the Canadian army, but was turned down. The reason given by army personnel was "anti-social behaviour."

Along the way, Marc Lepine built up a hatred towards

women. He rationalized that the army had turned him down because they had relaxed their rules regarding female recruits. In Marc's mind, his rejection by the army was directly caused by women. This phenomenon was nothing new to Marc. His warped reasoning laid all his rejections at the feet of one group—women.

The hatred in Marc's psyche festered until the thought of women taking what he considered men's rightful place in society became his all-encompassing focus. Slowly, a plan took form. Marc began dropping in to a north-end Montreal gun shop. Store employees say he made the usual customer inquiries and didn't appear strange or different in any way. He applied for a firearms-acquisition certificate from the police department. Since he had no criminal record, the permit was duly issued. The Ruger semi-automatic was purchased for $600.

Fifteen days later, unemployed 25-year-old Marc Lepine had chosen his target. This was no spur-of-the-moment decision made by an impaired individual. Marc neither smoked, drank nor used drugs. He had targeted the University of Montreal's L'École Polytechnique. Marc believed that engineering, traditionally a male occupation, was being infiltrated by women, who he perceived to be his personal enemies.

On a cold December day shortly after 5 p.m., Marc Lepine walked into the university building carrying a parcel wrapped in a green garbage bag. Only two days remained before the Christmas vacation would commence and this building would be virtually deserted. Now it was teeming with students, many of them chatting about the imminent Christmas recess.

Marc made his way to the second floor, where he met Maryse Laganière, a 25-year-old employee of the university. Marc shot her dead on the spot. Within a moment, wearing a wry smile across his face, he entered Room 303. Speaking in French, he requested that the women be separated from the men. No one paid much attention. Maybe this was someone's idea of a prank.

Marc, likely sensing that he wasn't being taken seriously,

fired two shots into the ceiling. He shouted, "You're all a bunch of feminists and I hate feminists." He went on to instruct the men to leave the room. Over 40 male students walked out of Room 303. As one of the women attempted to reason with Marc, he opened fire with the deadly Ruger. In minutes, the classroom was transformed into an enclosure of carnage. The wounded moaned. Six young women lay dead in crumpled heaps. Operating with cool determination, Marc descended to the first floor, entered the school cafeteria and opened fire. In an instant, three women were murdered.

The gunman's mission was still not complete. He climbed two flights of stairs to the third floor. Students and professors alike were unaware that a man with a rifle was on a rampage. When Marc entered Room 311 and opened fire, the terror-stricken occupants desperately attempted to find some protection under desks and behind anything that would afford them cover. There was no escape. Marc sought them out. Leaping from desk to desk, he kept on shooting. Four more young women lay dead among the wounded.

Then, according to those close by, Marc uttered an expletive and shot himself in the head, killing himself instantly. In his wake he left 14 young women dead and 13 wounded. The carnage he wreaked that day took the lives of Geneviève Bergeron, 21; Hélène Colgan, 23; Nathalie Croteau, 23; Barbara Daigneault, 22; Anne-Marie Edward, 21; Maud Haviernick, 29; Maryse Leclair, 23; Annie St. Arsenault, 23; Barbara Marie Clueznick, 31; Maryse Laganière, 25; Anne-Marie Lemay, 27; Sonia Pelletier, 28; Michèle Richard, 21; and Annie Turcotte, 21.

With the exception of Albert Guay, who was instrumental in placing a bomb on an aircraft in 1949, killing all 23 aboard, the Lepine rampage was Canada's worst mass murder. The city of Montreal and the entire country were aghast at the cold-blooded killings.

As the bodies were removed and the wounded were attended to, no one could even guess at the killer's motive. But Lepine had taken care of that detail. He had left a three-page letter outlining his reasons for the mass killings. His last message to the world blamed feminists for all his personal ills and indeed the ills of the world. It also contained a chilling future hit list of 15 women who had achieved acclaim, many of them in occupations traditionally held by men.

And so it was left for survivors to bury their dead—young talented women with a lifetime ahead of them, whose lives were so tragically taken away while attending school.

At Notre Dame Basilica, Paul Cardinal Gregoire described the horror best as his voice rained down over nine of the coffins of the slain. "Fourteen youths were brutally mowed down in the beauty of their youth. In a few moments, a hopeless and vicious act of another young person was sufficient to destroy all the dreams and all the promises. Your daughters, your sisters, your friends, the future engineers over whom we weep, chose to be builders of society—in memory of them, in solidarity with them, you must strive to build a world of friendship. I ask God to give them peace."

Among the thousands overflowing the basilica were the mayor of Montreal, the premier of Quebec and the prime minister of Canada.

# Elmer Lord
# THEY FOUND THE KILLER IN THE TRUNK

Murderers never seem to learn that steamer trunks are cumbersome things designed to carry clothing rather than bodies.

Aletha Patterson stared down at the ominous trunk giving off the strange odour. It had been a busy day for Aletha. She had received notice months earlier that one of the rooming houses she managed, a four-storey brick structure on Third Street in Washington, D.C., was to be demolished to make room for a parking lot. All the tenants had been given notice weeks earlier. Some had decided to move to another building Aletha oversaw, while others had informed her that they would be seeking accommodation elsewhere.

With the help of superintendent Elmer Lord, Aletha supervised the professional movers who were busily loading furniture to be removed to the new building on Twelfth Street. Elmer, who hailed from England, was an efficient, conscientious employee.

It was the movers who brought the trunk to Aletha's attention. She couldn't remember having seen the trunk before. It bore no tags, but had the words "This Side Up" printed on the top in white chalk. Aletha called police. At around 11 a.m., September 12, 1952, two officers arrived at the rooming house. They pried open the trunk and peered inside. There reposed the decaying body of an adult male.

The body was immediately transferred to the morgue, where an autopsy was performed. The dead man had been about 60 years of age. He had received three powerful blows to the head with a blunt instrument. Any one of the three blows could have caused death. There was nothing in the man's pockets to assist in identifying him. He had been dead for about three months.

Detectives questioned Aletha and Elmer. Both stated that none of their roomers had disappeared, but there were a few who had not made the move with them. These roomers were traced and cleared of any complicity in the crime. Aletha and Elmer viewed the body, but claimed they couldn't identify the badly decomposed corpse. They were asked to search their memories for any unusual event which had occurred three months earlier.

Elmer remembered a Marine, accompanied by his wife, who had inquired about a room about three months earlier. The Marine had required a room for one night only and had lugged along a trunk. This type of inquiry may be considered odd in other cities, but in Washington, where servicemen and government employees are constantly on the move, it is rather routine. Elmer recalled the Marine's name, William Schmidt, because he once had an employee by that name. Schmidt had left his trunk in his room and had told Elmer that he would send around a mover for it the next day. That's the last Elmer saw of the Marine or his trunk.

Detectives elicited the assistance of the military. They were soon informed that there were 11 William Schmidts in the Marine Corps and that two lived near Washington. Both these men were checked, but were able to establish their innocence. Neither matched the description of the William Schmidt who had rented the room from Elmer.

The empty house on Third Street was thoroughly searched. Police found a locked closet door on the third floor. Someone had nailed the door shut with new nails and sealed it with putty. Investigating officers had the premonition that more bodies would be uncovered behind that door, but such was not the case. When the door was broken down, the closet was empty, but a sickening odour similar to the one that had emanated from the trunk was evident.

Detectives were stymied. Why would someone go to so much trouble to secure an empty closet? Had the closet provided a hiding place for a body which had been removed? If so, why nail it shut and seal it with putty?

Once more, Aletha and Elmer were asked to try to remember anything out of the ordinary. Aletha mentioned that the man who had previously held Elmer's job had left suddenly three months earlier. Retired pensioner Frank Moore had told Aletha he was going to Baltimore. Moore had left without turning in some of the rent money he had collected.

A short time after Moore's departure, Elmer Lord had asked Aletha for the man's job. She was more than happy to have the rather aristocratic Elmer look after the place and collect the rents.

Was it possible that Frank Moore had killed someone and left for parts unknown? Moore was checked out. He had never been in any trouble and had been an upstanding citizen, well liked by all. His sister, living in Arlington, Virginia, was appalled that anyone would think her brother would steal rent money, let alone commit a murder. She had another theory. Her brother had been in the habit of phoning her every week, but had stopped abruptly about three months earlier. Maybe, he was the victim rather than the murderer.

Frank Moore's sister viewed the body. She positively identified her brother. She even recognized his shirt, which she had given him as a gift.

The murder victim had been identified, but police were no closer to solving the crime. They were convinced that the killer had lived in the Third Street rooming house. Every roomer who had lived in the house three months earlier was found and questioned again without concrete results.

At a police meeting concerning the case, one detective theorized that if the killer had been an occupant of the house, he may have purchased the putty and nails from a nearby store. It was decided to canvass every store that sold such items within a 10-square-block area.

It took two days before weary detectives hit pay dirt. An alert store clerk remembered selling nails and putty to a man earlier that summer. She recalled the sale because the man had asked a lot of questions about the relative merits of plaster of Paris and putty. He had wanted to know which product cracked more easily. He had also purchased a small hatchet. She especially remembered the man because he spoke so elegantly, with an English accent.

Bingo! Why had no one thought of him before? Elmer Lord. The man in the case who appeared to be above suspicion.

Detectives obtained a search warrant before speeding over to Elmer's new quarters on Twelfth Street. Elmer greeted the familiar officers in his usual polite way. "Now what can I do for you?" The detectives' reply was a bit of a shock to staid Elmer, "You can tell us why you murdered Frank Moore. That would help a lot."

The flustered man attempted to bluff his way out of his predicament. He accused the officers of being lunatics to even suggest such a thing, but they produced a search warrant and proceeded to search Elmer's rooms. From a cardboard box, they extracted what was left of a can of putty, some new nails, a pair of bloodstained cotton gloves and a blood-caked hatchet.

Elmer slumped into a chair, sighing, "I'm not an accomplished killer, I guess." He went on to confess that on June 2, he had gone to Moore's room to join him for breakfast, which he did often. According to Elmer, the two men had argued over a trivial matter. During the argument, Frank had thrown a hatchet at him, but missed. Elmer threw it back at Moore, striking him in the head and killing him instantly. The police listened, but discounted much of Elmer's story, which was not compatible with the autopsy report.

Elmer went on to say that he had dragged Moore's body to the hall closet, where it remained for three months. He had nailed the door shut and had sealed it with putty when the odour became noticeable. He then asked for and got Moore's job. In September, when Aletha informed him that they had to move to another house, he was beside himself with worry. All he could think of was that body in the closet. By chance, he had found an old trunk in the basement. Being superintendent of the building, he knew the times when he wouldn't be seen or disturbed. He had lugged the trunk to the closet, had broken open the door and had placed the body inside. Later, the trunk was put in the hall to be moved by professional movers.

Elmer had nailed back the closet door and sealed all cracks with putty, hoping that this would keep the odour in the closet. Unfortunately for him, the movers became suspicious of the trunk. He had planned on depositing it in the basement of his new home. Had he succeeded, his crime might never have been discovered.

On March 19, 1953, Elmer Lord stood trial for the murder of Frank Moore. He insisted that the killing was not premeditated and evidently the jury believed him. He was found guilty of second-degree murder and sentenced to 7 to 21 years' imprisonment. He has long since been paroled.

# Grace Lusk
# LOVE TRIANGLE

Let me introduce you to Grace Lusk. You will like her. Everyone did in Waukesha, Wisconsin.

Amazing Grace was an attractive schoolteacher who, in many ways, was perfect. She was intelligent, highly educated, a snappy dresser in the style of 1913 and a real looker. She also had the figure to go with her many admirable attributes. There was one thing though. Nearing 30 years of age, our Grace lacked an experience which many girls of far more tender years have taken part in and, yes, even enjoyed. You see, Grace Lusk was a virgin.

Grace was introduced to 50-year-old Dr. David Roberts at a dinner party. The veterinarian, in partnership with L.D. Blott, owned the David Roberts Veterinary Co., a flourishing local business whose main products were a line of medical remedies for cattle in distress. In addition, the doctor owned a breeding farm and a dairy. He also owned Mrs. Roberts. No one had a bad word to say about Mrs. Roberts. Nobody ever does. But let's get back to Grace and Dr. Dave.

The virginal schoolteacher found the handsome doctor nigh on irresistible. One day she required some information about various cattle breeds to impart to her students. She found the doctor most accommodating in this regard. That's how it started—a gently squeezed hand—a stolen kiss, and then that most intimate of all acts took place. I mean, over and over again.

Grace was thrilled and excited with this new sensual experience which had eluded her all of her 30 years. Dave told her he loved her dearly. It would be only a matter of time before he would divorce his wife, marry her and they would live happily ever after. But that time never seemed to roll around.

Dave the Knave was burning the candle at both ends, so to speak. He had no intention of leaving his wife. After all, the Roberts family was well respected. Mrs. Roberts was a wheel down at the church. No, a man of his looks, charm and sexual prowess would service both women; something like the stallions at his breeding farm.

But Grace had been put off for too long. When the sizzling affair was in its fourth year, she decided to have it out with Dave. One evening, while comfortably ensconced in a hotel room, she confronted him, stating that he had to tell his wife, Mary, of their love. Grace wanted to know then and there if she had been deceived. She explained that first her education and then her teaching career had occupied all her time and thoughts until she'd met him. Now her life had been terribly disrupted. If he didn't truly love her, she wanted to know now. If he did love her as he claimed, it was only fair to them all that he inform his wife of the truth and ask for a divorce.

Can't you just see Dave wiping the perspiration off his forehead? Once more, he told Grace he would tell his wife soon. Not good enough, said Grace. She pulled a revolver out of her purse and commanded Dave to put his hand on a Gideon bible and swear he would tell his wife of their love that very night. Dave's hand couldn't wait to spread-eagle on that bible.

Moments later, the lovers embraced and did what lovers do. Now in a somewhat better mood, Grace accepted Dave's latest proposition, namely, that he would tell his wife about them by June 15.

Dr. Dave Roberts had a problem. He had to get rid of Grace, but just how was another matter. Grace moved things along a bit when she wrote a letter to Mary Roberts, insinuating that Mary's husband would be approaching her shortly over a delicate subject involving Grace and the good doctor. Mrs. Roberts received the letter and was somewhat puzzled. She had never in her wildest imagination suspected that her husband had been unfaithful. She confronted Dave, who passed off the letter as being from a girl who was making a bit of a nuisance of herself.

Undaunted, Grace wrote another letter, a much more explicit letter. This time, Mary Roberts had to take notice. She insisted on meeting with this girl whom she thought was chasing her husband. Dave could no longer persuade her that their relationship was nothing more than an infatuation.

On June 21, 1917, Mary Roberts took the bull by the horns and visited Grace at her rooming house. The adversaries stood face-to-face, eyeball-to-eyeball. Mary's opening gambit was simple and to the point. She wanted the younger woman to withdraw. Grace countered with the claim that Dave truly loved her and that should be the deciding factor.

Despite Mary's pious nature, she let fly some very unladylike remarks. Regaining her composure, she suggested that the proof of the pudding is in the eating. She called Dave at home and told him to get right over there and repeat his words about Grace being a nuisance.

As had become his habit, Dave rubbed the perspiration from his forehead. He knew he had to do something. He picked up his business partner, L.D. Blott, and drove over to Grace's place. As they approached, they heard the loud reports of two shots. Dave, scared out of his wits, told Blott to go and see what was happening. Blott, also a tad apprehensive, peeked in through a window. There, on the floor, was Mary Roberts with two bullets in her side. Blott ran back to Dave, who quickly called a doctor and police. Dr. Davies was the first to arrive at the scene. He examined Mary Roberts and declared that she was dead.

The doctor, completely occupied with the dead woman at his feet, looked up to see Grace at the top of the stairs. Not quite grasping the situation, Dr. Davies told Grace that Mrs. Roberts was dead. It was only then that he noticed the trickle of blood seeping from Grace's left breast. Later, he would learn that the wound was self-inflicted, but at the time the doctor had other problems.

Grace, who he now figured had killed Mrs. Roberts and turned the weapon on herself, was loosely holding a revolver in her right hand. He made a gesture forward, as if to approach Grace, but stopped abruptly when she commanded, "If you come up, I'll shoot."

Dr. Davies talked quietly to Grace, attempting to calm her down. He succeeded somewhat as Grace rambled on about her reasons for the shooting. She related that Dave had told her repeatedly that he loved her only and how he had sworn on a bible that he would tell his wife everything by June 15. She even reminded Dr. Davies that it was the twenty-first, making Dave delinquent by six days. Grace said that she had given Dave an out. She had told him that if he really didn't love her, he could call off the whole thing. The cad had sworn that she was his true love and that he had no feelings for his wife.

At the conclusion of her yarn, Grace inquired of the doctor as to the location of the heart. Dr. Davies pointed to the area. Grace then turned and hurried to her bedroom. The doctor heard a shot and rushed to her side. Whatever qualities Grace possessed, accuracy was not one of them. She had missed killing herself for the second time that evening.

The semiconscious Grace was removed on a stretcher. She was able to say, "I am so strange. I love him still."

The love triangle and its tragic conclusion was the most exciting event ever to take place in Waukesha. People took sides. Some felt that Grace deserved the worst for killing churchgoing Mary Roberts, and even expressed disappointment at Grace's poor aim. Others felt that Dave Roberts was the culprit of the entire piece.

Grace stood trial for the murder of Mary Roberts. She was found guilty of murder in the second degree. When the foreman of the jury read out the verdict, Grace didn't swoon or burst into tears. She sprang from her seat and clutched the neck of the prosecuting attorney until court officials pried her hands from his neck. She had to be forcibly removed from the courtroom.

Grace was sentenced to 19 years' hard labour at the

Wisconsin State Prison at Waupun, with the stipulation that every June 21 be spent in solitary confinement.

In January 1923, after serving five years of her sentence, Grace Lusk received a pardon from Wisconsin governor John J. Blaine. She moved to a southern state where she died of natural causes in 1930. As for Dr. David Roberts, he remarried and lived out the rest of his days in relative comfort and contentment.

# Lee Roy Martin
# TERROR IN A SMALL TOWN

No one wanted to listen to Roger Dedmond. It was one of those cases where everyone was convinced he'd killed his wife.

Roger's strange saga began on March 1, 1967, when he and his wife were spending an evening in a nightclub near the town of Gaffney, South Carolina. Twenty-eight-year-old Roger was downing whiskey straight up with beer chasers. He and his wife, Ann Lucille, began quarrelling, which wasn't unusual. It seemed every time the young couple had a few drinks they would sort of agree to disagree.

Ann Lucille became so angry that, at one point, she flailed out at Roger and scratched his face. As the evening wore on, the couple reconciled and decided to get a bite to eat. They drove to a doughnut shop. Roger left his vehicle, purchased doughnuts and coffee and returned to find that his wife had driven off in the car. This might cause the average husband some concern, but Ann Lucille often pulled such capers, especially when she was a bit tipsy or angry or both.

Next morning, Roger Dedmond was informed that his wife had been murdered. Her body had been found in the centre of the highway, between the towns of Union, South Carolina, and Spindale, North Carolina. Roger was picked up as the logical suspect and tried for the murder of his wife.

He stuck to his story of her disappearance at the doughnut shop. It was an unlikely tale, especially since police officers swore that Roger had confessed his guilt to them when he was taken into custody. He admitted that he had argued with Ann Lucille and that she had scratched him, but swore that he had had nothing to do with her death. The jury preferred to believe the police and found Roger Dedmond guilty of manslaughter. He was sentenced to 18 years' imprisonment. Roger was hustled off to the Union County Prison Camp and that, to all intents and purposes, was that.

Two months passed. On February 8, 1968, Bill Gibbons, the managing editor of the local newspaper, the *Gaffney Ledger*, received a most unusual phone call. The caller assured Gibbons that this was not a crank call. He gave explicit instructions, informing the startled newsman where two female bodies could be found. He also stated that he was the killer of Ann Lucille Dedmond. Then the caller hung up.

Gibbons believed that the man was a crank, but stranger things have happened. He called the local sheriff and together they followed the phantom caller's instructions. Sure enough, near a bridge over People's Creek, just as the caller had said, lay the body of a nude female. The body was quickly identified as that of Nancy Parris, a 26-year-old housewife who had been reported missing while walking her poodle the previous day. The back of the body bore signs of having been burned by cigarettes. An autopsy revealed strangulation to be the cause of death.

Additional officers were requested to trace the second body. In the exact location indicated by the caller, police found the nude body of 14-year-old Nancy Rhinehart. She too bore cigarette burns and she too had been strangled. Nancy had been reported missing by her mother 10 days earlier. Both victims had been murdered within 24 hours of the time they had been found. Investigators theorized that Nancy Rhinehart had been held captive for 10 days before being killed.

The news that two female bodies had been found in the Gaffney area spread terror throughout Union County. There was also the distinct possibility that the same man had killed Ann Lucille Dedmond.

Was some maniac on a killing spree and was he now playing a macabre game? Most serial killers distance themselves from their victims and make every effort to escape detection, but there have been exceptions. David Berkowitz, also known

144

as Son of Sam, wrote to a newspaper. Jack the Ripper wrote letters to the police. Did their counterpart in peaceful Gaffney demand recognition for his kills? Had he not made the phone call to the newspaper, the bodies of his two latest victims might never have been found.

Citizens in the area bought locks and guns. In the two days after the bodies were discovered, the main hardware store in Gaffney sold 200 guns, all they had in stock. Five days later, on February 13, 1968, 15-year-old Opal Buckson was walking the quarter mile from her home to the bus stop to catch her lift to school in Gaffney. Her brother and sister, Gracie, had not been as fast as Opal in completing their chores, and as a result trailed along behind their sister.

It was Gracie who noticed the man who grabbed Opal and forced her into the trunk of his blue sedan. Gracie was about 50 yards away. She couldn't believe her eyes. Opal screamed and so did Gracie, but the man managed to slam his trunk closed and drove away with the teenage schoolgirl. Gracie's brother ran home and told his father what had happened.

Emanual Buckson ran down the road and found his daughter's schoolbooks spread across the highway. He also recovered one of Opal's shoes. Investigators interviewed all the principals involved and concluded that this latest abduction was most probably connected to the man who had committed the two previous murders.

Police revealed to the public that Bill Gibbons had received another call from the alleged killer on the day before Opal's kidnapping. Gibbons was certain it was the same voice that had directed him to the two bodies. This time the mystery caller said, "If they don't catch me, there will be more deaths." He also emphatically stated again that he was the killer of Ann Lucille Dedmond. When Gibbons attempted to talk the man into giving himself up, the caller responded, "It's no use. I'm psycho and I'd get the chair. They'll have to shoot me like the dog I am. The only reason I'm telling you all this is to get that other boy out of prison. He's serving my sentence."

Gibbons kept the man on the line. He inquired about the

fate of Nancy Parris's poodle. The caller claimed he had killed the dog, but not at the location where the body had been found. He had killed Nancy and her poodle in one location, but had moved her body. He would not say where the dog could be located because he had left tire tracks there that could be traced to him.

During the same call, the killer told Gibbons how he had stopped Ann Lucille Dedmond as she drove erratically down the road. He had been trailing the Dedmonds from the time they had left the nightclub. He also described what she had been wearing and gave several details only the killer could know. Once detectives heard Gibbons's story, there was no doubt whatever that an innocent man was in prison serving time for a crime he had not committed.

On February 15, two days after Opal's kidnapping, hundreds of citizens of Union County were searching for the girl. Two of the searchers, Theodore Lang and Frank Henders, were cruising the back roads of the county looking for anything suspicious. They spotted a man standing beside a vehicle. The stranger quickly drove away. Lang and Henders thought he was behaving suspiciously and managed to obtain the licence number of the vehicle. They passed along the information to the sheriff's office.

That same day, detectives drove out to the spot where Lang and Henders had observed the man standing beside his car. One of the officers noted a quantity of fresh pine needles protruding from under a dead log. To the trained officer, the scene didn't look natural. Debris and branches were removed, uncovering the bare legs of Opal Buckson. Her body bore the telltale cigarette burns. Opal, like the other victims, had been strangled.

By the time Opal's body was found, the licence number of the suspect's vehicle had been checked. The car belonged to a local man, Lee Roy Martin, a 30-year-old textile worker. Martin seemed to be an unlikely serial killer. He was a steady, hard-working family man, whose wife refused to believe that her husband was anything but what he appeared to be. But Lee

Roy Martin heard voices. He claimed it wasn't him who had killed the four women, but another Lee Roy. Martin led police to the victims' clothing and to the corpse of Nancy Parris's poodle. He was found guilty of four counts of murder and received four life sentences. After serving three years in prison, he was murdered by a fellow inmate.

Roger Dedmond was released from prison after serving one year. Today, he is in the construction business in North Carolina.

# Marcus Marymont
# TORRID AFFAIR LED TO MURDER

Marcus Marymont had always wanted a military career. As a teenager he was a member of the California National Guard. In 1937, he joined the U.S. Army and later transferred to the air force.

Mark was born in Oakland, California, the product of an average home. He did well in school and was never in any trouble. Mark's decision to make the military a lifelong career appeared to be a wise one. He served in the United States, Japan and Korea before being transferred to the U.S. air force base in Scunthorpe, England.

Mark's career in the service was distinguished. In all, he was the recipient of 13 medals, the most notable being the Soldiers Medal. In 1941, while serving in Alaska, Mark had saved a man from a burning ship without regard for his own safety. Along the way, he married, had three children and received several promotions before achieving the rank of master sergeant.

In 1956, we find Master Sergeant Marcus Marymont, a family man approaching middle age, stationed in England with his stable, rewarding career well established. Wouldn't you just know it, Mark walked into a shop in Maidenhead one day and met Mrs. Cynthia Taylor. Cynthia was a cute 23-year-old with a charming smile and a gorgeous figure.

There stood the sarge, resplendent in his crisp uniform, fit as a fiddle. Thoughts of his 43-year-old wife, Mary, and the three young ones at home didn't enter his head. Whatever chemistry takes place between members of the opposite sex boiled and seethed within Mark and Cynthia on that fateful day. As luck would have it, Cynthia was separated from her husband.

Let me spare you the titillating details. Suffice it to say, Mark, who was 37 when he met Cynthia, should have known better. Within weeks, they were lovers. The opportunities for lovemaking posed something of a problem. After all, Mary and the three kids lived close to the base. Despite this inconvenience, Mark and Cynthia never let two weeks pass without bedding down, either at her digs or at a convenient hotel.

We all know that such a relationship cannot last forever. In the normal course of human endeavour, something usually has to give. The lovers managed to continue their affair for two years before things came to an abrupt end.

On June 9, 1958, Mary Marymont died in hospital. A little over a month later, Mark was charged with her murder. Being a member of the U.S. Armed Forces, he was tried by a U.S. general court martial at Denham, England. It was alleged that he had poisoned his wife with arsenic because he was in love with Cynthia Taylor.

A doctor testified that Mary had been brought to the hospital in critical condition. Mark had told the doctor that his wife had taken ill at about 9 p.m. the previous evening. He had fetched her some medicine from the hospital, but in the morning she was much worse and he had her removed to hospital. Another doctor who had attended Mary before she died was aware that she had been sick off and on for the past year. He suspected that she had been poisoned, but when he mentioned it to another doctor, he was told, "You have been reading too many magazines."

After Mary's death, the doctor spoke to Mark about an autopsy. Initially, he agreed, but later said that in deference to his children he didn't want his wife's body disfigured. Nevertheless, an autopsy was performed. It indicated that Mary had received a large dose of arsenic within 24 hours of her death, as well as quantities of arsenic a month or two before her death. Marcus was arrested and charged with her murder.

Renowned pathologist Dr. Francis Camps was called as an expert witness at the trial. He confirmed that there was no doubt whatever that Mrs. Marymont's death had been caused by arsenic poisoning.

At this stage of the trial, the prosecution had firmly established the cause of death. They then went about proving that the accused had had access to arsenic. Two civilian cleaners at the air force base testified that about a month before the murder, they had seen a master sergeant in the base's chemical lab, where arsenic was kept. According to the cleaners, the sergeant had said, "There's a lot of chemicals on these shelves. There's even arsenic." The cleaners had agreed. The sergeant inquired, "Don't they lock this stuff up?" The cleaners told him that they didn't. They identified the sergeant as Mark Marymont.

A pharmacist in Maidenhead, Bernard Sampson, testified that on May 23, only weeks before Mary Marymont's demise, Mark had attempted to purchase arsenic from him. When Sampson told the sergeant that he had to have a police form made out before he could sell Marymont the poison, the sergeant thanked him and left the shop.

Brick by brick, the prosecution was building a formidable case, but the juicy motive for murder was left for the principals to reveal from the witness box. Mark took the stand and admitted to his prolonged affair with Cynthia. He told the court that he had met and made love to her at every opportunity.

Whatever else Mark said, nothing had the impact of his statement that he had left his wife and children over the Christmas season of 1957 to spend it shacked up with Cynthia. Honestly, folks, you just don't do that. But wait, there was more. After Mary had gone to her great reward, Mark had waited only four days before rushing to the ever-loving arms of Cynthia Taylor. For shame!

Sixty-nine letters written by Cynthia to Mark were introduced into evidence. They smouldered with expressions of undying love. These letters had been found in Mark's desk at the air force base. A prosecution lawyer made much of the fact that Mark hadn't destroyed them. He theorized that the accused had had no reason to destroy the letters because he had firmly believed he would never be accused of murder.

In summing up, the prosecution further theorized that Mark had been feeding arsenic to his wife for months to establish the fact that she was in ill health. On June 9, he had gone to the hospital to procure medicine, into which he had mixed a fatal dose of arsenic.

It must be pointed out that Cynthia Taylor did not know Mark was a married man. They had often talked about marriage, but not too seriously, because her estranged husband wouldn't grant her a divorce. She claimed that Mark had promised to adopt her baby son, Chris, when they did marry.

Defence attorneys acknowledged Mark's affair with Cynthia, but presented another theory in regard to Mary's death. They produced a witness, Marion Conway, the wife of another master sergeant. She swore that Mary had confided in her that she was aware of her husband's affair. Mrs. Conway told the court, "She was under a terrific emotional pressure because, she said, she minded terribly to think of her husband making love to someone else, then coming home and making love to her. She felt she almost couldn't stand it." In this way, defence counsel put forth the theory that Mary Marymont had become despondent and had committed suicide.

Mark admitted to having chatted with the cleaners in the chemical lab, but surely that was not proof of guilt. He swore he had never been in Bernard Sampson's pharmacy and claimed that Sampson must be mistaken. Under cross-examination, the pharmacist admitted that the sergeant had not been in his shop more than 10 seconds.

In the end, Sergeant Marymont was found guilty. He stood at attention and heard the sentence read by Colonel Albert Snider: "It is my duty as President of this Court to inform you that the Court in closed session and upon secret written ballots, three fourths of the members present concurring, sentences you to be dishonorably discharged, forfeit all pay and allowances and be confined to hard labour for the term of your natural life." Master Sergeant Marcus Marymont was returned to the United States and incarcerated at Fort Leavenworth Prison to serve his sentence.

# Donald Mason
# PROPER YOUNG MAN KILLED HIS WIFE

Donald Mason was a proper young man raised in a proper religious family. Smoking, drinking and cursing were what other boys did, not Don. The Bible was the word of God and the Good Book was the most influential factor in his life. Sex before marriage was unthinkable.

Don met Ruth Ragatz, a stunning blond, at a church convention. Don was smitten, but there was a complication. Ruth was seeing another boy. However, she and Don continued to see each other at church functions until finally Ruth terminated her relationship with Don's rival. The pair married in July 1983.

The honeymoon preyed on Don's mind. Although he had been a virgin, he discovered that Ruth was not. The thought of his wife in bed with another man festered in his mind. He couldn't get it out of his head. As the months wore on, he began to worry that since Ruth had not been chaste before their marriage, how could he be sure she had been faithful since their wedding day.

Three years of doubts and suspicions passed. Don thought of divorce, but with his religious background that was out of the question. There was another way; he would murder his wife. (Apparently, his religious background didn't hinder that decision.) Lesser men than he had committed murder and avoided detection. Murder was definitely the answer to his dilemma. He would plan the details and he would kill his wife. It would be the perfect murder.

In October 1986, Don took out a life insurance policy for $100,000 and one on Ruth's life for the same amount. The scheme would not only be perfect, it would pay handsomely as well.

Don was 27 years old. He and Ruth lived in a trailer park in Plattekill, New York. Both worked at the AT&T complex in Ramapo. They were well liked, conscientious employees. No one knew what dark thoughts Don Mason harboured in his warped mind.

In March 1987, Don underwent a hernia operation and was off work for a couple of weeks. What an opportune time to put his well-thought-out plan into action. He would use a belt to strangle Ruth. No gun, no knife, no discernible murder weapon. How clever, Don thought. It would look like a robbery with sexual assault as an afterthought. He would receive sympathy from friends and co-workers, even some police officers, whom he knew personally.

On Tuesday, March 24, after Ruth came home from work, Don playfully told her, "Turn around and close your eyes." Ruth may have thought she was about to be given an unexpected present. When she turned her back, he quickly looped a belt around her neck and pulled tight. Ruth, eyes bulging, managed to turn around. She scratched at Don's face, but it was no use. He pulled tighter until Ruth stopped breathing.

Don bent over his wife and ripped jewellery from her body. Then he dragged her out to her car. It was tough sledding. After all, Don had recently had a hernia operation and he didn't want to dislodge his stitches. Soon, he was speeding along the thruway. As far as any onlooker was concerned, it seemed as if Ruth was catching a few winks in the passenger seat. At the toll booths, no one gave them a second glance.

Don pulled into the Caldor Shopping Centre in Ramapo and drove up beside a trash-disposal unit behind the Shop-Rite Supermarket back door. He dragged his wife's body out of the car. Don realized one thing had gone wrong, but there was nothing he could do about that now. Ruth had managed to scratch his face. Systematically, Don went about breaking Ruth's fingernails, knowing that it was his flesh under those nails. It was a tedious task and dangerous, too. Someone could walk out of the Shop-Rite at any moment. Don quit breaking the nails. He ripped at Ruth's blouse and tore away her brassiere. Then he pulled down her pantyhose. Working frantically now, he removed her coat and purse before driving away.

It had all gone smoothly. Don drove Ruth's car to the parking lot of a King Kullen Supermarket in Suffern, where he transferred to a rented car he had previously placed there. As he approached his home at the trailer park, he threw away Ruth's coat and purse along with the belt he had used to kill her.

Don washed his hands and face. It was time to prepare a hot meal for Ruth. After all, since he was recuperating from his hernia operation, he had been in the habit of preparing the evening meal. It was the least he could do.

That evening, Don called a friend, Bob Parks. Don was concerned. Ruth hadn't come home from work. He and Bob drove around looking for Ruth's Chevy Sprint, but couldn't locate it. The folks at AT&T told him she had left the facility at 5:30 p.m. Don called the police, but they said they couldn't do anything for 24 hours.

Next morning, Don Mason was beside himself with worry. Tearfully, he reported his wife missing to the Ramapo police. Within an hour a truck driver making a delivery to the Shop-Rite Supermarket came across the body of Ruth Mason. As soon as she was identified by an AT&T employee, a detective informed Don that his wife had been murdered. He burst into tears.

That night, Ruth's car was found. Nothing of importance was discovered in the vehicle, but its location puzzled investigators. Who would dump a body where it could be found at any moment and then abandon the victim's car some miles away? It appeared to investigators that the killer would have to have had a second car in order to get away from the shopping centre where Ruth's Chevy was found. It just didn't add up. Was rape the motive or was it robbery, or as sometimes happens, a combination of both? Why take the dead woman's purse? Where had she been attacked?

Don Mason, understandably distraught, was requested to visit the Ramapo police station to assist police. Detectives couldn't help noticing the scratch on his face, but didn't comment about it at the time. An autopsy performed that same day indicated that Ruth had not been raped. Death was attributed to asphyxiation due to ligature strangulation. It was believed that the murder weapon was something smooth, like a belt.

One of the detectives mentioned that Don would be wise to have the doctor who had just performed the autopsy take a look at that nasty scratch on his face. Don agreed. The doctor treated the scratch and informed detectives that it had been made by a fingernail and was surrounded by cosmetic makeup. Don told police he didn't remember how he had received the scratch, but admitted that he had applied makeup so the scratch wouldn't be so noticeable.

Detectives believed that Don Mason had killed his wife. They asked him to agree to a polygraph test and were surprised when he quickly acquiesced.

While waiting for arrangements for the test to be finalized, one of the detectives informed Don that his version of his wife's disappearance didn't make sense. Don surprised those present by blurting out, "I killed her. I did it in our trailer as soon as she came home from work." He went on to tell of his obsession that his wife was unfaithful. The thought had eaten away at his mind until he had turned to murder to solve his problem. He told detectives that he had hidden his wife's jewellery and a $100,000 life insurance policy under his bed.

Don wondered out loud whether he would have gotten away with murder had Ruth not scratched him. No one told him that his credit card had already been traced to the agency where he had rented the getaway car.

Don Mason pleaded guilty to his wife's murder. He was sentenced to a term of 22 years to life in prison.

# Mary Kay McKinley
# LITTLE SISTERS

It's sort of an unwritten law and is in decidedly poor taste to make love to two sisters at the same time. John Cassidy of the western Pennsylvania town of Monongahela didn't believe in written or unwritten laws. He had known Mary Kay and Bonnie McKinley all their lives. While they were still in their early teens, he had had intercourse with both sisters. John married Mary Kay when she turned 17.

Despite the wedding, complete with whiskey and dainty sandwiches, John simply couldn't get Bonnie out of his mind. Darn it all, what's so wrong about a man bedding down with two women? The more he thought about it, the more it made sense. John sat Mary Kay and Bonnie down and told them his plan. He would stay legally married to Mary Kay, but wanted Bonnie to move into their home and share their bed. Well, son of a gun, the girls didn't think the idea half-bad. Just as they had shared treats as little girls, they would now share a husband. Bonnie moved in and everyone was as happy as a lark.

Both sisters proceeded to have children. Mary Kay had five and Bonnie, four. John, the rascal, fathered an additional child by a third woman who doesn't enter our racy tale other than to provide a tenth child to the Cassidy household. It got so crowded around the house that John purchased a second home, in which he installed Bonnie and their four offspring. John split his lovemaking between the two homes on a time-sharing basis. This rather pleasant arrangement continued for 12 years and might have gone on indefinitely, except for one thing. John committed suicide.

On February 12, 1991, the sisters and the 10 children were

saddened by this untimely circumstance. Mary Kay found John with half his head blown off. Evidently he had placed the barrel of a shotgun under his chin and fired away. Both wives, er... sisters, attended the funeral, as did all 10 children. Everyone wept.

The local coroner officially labelled the death as suicide, although he was puzzled after receiving an anonymous call from a woman who insisted John's demise was something more than suicide. Without evidence to the contrary, the coroner stuck to his original cause of death.

A month after the funeral, Bonnie drove to the closest state police office in Belle Vernon with a story to tell. It was she who had called the coroner. She had something on her mind and had to tell someone. Bonnie said that some time before John's death, he and she had purchased a telephone tape recorder and had installed it on his own line in the basement of his and Mary Kay's home. John had told her that he suspected that his 29-year-old wife was having an affair with a 17-year-old local boy, David Bowers. Bonnie passed over the tape, which was played then and there. It was a conversation between young Bowers and Mary Kay in which they expressed undying love for each other and plotted to kill John.

The police well realized that under Pennsylvania law recorded conversations cannot be used as evidence, yet they had no intention of letting a murderer go unpunished. They asked Mary Kay to drive over to the police station. Once there, officers explained the situation to her and played a couple of minutes of the tape. Mary Kay burst into tears and confessed to her husband's murder.

According to Mary Kay, she had often been abused by John, particularly when he was in his cups. On the night of the murder, he had been drunk and had passed out on a couch in the living room. Mary Kay believed that she had only one chance at happiness and that was to kill her abusive husband and latch on to her 17-year-old lover. She would begin a new life. Mary Kay thought of the ramifications, but all things considered, decided to go through with the murder. David had agreed that it was the only sensible thing to do and had instructed her on how to murder her husband.

Mary Kay pulled the trigger. Then she did what many self-respecting killers have done before her. She dialled 911. Based on Mary Kay's story, she and David Bowers were arrested.

The district attorney had a problem. In custody were two individuals who had planned and carried out a cold-blooded murder, yet the prosecution's case was flimsy because the tape recording couldn't be used as evidence. Since the subsequent confession had been given based on the few minutes the tape had been played for the accused, it too might very well be inadmissible as evidence.

It was plea-bargaining time. In the case of Mary Kay, the D.A. agreed that in return for a guilty plea, the charge would be reduced from first-degree murder to third-degree, which carried only a 5- to 10-year prison sentence. In addition, Mary Kay agreed to testify against David Bowers.

She revealed that her romance with David began years before when he used to call early in the morning to go hunting with her husband. A little kiss led to a little hug and a little hug led all the way to bed or a convenient haymow. Mary Kay stated that she never had intercourse with David in her home. She was too afraid of John, and besides, those children were underfoot all the time.

And why did Bonnie turn in her sister? Well, according to Bonnie, Mary Kay had no right to knock off John. After all, he was her man too, and she didn't have a spare like David waiting in the wings to take up the slack, so to speak.

In the end, Mary Kay was found guilty and received the agreed-upon sentence of 5 to 10 years' imprisonment. David Bowers stood trial in January 1993. Mary Kay testified that he had instructed her on how to murder her husband. He had told her the best time to do it would be when John passed out. He allegedly had even told her how to place the shotgun to make it look like suicide.

Despite the damaging testimony given by David's former lover, the Pennsylvania jury chose to believe that the older woman had been the driving force behind the love affair and the murder plot. David Bowers was found not guilty.

David walked. Mary Kay went to jail. Her children now live with their maternal grandfather. Bonnie lives with her brood and no doubt pines for the good old days when she had half a husband.

# The Menendez Brothers
# THE AMERICAN DREAM SHATTERED

On the night of August 20, 1989, around 10 p.m., Jose and Kitty Menendez sat watching TV, eating vanilla ice cream and strawberries in the family room of their $5-million home in Beverly Hills, California. Two intruders lugging 12-gauge Mossberg shotguns walked into the room through open French doors. One raised his shotgun and fired directly into the back of Jose's head.

It is believed that Kitty rose from the sofa and, for a split second, may have seen her attacker. A shotgun blast tore into her face. The killers stood there amidst the blood and human tissue. They continued to fire shot after shot into the two bodies. Jose was struck six times. Kitty received 10 blasts. Their bodies were literally blown to pieces. The two killers gathered up the 16 casings from the pools of blood on the floor. Officials later stated there was nothing left of the victims' faces to distinguish them as human beings.

Who were these people whose bodies lay in pieces amidst the opulence of their Beverly Hills mansion?

Jose Menendez was born in Cuba in 1944. When Fidel Castro came to power, the affluent Menendez family sent their 16-year-old son to the United States to live with a relative. Jose, an excellent swimmer, entered high school in Hazelton, Pennsylvania, where he soon earned an athletic scholarship to Southern Illinois University. While attending university, the ambitious young Cuban met and fell in love with beauty queen Mary Louise Anderson, known to everyone as Kitty. Kitty and Jose married. Jose was 19, Kitty, 21.

The young couple moved to New York, where Jose

completed his education at Queens College. To make ends meet, he held several jobs, including washing dishes in a restaurant. He obtained his first real job with Lyons Container Services. In three years, he was president of the company. Jose moved from executive position to executive position, always advancing and always excelling. By the age of 35, he had become chief operating officer of RCA/Ariola at an annual salary of $500,000.

Jose and Kitty had two strapping sons, Lyle and Erik, a pleasant home in Princeton, New Jersey, and all the trappings of wealth and success. The two boys exhibited the athletic skills inherited from their parents. Tennis became their major sport. Jose saw to it that both boys received private instruction.

In 1986, Jose retired from RCA, walking away with a cool $1 million. He was hired to reverse the sagging fortunes of International Video Entertainment Inc. at the whopping salary of $1 million a year. His new position required the family to move to Los Angeles, the centre of the entertainment industry.

Jose purchased a new home in Calabasas. Kitty busied herself remodelling the house. Erik attended high school, where he was a star on the tennis team. Lyle was accepted at Princeton University, where he too excelled at tennis. Jose characteristically plunged himself into his new job. He was extremely successful at turning around a company that had lost $19 million the previous year into a cash cow producing a $20-million profit two years later.

On the surface, the family appeared to have attained the American dream. But there were bumps. At Princeton, Lyle was caught copying a classmate's assignment paper and was summarily suspended from university. He returned home. His parents were deeply hurt by their son's suspension.

The offspring of the wealthy, born into material riches, often become bored with their lives. So it was with Erik and Lyle. Fast cars and tennis weren't enough. To break the monotony, they burglarized homes together with other wealthy boys, not for the loot, but for the thrill. Erik confessed to being involved in a burglary. Many believe Lyle was also involved. Jose used his influence and managed to have Lyle exonerated, while Erik was put on probation. The court ordered both boys to undergo psychological counselling. Their mother set them up with psychologist Jerome Oziel.

The disgrace of their sons' actions was too much for Jose and Kitty. They decided to move up to Beverly Hills, to the never-never land of the very rich. Jose purchased a $5-million Spanish estate complete with swimming pool and tennis court on North Elm Drive. The family had arrived in every sense of the word.

Lyle, now 21, was accepted back at Princeton, but things didn't go well at university. He often argued with lecturers and other students. Lyle and his roommate, Donovan Goodreau, had a heated argument over some money that Lyle claimed was missing from their room. He threw Goodreau out. Donovan left without his wallet. Later, Lyle showed friends the wallet, which contained Goodreau's California driver's licence. That summer of 1989, Lyle was back in Beverly Hills living with his parents.

About two hours after the roar of the shotgun blasts echoed through the Menendez home, Lyle and Erik allegedly drove home from a movie and discovered the bodies of their parents. Erik, 18, dialled 911 and sobbed hysterically, "They shot and killed my parents." When police arrived, they found Erik curled in the foetal position on the front lawn.

Who committed this terrible crime? For a while there, many believed that the Mafia had been hired to rub out a business competitor. The police had little to go on as nothing incriminating had been been found at the scene of the killings. No murder weapon has ever been found.

In the weeks immediately following the murder of his parents, Lyle is reported to have gone through $700,000, which tended to attract the attention of the police. He rented a limo and hired a bodyguard, ostensibly to protect him from the assassins who had killed his parents. He also picked up a Porsche Carrera and a Rolex watch, as well as clothing costing $40,000. Lyle always favoured a Princeton hangout, Chuck's

Spring Street Café. He must have fancied it a great deal. Immediately after his parents' deaths, he bought the café.

Six months passed. The two sons of the victims stood to inherit $14 million. Unexpectedly, Lyle was picked up by Los Angeles police and charged with his parents' murders. Erik, who was attending a tennis tournament in Israel, was taken into custody when he returned home.

Judalon Smyth was a 37-year-old former lover of psychologist Jerome Oziel, the doctor who was Erik's and Lyle's counsellor. Smyth had called Los Angeles detectives with a most amazing narrative. She swore that two months after the murders, she had been in Dr. Oziel's office and had overheard Erik confess to the murder of his parents.

Smyth went on to tell the detectives that when Lyle heard that his brother had confessed he threatened to kill the doctor if he reported the confession to police. She also claimed that Oziel had tapes in which both Erik and Lyle had discussed the murders with him. Smyth said that the murder weapons had been purchased at a sporting goods store somewhere between Los Angeles and San Diego.

Smyth's story was taken seriously. Certain facts revealed by her checked out. Police opened Dr. Oziel's safe-deposit box and confiscated 17 audiotapes concerning the murder. Detectives found the sporting goods store in San Diego where two 12-gauge Mossberg shotguns had been sold to a young man using Donovan Goodreau's California driver's licence for identification two days before the murders. You may recall that Lyle had shown friends Goodreau's licence after he threw him out of his room in Princeton.

Dr. Oziel has claimed that his controversial tapes were discussions between doctor and patient and are therefore confidential. At a closed-door preliminary hearing, a judge ruled that since Lyle reportedly threatened to kill Oziel if the doctor revealed the contents of the tapes, the doctor/patient confidentiality had been broken and the tapes could be introduced at a future trial.

This ruling was appealed and it was left for the Supreme

Court of California to decide whether or not the tapes would be admissible. Eventually, the Supreme Court ruled that Dr. Oziel's taped notes, which reportedly relate in detail how the two brothers had killed their mother and father, would be admissible as evidence.

On July 20, 1993, the two brothers were to stand trial, but a week before their date with justice, their lawyer, Leslie Abramson, arguably the best criminal defence lawyer in California, admitted her clients had killed their parents. All the protestations of innocence during the last four years were out the window. Now the defence would go about attempting to prove that Lyle and Erik had been sexually molested for years by their father with their mother's knowledge. They had killed in self-defence.

On the other side of the coin, the prosecution contended that the brothers killed for greed, their motive being to get their hands on a $14-million estate. If found guilty, Erik and Lyle, 22 and 25 years of age, could have received the death penalty.

The trial, carried live on TV, was gripping and emotional, but no one knew if the boys' testimony was true or not. Lyle, complete with choked-back controlled tears, related how his father started massaging him at age six. Eventually, this led to oral sex, which Jose supposedly believed was a true form of father/son love. Lyle claimed that life was a constant round of rapes and other depravities. When the boys complained to their mother, she told them that their father knew best. Yes, they claim they feared for their lives and that led to killing their parents. In California, that can be construed to be self-defence.

Some correspondents who covered the bizarre trial called this the chutzpah defence. It was not easy to believe that two privileged young men, who had lied for years, were telling the gospel truth.

Evidence had been brought forth indicating that Jose was a hard-driving executive who was equally demanding on his sons. He pushed them to excel at tennis and life in general. Did he sexually molest his sons, as Lyle and Erik claimed? Perhaps we will never know. Meanwhile, the family that acquaintances thought exemplified the American dream was certainly something less than that. Mother and father are dead.

In 1994, the two sons stood trial, their lives hanging in the balance. When the jury failed to reach a verdict, the presiding judge declared a mistrial. Two years later, and after a five-month trial, Erik and Lyle Menendez were found guilty of murdering their parents. They were sentenced to life imprisonment, a sentence they are presently serving.

On the day of the sentencing, Lyle married his girlfriend, Anna Eriksson, who he came to know by correspondence. The ceremony was carried out by conference call. Lyle and his best man, Erik, were eight miles away in prison while the bride was in Lyle's lawyer's office in Los Angeles.

# Roland Molineux
## A DEADLY GIFT OF POISON

Let's face it, poison is the most insidious method of disposing of the unwanted. Oh, sure, you can chop, strangle or shoot friends and enemies, but employing these pedestrian methods necessitates being in relative proximity to the victim. Poison allows the perpetrator to put distance and, in many cases, time between himself and the recipient of the fatal white powder or deadly vial.

The Knickerbocker Athletic Club of New York was one of the most prestigious clubs in the Big Apple at the turn of the century. It catered to the sporting crowd, but was also a home away from home where gentlemen could discuss accumulative preferred stocks, the state of the Union and what trinket to pick up at Tiffany's for their current mistress.

In 1898, the club was saddened by the loss of Henry C. Barnet, an executive of the Knickerbocker Club. Henry had suffered a bout of diphtheria and had been confined to bed at the club for a week. Doctors said he had resumed his normal activities prematurely and, as a result, had died of a heart attack.

Six weeks after Henry's demise, a seemingly unrelated event occurred at the club. On the day before Christmas, athletic director Harry Cornish opened his mail and was pleased to see that someone had sent him an attractive Christmas present. It was an ornate silver bottle holder complete with a sealed blue bottle of Bromo-Seltzer. An envelope accompanied the gift, but there was no card inside the envelope. Someone had forgotten to enclose the card, thought Harry. He was curious enough to tear away his name and address from the wrapping paper.

A few days later, he took the gift to his home. Harry was divorced. He lived with an elderly aunt, Katherine Adams, and her married daughter, a Mrs. Rogers. They teased the 32-year-old Harry about a secret female admirer who was sending him anonymous presents.

On December 28, Katherine Adams awoke with a violent headache. She suggested that some Bromo-Seltzer might do her the world of good. Harry remembered his recently acquired gift, broke the seal and poured some of the powder into a glass of water. Katherine drained about three-quarters of the glass and remarked that the potion tasted bitter. Harry took a sip and said that it tasted fine to him.

Minutes later, Katherine took ill and called out for Harry to come to her aid. Harry jumped up, staggered and fell to the floor. He managed to get outside, where he violently vomited, which probably saved his life. Meanwhile, Mrs. Rogers had summoned a doctor for mother, but there was little the doctor could do. Katherine Adams died shortly after his arrival.

The Bromo-Seltzer was analyzed and found to contain cyanide of mercury, a deadly poison. The doctor who ministered to Harry was the same medic who had attended the late Mr. Barnet only weeks earlier. He remembered that Barnet had mentioned something about receiving a gift through the mail.

Katherine's murder was covered extensively in the New York newspapers. Harry provided them with the sample he had kept of the handwriting on the wrapping of his gift. It was reproduced in the paper. Two officials of the Knickerbocker, John D. Adams and Andre Bustanoby, recognized the sample handwriting. After checking some correspondence on file, they came to the conclusion that the man who had addressed the poisonous gift to Harry was club member Roland Molineux. New York's finest were immediately informed of their discovery.

An investigation into Roland's history was most enlightening. Detectives learned that back in 1897 Roland had introduced his girlfriend, Blanche Cheeseborough, to Henry

Barnet. Henry had taken a shine to Blanche and had become Roland's rival for her affection. Henry's pursuit of Blanche had come to an abrupt end when he had taken ill and died at the club. Nineteen days after Henry's untimely death, Blanche and Roland were married at the appropriately named Church of the Heavenly Rest.

But why oh why had poor Katherine Adams been poisoned? The poison wasn't meant for her at all. In 1897, Roland had had a bitter argument with Harry Cornish concerning the running of the Knickerbocker Club. The dispute had ended up before a committee of the club's officials, to whom Roland stated, "Discharge Cornish or lose me." Cornish stayed. Roland had no way of knowing that Harry would take home the silver holder and the bottle of poison, nor did he have the slightest idea that Harry's Aunt Katherine would be the victim of his diabolical scheme.

When Henry Barnet's body was exhumed and found to contain cyanide of mercury, Roland was taken into custody and charged with the murder of Katherine Adams and the attempted murder of Harry Cornish.

At the trial the prosecution paraded an array of the obligatory handwriting experts, who had compared the writing on Harry Cornish's poisonous gift to that of Roland Molineux. The two samples were a match. No amount of cross-examination could change the experts' opinion. There was no doubt that Roland Molineux had addressed the fatal parcel.

Investigators traced the bottle holder to a store in Newark, not far from Roland's place of business. One of Roland's employees swore that the paper used to wrap the poison was exactly the same as the kind used in Roland's office. Cyanide of mercury was readily available to the accused at his workplace.

The Molineux trial lasted three months, but the jury took only eight hours to find the rogue guilty as charged. Roland was sent up the river to Sing Sing, where he awaited his execution on death row. Using his father's money, he fought for his life for the following two years. In October 1901, the Court of Appeals reversed the previous court's verdict and ordered a new trial.

The passage of time often has a strange effect on the public's attitude towards a murder suspect. Almost four years after the murder, Roland Molineux again stood trial for murder and attempted murder. This time, no details of Barnet's murder were admissible. Roland was allowed to testify and, all in all, gave a good impression. The defence came up with a witness who swore she had seen another man, not Roland, mail an identically wrapped parcel addressed to Harry Cornish.

The jury deliberated only four minutes before acquitting Roland. Unlike many a man who narrowly escapes an appointment with the electric chair, Roland didn't fade into obscurity. He wrote several books about his experiences and was relatively well known in the New York area.

In 1913, Roland Molineux suffered a nervous breakdown and was confined to the New York State Hospital for the Insane. He died there in 1917.

# Dan Montecalvo
# A HIGHLY UNLIKELY PAIR

They met, wed and, ultimately, one was to kill the other.

Carol was born to hard-working blue-collar parents in Buffalo, New York. She grew up to be an attractive young woman who thirsted for higher education. With the support of her family, she attended and later graduated from State University of New York with a Bachelor of Science degree. In 1970, she earned her master's degree from the same university.

An unsuccessful marriage to a foreign student lasted only one year. Carol's father had been opposed to the marriage, and from that time father and daughter were never on what you would call friendly terms.

Single and alone, Carol remained in her position as a student counsellor at the University of Wisconsin at Madison. In time she became deeply involved in religious life and attended bible classes regularly. One of her religious friends asked her to be a pen pal of bank robber Dan Montecalvo, then serving time at the Federal Correctional Institution in Oxford, and Carol agreed.

Letters flowed between the two very different personalities. Soon Carol was visiting Dan at every opportunity. To her, Dan Montecalvo was a charming, sensitive man who had been led down a path of crime through no fault of his own.

Dan's father had been a small-time thief in Chelsea, Massachusetts. He had been shot to death by police during the commission of a robbery. His mother, a part-time prostitute, often brought clients to their two-room apartment when her little son was at home. Dan started stealing at the age of nine and spent the next nine years of his life in and out of reform schools and foster homes.

As a kid, Dan acquired a lengthy police record. As a young man, he was a hard-drinking, gun-toting gambler who specialized in robbing banks. Whenever he did pull off a successful robbery, he blew his take on gambling. It was a no-win situation. He was caught and stashed away in penitentiary. This was the man whom religious, trusting Carol had taken to her heart.

Dan professed that he too was madly in love. Most of Carol's visits to the penitentiary were spent praying with Dan. Within a short time he converted to Carol's evangelistic sect. Although he had 10 more years to serve, the lovers thought that prayer would be instrumental in obtaining his early release. In the meantime, they decided to marry. It took some time, but eventually they received permission from prison authorities. On July 14, 1980, they were married in the prison yard. Six months later, their prayers were answered. Dan was released and the happy couple moved to California to begin a new life together.

The Montecalvos settled in Burbank, where Carol obtained a position with a telephone company, selling Yellow Pages ads. Soon after landing the job, it was apparent that she had an unusual aptitude for that type of work. Carol was the ace of the sales staff. Later, she switched to Pacific Bell, where she made a fine living. Things didn't go as well for Dan. He moved from job to job, drank heavily and often lapsed into deep depression. In 1986, a bleeding ulcer made working impossible for him. Dan took to the bottle with a vengeance.

Carol, with her simple faith that prayer could solve all problems, prayed that her husband would turn his life around. Once again, as if by a miracle, she received the good news that she had won a sales contest at her place of employment. The prize was an all-expenses-paid trip to Hawaii. Just what Dan needed: a full week's escape from the troubles of the world. He would return a new man, the charming soft-spoken, considerate Dan she had married years earlier in the prison yard.

On March 31, 1988, Carol was busy preparing for their trip. Next day, they would take off for beautiful romantic

Hawaii. That night, around ten-thirty, Carol and Dan went for a walk, as they did most nights that Dan was home.

The call was received by the 911 operator a few minutes after 11 p.m. The caller was a man who implored, "Please help, hurry up. We've been shot." One minute later, the first police car arrived at the scene. From the information given by the desperate caller, there was some concern that an armed burglar might still be in the house or on the premises.

It was nine minutes after the initial call before Dan came out of the house. Only then did police rush to his aid and into the house, where they found Carol on the floor of the hallway. It was too late. Carol was dead, apparently shot to death by a burglar. Dan had been shot in the back by a single .25-calibre bullet, which had lodged in the front of his body near the small intestines. He was rushed to hospital, where he successfully underwent an operation.

Detectives listened as Dan told his story of the shooting. When they left the house for their walk, he and Carol locked up as usual. Upon returning, they strolled up the driveway. Dan noticed that their vehicle licence plates were to expire the next day. He had the sticker to place over the old plates in the glove compartment of the car. He fetched the sticker while Carol went inside to get a wet towel to clean the plates. Suddenly, Dan heard her shout, "What are you doing here?," followed by the sound of two shots. Dan ran into the house, only to be grabbed from behind. He was shot and fell to the floor. He heard a male voice say, "Let's get out of here," or words to that effect. Dan was able to get up. He saw Carol lying in the hall bleeding profusely as he made his way to the den to use the phone. It was then he noticed that their safe had been burglarized. A cash box had been pried open. About $800 in change and loose bills were missing. Dan dialled 911.

Detectives looking for signs of forced entry found a slit in the back-door screen, which had apparently allowed the intruders to reach inside and open the door. There seemed little doubt that Carol and Dan had been unfortunate enough to surprise armed burglars in the process of robbing their home.

Dan received the sympathy of investigating officers and his wife's religious friends.

It took only a week for the situation to change dramatically. A check of Dan's past disclosed his criminal record. A man with such a record deserved a closer look, police decided. As they delved deeper, they found out that Carol had been insured for $600,000. Dan had already collected $400,000, but a few of the insurance companies held back their payments when they learned he was a suspect in his wife's murder. Still, $400,000 isn't bad. Dan visited Las Vegas and proceeded to lose thousands of dollars a night. Authorities also learned that before Carol's death, Dan had been gambling on credit at the Las Vegas casinos. When he failed to honour his markers, the casinos threatened to deposit them at his bank, a normal procedure when clients can't pay up. In Dan's case, he had no hope of covering the markers, which would have been treated as rubber cheques. Being a parolee, this offence could land him back in prison. As soon as he laid his hands on Carol's insurance money, he paid off the threatening casinos.

Police were sure they had their man, but one thing bothered them. Carol had been shot with a .38 weapon, while Dan had been shot with a .25. How had he disposed of the two weapons after shooting his wife and himself? A search of Dan's belongings uncovered an empty hollowed-out book, which could have held the two weapons until he was able to get rid of them.

Based on overwhelming circumstantial evidence, Dan Montecalvo was arrested and charged with his wife's murder. He was tried and convicted. Protesting his innocence to the end and acting as his own co-counsel, he was sentenced to 27 years' to life imprisonment. He is currently serving that sentence.

# Joe Nail
# NAILED

If ever two people were completely different, they were Carolyn and Joe Nail. Carolyn, 48, was a dark-complexioned brunette with a stunning figure. A graduate nurse, she had risen in the ranks of the Marshall Memorial Hospital in Madill, Oklahoma, to become director of nursing. Her husband, Joe, was an oilfield roustabout who drank heavily between jobs. He was constantly fearful that Carolyn, more often than not the family breadwinner, would leave him.

Joe's fears were well-founded. Carolyn couldn't abide the drunkenness and abusive threats indefinitely. In August 1989, she obtained a divorce. Joe didn't take the divorce well. He drank more than usual and often confided to acquaintances that he would get even with " that bitch."

Carolyn went about restructuring her life. She dated 60-year-old Don Hofferber, a successful contractor. Although Don had divorced his wife in 1976, they continued to have an off-and-on relationship until 1990, when they permanently parted. He liked and admired Carolyn Nail. With both of them free, it was a foregone conclusion among their friends that the pair would eventually marry. Meanwhile, Don was Carolyn's constant companion.

Madill is a small Oklahoma town with a population of about 3,000. Violence is not an everyday occurrence there. Murder and its ugly ramifications are practically unknown in the peaceful little community. That's one of the reasons the desperate call to the hospital received immediate attention.

On Saturday, June 2, 1990, the Marshall Memorial switchboard received an ominous call pleading, "Help me." There followed a fading partial address. In minutes, an ambulance and police were speeding to Carolyn Nail's home.

The first officers at the scene noted the glass patio door at the rear of the house was broken to pieces. Proceeding with caution in case the intruder or intruders were still in the house, police made their way to the master bedroom. There, at the foot of the bed, clad only in shorts, was the body of Don Hofferber. He had been shot in the neck, abdomen and arm. Carolyn lay dead beside the bed. She had managed to dislodge a white telephone from the night table and call the hospital before she died. She had been shot five times. Three bullets had entered her back, causing her death.

It was later determined that both Carolyn and Don had been murdered with the same weapon, a .22-calibre semi-automatic rifle. From the position of the bodies, it appeared the killer had opened fire at the couple from the bedroom doorway. Carolyn's pit bull cowered in a corner amidst the blood and chaos. Police found $1,700 in Don's wallet, which ruled out robbery as a motive for the killings.

An autopsy indicated that the pair had engaged in sexual intercourse shortly before being shot. Don had died instantly, but Carolyn had lived long enough to make her desperate phone call.

Initially, police speculated that one of Don's many competitors in the construction business, envious of his success, may have been responsible for the killings. Don had a reputation for being a ruthless businessman. It didn't take long, however, for police inquiries to turn up the bad feeling Joe Nail harboured for his former wife. It was learned that Carolyn had told Don of her fear of Joe. Don had given her a .25-calibre handgun for her protection and had purchased a .380-calibre weapon for his own use. Both guns were located, but neither played a part in their owners' deaths.

Joe, who lived in a trailer 40 miles from Madill, was questioned. He readily consented to have his trailer searched. Nothing incriminating was found. Joe admitted he hated his ex-wife, accusing her of running around on him before they were divorced. He wasn't sorry someone had blown her away, but swore he wasn't the guilty party. Joe said he had been fishing alone at the Lake of the Arbuckles at the time of the murders. He had last seen Carolyn a few days before her death, when he had gone to her house to pick up the pit bull, which they owned jointly. He had returned the dog the same day. That was Joe's story and he stuck to it.

Investigators believed that Joe Nail, probably intoxicated, had committed the double murder. Despite their suspicions, there was no eyewitness and no murder weapon. Their case had to be built on circumstantial evidence and that's exactly what they set out to do.

In a small town the size of Madill, rumours spread like weeds. Many of these stories reached the ears of the police. Everyone in town realized an aggressive pit bull would never allow a stranger free access to the house without offering some resistance. Surely the killer was well known to the dog. A neighbour of Carolyn's contacted police, saying that on the evening of the shooting, while standing in her front yard, she noticed a white pickup parked in front of Carolyn's house. She went into her home for a few minutes and then came back outside. As she did so, she watched the pickup drive away. When it was directly opposite her, the driver stared at her. Their eyes met. She was sure he was Joe Nail.

Although Joe had stated he had been fishing at the time of the crime, a security guard at his trailer park swore that Joe had driven out of the park in his white pickup about two hours before the murders and had returned about an hour after the murders, allowing him plenty of time to drive the 40 miles to Carolyn's house and back. In addition, several of Joe's acquaintances came forward, stating that he had often verbally threatened to kill his ex-wife. Carolyn's friends volunteered that she lived in fear of Joe.

Detectives believed this was a case of murder without any great intrigue or plot, simply a man enraged at his ex-wife and her lover, enraged enough to kill them both.

In October 1990, Joe was taken into custody and charged

with the double murder. The prosecution proved that Carolyn had once given Joe a .22-calibre semi-automatic rifle as a birthday present. They produced a witness who placed Joe in his truck about nine miles from Carolyn's home, as well as the neighbour who placed him in front of Carolyn's home on the night of the murders. The security guard from Joe's trailer camp also gave his damaging evidence.

Joe's defence attorney pointed out that Don Hofferber had business enemies who wanted him out of the way. In addition, several members of his family stood to inherit large sums of money and a prosperous business. Wasn't it just possible that Don was the main target and Carolyn an incidental victim? The Oklahoma jury thought not.

Joe was found guilty on two counts of first-degree murder, placing him in jeopardy of receiving the death penalty. However, his attorney pleaded that the murders were crimes of passion. He was successful in having Joe Nail sentenced to two life terms without possibility of parole.

# Hank Nguyen
# REJECTED SUITOR

When Saigon fell in 1975, Tina Pham fled her native Vietnam in a desperate effort to find a safe haven. Like many other boat people, she made her way to Indonesia. Tina married and had two children. She and her husband eked out a meagre living for years before deciding to emigrate to the United States. In 1980 they settled in Orange County, California, where their third child was born.

By 1985, Tina's marriage had deteriorated and ended in divorce. However, she and her ex-husband were on good terms. Both contributed to their children's support and spent an equal amount of time with them. Tina worked as a hair-dresser. She lived in a comfortable apartment with relatives in Garden Grove, California, not far from Reverend Robert Schuller's famed Crystal Cathedral.

Each morning Tina reported for work at precisely 11 a.m. On October 24, 1990, when she failed to show up or phone in ill, her employer called her home, but received no response. Tina and all her relatives were apparently not in.

That night, one of Tina's relatives tried her bedroom door and found it locked. She assumed Tina was asleep, but when there was no sign of Tina after several hours had elapsed, she decided to unlock the door with a spare key kept in the apartment. The bedroom was in darkness and there was no sign that anything in the room had been disturbed. More important, there was no sign of Tina.

The relative gingerly made her way to the bathroom. There lay Tina Pham on the floor. The 42-year-old woman was on her back, her black dress pushed up around her waist. Her panties were pulled down halfway to her knees. Dried blood had oozed from her mouth onto the bathroom floor.

An ambulance was at the scene in a matter of minutes. Medical attendants confirmed that Tina was dead. A police photographer arrived at approximately the same time and took photos of the body before a relative lifted Tina's panties and rearranged her dress. Later, this relative would explain that she had done so in order to spare the victim unnecessary embarrassment and had no idea she was contaminating a crime scene.

Initially, there was no indication that a crime had been committed. Relatives of the dead woman told police that Tina had suffered from heart disease and was taking medication, which was found in the bathroom. There was no reason to believe that Tina's death was due to anything but natural causes, although police noted that her bedroom window was open about 12 inches. Since nothing was missing from the bedroom, it was assumed that Tina had opened the window herself.

An autopsy was performed to verify the cause of death. Dr. Ronald Katsuyama noted petechial haemorrhages in the eyes, which indicated to him that strangulation was the cause of death. The interior of the victim's throat revealed several bruised areas. Tina had received a blow to the mouth which had split her lower lip. The blood found on the bathroom floor had emanated from this wound. After hearing from the coroner, police realized they had a murder on their hands. In addition, when they scanned the photos taken at the scene by the police photographer, they learned that someone had rearranged Tina's panties and dress.

Police immediately mounted a full-scale murder investigation. Tina's bed was examined. When the bedspread was removed, a small quantity of blood was found on one of the sheets, leading police to surmise that Tina had sustained the split lip while on the bed.

The time of death was established at between 9:45 a.m. and 11 a.m. on the day the body was found. A friend had talked to Tina on the phone at nine forty-five and, as she had not turned up for work at 11 a.m., it was reasonable to assume that she had been murdered between these times.

Police learned that Tina had dated three different men

since her divorce. Two of her boyfriends were checked out and eliminated as suspects. The third, Hank Nguyen, was located on the day following the murder. Detectives were shocked when, unlike the other Vietnamese who had been questioned, Hank proved to be most uncooperative. He would not discuss the case without having his lawyer present, but was willing to set up an appointment for the next day. Then, just as the detectives were about to depart, he changed his mind.

Hank told police he had nothing to fear. He had been busy supervising a construction job in Huntington Beach on the morning of the murder. He said he had been on the site until 9:30 a.m. when he left to purchase some supplies at a hardware store, returning to the construction site at 11:20 a.m. For emphasis, Hank used hand movements. That's when police noticed his bandaged thumb. When the detectives suggested they take a photo of his injured thumb, Hank refused.

Next day, Hank Nguyen showed up at police headquarters with his lawyer. He insisted that he had hurt his thumb in the hardware store and consented to remove the bandage. The thumb was examined and photographed. It was noted that the skin was broken on both sides. For all the world, it looked like a bite. Hank was quickly becoming a prime suspect.

Tina's relatives were questioned extensively. Slowly, authorities were able to piece together the relationship between Tina and Hank. One relative reported that she had taken Tina to a doctor to close a cut on her scalp. Tina claimed she had passed out, fallen and cut herself, but the relative believed Hank was responsible for the head wound. It had happened just before they broke up.

Police contacted an odontologist, who examined the photographs of Hank's thumb. He compared the photos with plaster casts of Tina's teeth. They matched. The doctor suggested that the position of the bite mark was compatible with the thumb having been placed over the victim's mouth, but he admitted that the teeth marks, while consistent with Tina's teeth, could also have been made by thousands of other people with the same dental characteristics.

Detectives dusted the window sill of the open bedroom

window. They were able to lift a single print, which matched Hank's index finger. While incriminating, it proved nothing, as Hank had often been in the bedroom and could have left the print at any time.

A search of the suspect's home was most revealing. Police found colour photographs of Tina taken in happier times. One picture featured Tina posing with her dress crumpled around her waist and her panties dropped halfway down to around her knees. Police did a double take. The photo matched the first photo taken of Tina's body. Hank had posed Tina's corpse in the exact position she had assumed when she had allowed him to take the erotic photo.

Investigating officers did one final check. At 9:30 a.m. they left the Huntington Beach construction site where Hank had been working. Driving as slowly as they dared, they proceeded to the hardware store and purchased the very items he claimed to have purchased. They then drove to Tina's apartment, allowing time for the murder and time for Hank to return to the construction site. At 11:20 a.m., Hank could easily have been back to work. Their suspect had had plenty of time to commit the murder.

The pieces fell into place. Hank was a rejected suitor. He and Tina had argued. He had probably punched her while she was in bed, splitting her lip, which bled onto the sheet. Tina ran away from her lover into the bathroom. As he strangled her, she bit him. Once she was dead, in a hateful symbolic gesture, he had positioned her body in the same pose as during a previous sexual encounter.

Hank Nguyen was arrested and stood trial for Tina's murder. On May 28, 1991, after deliberating for just five hours, the jury found him guilty of first-degree murder. He was sentenced to 25 years' imprisonment. At a later sentencing hearing, the conviction was adjusted to second-degree murder. The presiding judge ruled that the crime had not been premeditated and reduced the sentence to 15 years to life. Hank Nguyen is presently serving his sentence.

# Willie O'Shea
# IRISH JUSTICE

Willie O'Shea was a native of Ballyhane, County Waterford, Ireland. To say that he was a bright lad would be to overstate the case. No, Willie was a young man with below-average intelligence who worked as a farm labourer when the mood struck him, which wasn't often. He much preferred to snare rabbits and sell them for a living. Willie didn't need much to sustain himself, as he lived with his mother and stepfather, Michael Byrne.

In 1940, at age 20, Willie married 17-year-old Maureen Clavin. The marriage wasn't a happy one right from the beginning. Willie and Maureen lived in a three-room thatched cottage, but Willie was hardly ever home. He preferred the company of 16-year-old Thomas White, a fellow aficionado of the rabbit-snaring game. Thomas also had a distinct aversion to manual labour.

Maureen was forever complaining that her husband didn't earn enough money to provide her with the necessities of life. He often left her alone at night without oil for her lamps or even candles. Maureen was afraid to be alone in the darkened cottage at night.

In 1942, when Maureen became pregnant, it was not a joyous occasion in the O'Shea household. Willie didn't change his argumentative, neglectful ways one little bit. In February 1943, Maureen gave birth to a healthy baby boy. Four days after returning home from the hospital, she was awakened by the smell of smoke emanating from the roof of the cottage. As usual, Willie wasn't home.

Maureen had time to dress herself and the baby before

making her way to her mother-in-law's home while her cottage burned to the ground. Willie, the no-goodnik, arrived home to his burned-down house a little after 1 a.m. He walked to his mother's home and joined his wife and baby. There was some suggestion that arson had been involved, but nothing came of the rumours.

For three weeks the O'Sheas stayed with the Byrnes. There was a dramatic change in Willie's treatment of his wife. He was more attentive and there was no more quarrelling. Willie even took Maureen out for a walk each evening after tea. They would stroll arm in arm for about a mile down the dark road. The situation became so rosy that Willie actually secured a job working in a quarry.

Then it happened.

Willie and Maureen had gone for their usual evening walk. Suddenly, his mother was surprised to see her son running towards the house. Maureen was nowhere to be seen. Willie was crying and trembling. When Mrs. Byrne could get no information out of him, she ran down the lonely dark road screaming Maureen's name. Unable to locate her daughter-in-law, she returned to her home and implored Willie to tell her what had happened. Finally, Willie blurted out, "Somebody fired a shot at us." Mrs. Byrne ran down the lonely road once more. This time she came across Maureen's body. The young mother had been killed by a single shotgun blast in the back.

What in the world had happened? That's what the police wanted to know. They questioned Willie, who explained that he and Maureen were walking arm in arm along the road when a shot rang out. He felt her slumping to the road and gently lay her down. He saw nothing in the dark, but ran home in fear for his life. He told police he was sure the shot was meant for him.

The police paid a visit to the home of Willie's good friend, Thomas White. While there, they confiscated a shotgun which obviously had recently been cleaned. When Thomas was told of the tragedy, he returned to Willie's home with the police.

Willie was questioned about the fire that had burned down his home. Did he think there was any connection between the two incidents? Willie was confused, but although he swore he had nothing to do with his wife's death, he insinuated that he knew the identity of the killer. When asked if Thomas White was implicated, Willie broke down and told his fantastic story.

Willie had asked Thomas White to shoot his wife. Thomas agreed to do the job. Each night Willie walked with Maureen with the sole purpose of leading her to her death. As an aside, Willie told police that Thomas had set fire to the cottage, as well, in a failed attempt to kill Maureen. Willie knew the exact spot where Thomas would fire the fatal shot. On one occasion, Thomas didn't fire because someone happened along the road, but finally conditions were perfect.

To warn Willie that all was set, Thomas tapped his friend on the shoulder with the barrel of the shotgun. Then he shot Maureen from a distance of about three inches. Maureen said, "Oh, Jesus" as he let her slide to the road. Willie didn't even turn to see Thomas. He explained there was no need; he knew very well who had fired the shot.

The police questioned Thomas, who said he had seen Willie and Maureen walking on the night of the murder. He had ridden past them on his bicycle and had gone straight home. When his mother arrived home, she informed him of the tragedy. Thomas claimed that he hadn't used his shotgun for a few days and always cleaned it after each use.

Detectives confiscated Thomas's boots and socks, which were soaking wet and covered with mud. This was rather strange as the weather had been unusually dry for several weeks. When Willie led police to the exact spot where Thomas had stood to fire the fatal shot, they noticed a bog which never dried out. They made out the faint impression of Thomas's boots in the mud.

Both men were arrested. Willie was the most vocal, admitting his guilt over and over. He explained that he felt as if he was in prison being married. When the baby came along, he couldn't even go snaring rabbits when he felt like it. When he suggested to Maureen that he go away to join the army in England, she wouldn't hear of such a thing. There was no other way. Maureen had to go. Now he was dreadfully sorry about the whole thing.

On June 7, 1943, Willie and Thomas stood trial for murder. On the very first day of the trial, Thomas's lawyer applied for a jury to judge whether his client was mentally fit to stand trial. Renowned Irish doctors testified that, after interviewing Thomas, it was their opinion that he was mentally subnormal and could not follow the judicial procedures, nor could he give instructions to his lawyer. It took the jury only 10 minutes to find him unfit to stand trial. Thomas White was confined to hospital.

Willie wasn't as fortunate. He stood trial and was found guilty of his wife's murder. He too was examined by doctors, who agreed that although he was not a mental giant, he did know right from wrong. On August 12, 1943, Willie O'Shea was executed.

The old Irish trial is a rare example of the unusual circumstances that can take place in a murder case. The man who did not fire the fatal shot was executed, while the man who pulled the trigger never stood trial.

# Pell, Royal and Morey
# SENSELESS KILLING

Various studies have been conducted on the home life of men and women who have committed murder. A disproportionate number of these killers seem to come from broken homes, where alcoholism, and child, wife and drug abuse were prominent. None of the above applies to the Morey family of Ypsilanti, Michigan.

The Moreys lived in a white clapboard house on Pearl Street. Bill Morey worked all his life for the United Stove Co. Over the years he had managed to pay off the mortgage on his home. Mrs. Morey taught school for the first six years of her married life. The family attended church every Sunday.

On January 27, 1933, the Moreys were blessed with their first child, a son. Bill was their pride and joy. As he grew up, he achieved good marks in school, sang in the church choir and regularly attended Sunday school. Eight years after Bill's birth, a second child, a daughter, was born to the Moreys. Young Bill was a loving, protective big brother. In high school, Bill's marks seemed to level off. Some of his teachers felt he was an underachiever when it was learned that his IQ was 123.

During his junior year in high school, Bill took his first drink of beer. Soon it became customary for him and his friends to pick up a case of beer a couple of times a week and to cruise the town looking for girls. Bill had no trouble finding girlfriends. He stood an inch over six feet, had a shock of thick black hair and the slim build of an athlete.

When Bill graduated from high school, his marks were below admission standards at the University of Michigan. He was told to apply to another college and reapply in a year's time. Bill was accepted at Michigan State Normal College, located only a few blocks from his home. That summer of 1951 he looked forward to his first semester at Michigan State.

If a cross section of 18-year-old young men had been taken, it is conceivable that Bill would have been hailed as your average all-American boy. He wasn't a slacker; he wasn't outstanding. Bill was an average boy from an average home. Yet Bill Morey would kill before the summer was over.

On September 11, Bill and two friends, Dan Myers and Max Pell, went for a drive in Dan's car. The boys purchased a case of beer and cruised around town looking for girls to pick up. They drove to Ann Arbor, but didn't have any luck finding girls. Finally, they parked near University Hospital.

For reasons never really explained, the conversation centred on how easy it would be to grab a purse from one of the several nurses going to and from the hospital. One of the boys thought it was a crazy idea. Bill thought it would be cool. Evidently he said, "Let's hit someone over the head and rob them." Dan piped up that the whole thing was silly. Bill insisted. He would hit a nurse over the head, rob her and drag her into the car.

Bill picked up a 12-inch wrench and watched for a likely victim. Nurse Shirley Mackley left the hospital. For a few minutes, she was alone on the street. Bill walked hurriedly up behind her and swung the wrench at her head. Shirley felt the glancing blow, screamed and ran for her life. Bill dashed back to the car and the three boys drove away. Max and Bill laughed at the botched robbery attempt.

The boys enjoyed reading about the attack on the nurse in the local newspaper. During the week following the assault, Bill, Max and another boy, Dave Royal, were driving around town. They picked up a fourth boy, a preacher's son, Dan Baughey. Bill bragged to Dan that it was he who had attacked nurse Shirley Mackley. Dan didn't know what to do. Maybe the guys were just pulling his leg. He decided to discuss the matter with his father.

Next evening, Max, accompanied by Bill and Dave, drove

to University Hospital. Thirty-four-year-old nurse Pauline Campbell left the hospital after completing her shift. Pauline was a pretty woman, well-liked, quiet. She didn't deserve to die on the streets of the city.

Bill picked up a mallet from the floor of the car. It was a rubber-headed one used to take dents out of cars. He stuffed it into his belt and got out of Max's car. Pauline had no idea that she was being stalked by an 18-year-old student. Bill was wearing moccasins and made very little noise as he closed the distance between himself and Pauline.

Max turned on the headlights of the car and slowly followed. Bill was finally in range. He brought down the mallet with all his might on Pauline's head. Again and again the mallet crashed against Pauline's skull until she was dead. Bill shouted to Dave to come and give him a hand. He was attempting to drag Pauline into the car. Dave jumped out to assist with Pauline's limp form, but Max objected. The interior of the car had just been cleaned. He didn't want blood all over the seats and floor. The boys took Pauline's purse, left her body on the road and drove off.

A few minutes later, Bill examined the contents of Pauline's purse. It contained the usual things, as well as $1.50 in cash. Bill kept the money, but threw the purse and its contents into the Huron River. The three boys stopped for sandwiches and coffee.

Bill returned home at 1:30 a.m., in time to make his curfew. His mother let him in. She noticed nothing unusual in his behaviour and went to bed. Bill went up to his room, crawled out a window and rejoined his buddies. At 4:30 a.m., the three friends returned to their respective homes.

On Monday, Bill registered at Michigan State Normal College. The following day he delivered an address at his high school, advising students on the complications of enrolling in an institution of higher learning.

Over the weekend, Dan Baughey heard about the murder on the radio. He recalled the conversation he had had with Bill about the attack on Shirley Mackley. He wondered if Bill and his friends had had anything to do with the murder, which was the main topic of conversation in Ypsilanti and Ann Arbor. Dan asked his father for advice and was told to go to the police with his suspicions.

Bill, Max and Dave were picked up. Initially they denied any involvement, but when asked to take lie detector tests, they lost their nerve and confessed.

Dan Myers, the boy involved in the first attack, was sentenced to one to ten years' imprisonment for his part in that incident. Dave Royal was found guilty of murder in the second degree and was sentenced to 20 years to life. Max Pell and Bill Morey were found guilty of murder in the first degree. Both were sentenced to life imprisonment.

In the state of Michigan, which has no death penalty, a sentence of life imprisonment means natural life, unless the sentence is commuted. There is no parole granted in the case of a life sentence for first-degree murder.

The murder of Pauline Campbell is remembered not because of its convoluted plot or the evil background of the participants. It is remembered because no one, including the perpetrators, has ever given a logical reason for this senseless killing.

All three men involved have been released from prison. Max Pell had his sentence commuted by the governor of the state in 1967, after serving 16 years. Dave Royal was paroled in 1970 after serving 19 years. Governor W.C. Milliken commuted Bill Morey's sentence in December 1970, after he'd served just under 20 years in prison.

# Valerie Percy
# SENATOR'S DAUGHTER MURDERED

Charles Percy was in the midst of his campaign for the U.S. Senate. The former president of the Bell and Howell camera empire had retired from the world of business and finance to enter politics.

Percy, a self-made millionaire, was a man who had it all. He and his wife, Lorraine, lived in the small exclusive community of Kenilworth, a suburb of Chicago, on an estate bordering Lake Michigan.

On the night of September 18, 1966, 11-year-old Mark Percy was staying overnight with friends. Roger Percy, 19, was away at university. At home that night were Charles, Lorraine and three of their children, Gail, 13, and the 21-year-old twins, Sharon and Valerie.

Sharon chatted with Valerie in her sister's bedroom at around eleven-thirty after returning from a date. Valerie was sitting on her bed watching TV when the twins bade each other goodnight. Sharon retired to her room. Gail was already asleep. Charles had come home late and had watched TV with Lorraine. The couple retired about 1:30 a.m.

Some hours later, Lorraine woke up. She thought she heard glass breaking but wasn't concerned enough to investigate. Later she said that she thought one of the girls had toppled a glass from a night table. She turned over and went back to sleep. In an instant, another noise disturbed Lorraine. She called out, "Valerie, Val," but received no response.

Lorraine left the master bedroom and opened the door to Valerie's room. There in the dark she saw the form of a man bending over her daughter's bed. She didn't see the man's face, but believed he was wearing a shirt or jacket. He carried a flashlight, which he pointed at the terrified woman as she opened the door. Lorraine Percy later told police, "I took a step backward, turned and ran back to our bedroom. I awakened my husband and pressed the central burglar-alarm button that activated the siren on the roof."

The assailant ran past Lorraine and down the stairs. He fled through French doors and out into the night. At precisely 5:05 a.m., the siren broke through the silence of the early morning. Charles Percy called his neighbour and friend, Dr. Robert Hoft. In a matter of minutes, the doctor was bending over the blood-spattered body of Valerie Percy. The young girl, who had just graduated from Cornell University and had come home to assist her father in his political campaign, was beyond help. She had been bludgeoned about the head and had been stabbed 10 times in the throat and chest.

Charles Percy called the Kenilworth police. Realizing they were ill equipped to handle the first homicide ever to take place in their community, they immediately called Chicago police for assistance.

Detectives ascertained that the assailant had gained entrance through the French doors. He had used a glass cutter to cut away a small section of glass, enabling him to reach in and open the door from the inside. It was this piece of glass falling to the floor that had disturbed Lorraine's sleep.

Due to the prominence of the murdered girl's father, the homicide caused a sensation. The Percys moved out of their home and went into seclusion as police mounted an extensive investigation into the killing.

Several things puzzled investigators. It appeared that the assailant had gone directly to Valerie's room where he had instituted the vicious assault. Yet the dead girl's friends and acquaintances could come up with no one who would want any harm to come to Valerie, let alone kill her. Robbery didn't appear to be the motive as nothing had been taken from the estate. Conversely, some investigators reasoned that the killer had ventured into Valerie's room by chance and had been interrupted by the girl as he cased her room for anything of value.

For a short while police couldn't understand why the Percys' Labrador retriever hadn't barked at a stranger entering their home at five in the morning. However, they soon realized that because Charles was in the midst of a major political campaign, strangers were constantly entering and exiting the house. The dog paid them little heed.

As the weeks passed, it became clear that Valerie's murder wouldn't be quickly solved. For some strange reason, the high-profile murder attracted a series of confessions. In all, 19 men confessed to the crime. Each confession had to be checked out. After time-consuming investigations, all the men were cleared of any complicity in the Percy killing.

In 1967, a professional burglar, Fred Malchow, was drawn into the web of the investigation. Malchow was no ordinary thief. He and other members of a gang would rob a residence, hop a plane and be in another part of the country that same day. He was questioned in the Norristown Pennsylvania Jail. Although he was known to have been in Chicago at the time of the murder, he steadfastly denied that he had had anything to do with Valerie's death.

Later, a fellow inmate informed police that Malchow had confessed the Percy murder to him. Totally unexpectedly, Malchow escaped from jail before he could be questioned further. The desperate career criminal was killed when, surrounded by police, he jumped to his death from a trestle into the Schuylkill River.

Three years after Malchow's death, another convict, Jimmy Evans, who had spent time in jail with him, came forward and told authorities that Malchow had also confessed to him that he had killed Valerie Percy. According to Evans, Valerie had awakened while Freddie was in her room. Freddie had held her down with one hand, while he stabbed her with the other.

Seven years after the murder, the name Fred Malchow came to the forefront once again. Harold Hohimer told detectives that his brother Francis had confided in him on the day after the murder, telling him, "I've been on a score. There was some trouble, and I had to do somebody in. I had to 'off' somebody."

Francis Hohimer, a burglar serving a 30-year sentence in the Iowa State Prison, was questioned by police. He told them that back in 1966 he had headed a gang of robbers. He disagreed with his brother's story. He claimed that he himself hadn't been in the Percy residence on the night of the murder. One of his gang, Fred Malchow, had been the killer. Francis went on to tell police certain details concerning the interior of the Percy home, which he could know only if he'd been there or if the killer had described them to him.

With the chief suspect in the case long dead, authorities felt that the Valerie Percy murder was unsolvable.

In 1966, after staying in seclusion for two weeks, Charles Percy announced that he was continuing his political campaign. He was successful in his bid for the U.S. Senate. In his victory speech, he said, "There is one person who is not here. She would have been happy to be here." Those present knew he was referring to his daughter Valerie.

# Peter Queen
# WAS CHRISSIE'S DEATH MURDER OR SUICIDE?

The demon rum has played a major role in many a murder case. Certainly, Chrissie Gall's alcoholism caused her death. Whether her life ended by means of murder or suicide is another matter.

Chrissie was the daughter of a shoemaker in Glasgow, Scotland. One of six children, she was forced, for financial reasons, to leave school at age 14 and obtain employment as a domestic. For years Chrissie worked to help support her family. In 1925, when she was 21, she was employed by the Queen family. It was while thus employed that she met the Queen's 24-year-old son, Peter. Peter had been married at age 18 to a young girl who was an alcoholic. After two years of marriage, Mrs. Queen was placed in an institution. The couple never lived together from that time on.

Peter fell in love with Chrissie. When she left his parents' employ to take care of her own seriously ill mother, he often called on her. After her mother's death, she stayed on to take care of her father.

Chrissie was a pretty girl of average intelligence. There is little doubt that, as Peter loved her, she in turn loved him dearly. Strangely for one so young, Peter had fallen in love for the second time with a girl who was addicted to alcohol. Peter, who didn't drink at all, was kind to Chrissie and always treated her with affection.

Three years after the death of his wife, Mr. Gall moved in with one of his other daughters and Chrissie left home. Peter saw to it that she was comfortably placed in rooms at the home of two of his friends, Mr. and Mrs. James Burns. By this time, Chrissie was drinking every day and was intoxicated half her waking hours. Three months later, Peter moved in with her and they lived together as husband and wife.

The year was 1931. Peter was 30, Chrissie, 27. Peter was still a married man. Chrissie was extremely sensitive to the situation and went out of her way to make sure none of her relatives knew she was living with a married man. She often said that this guilty knowledge had driven her to drink.

The drinking continued. Mr. and Mrs. Burns were sympathetic to Chrissie's condition and often had long talks with her in an attempt to get her to stop drinking. Chrissie always promised that she wouldn't drink anymore, but always returned to the bottle. She often threatened to commit suicide. Throughout it all, Peter was an understanding companion and lover.

In the summer of 1931, Chrissie turned the gas on in the kitchen and retired for the night in a drunken stupor. It was only by good fortune that Mrs. Burns managed to save both their lives. Shortly after this incident, Peter and Chrissie moved to their own home at 533 Dunbarton Road. Her family was still under the impression that she was a domestic. They had no idea she was living with Peter Queen.

Chrissie continued to drink heavily. Peter came to the conclusion that a change of scenery would do Chrissie good. He made arrangements for her to vacation in Aberdeen with her young niece Nessie. Chrissie would have to look after the little girl and Peter felt that keeping busy might assist her in staying away from alcohol.

On Thursday, November 19, Chrissie met her brother Bert. The two went pub crawling and Chrissie proceeded to get very drunk. When she returned to the house on Dunbarton Road with her brother, a worried Peter was waiting up for her. For the first time Chrissie had brought a member of her family to her home. Drunk as she was, she was able to tell Peter to please let on it was his aunt's house. Peter went along with Chrissie, and her brother left the house believing that she was a domestic to Peter's aunt. He would never see his sister alive again.

Next day, Chrissie woke up and proceeded to drink all day. That evening, two friends, Mr. and Mrs. Johnston, visited and found Chrissie in bed. They stayed some time and helped Peter feed her sandwiches and tea. The Johnstons left at 10:45 p.m. Four hours and 15 minutes later, at 3 a.m., Peter Queen rushed into a Glasgow police station and informed police that Chrissie was dead.

Police officers entered Chrissie's bedroom. She lay dead in her bed with the bedclothes pulled up, covering her chest. A rope, tied in a half knot, was around her neck. Her upper denture was still in place. Chrissie was dressed in her nightclothes. The rope, which proved to be part of a clothesline, was removed by a police officer, who would later state that the knot was very tight. The bedroom itself was eerie, in that nothing was disturbed. There was no sign of a struggle.

An autopsy indicated the obvious, that death was due to strangulation. Within two hours, Peter Queen was taken into custody and charged with murder. When charged, he said only, "I have nothing to say."

Peter Queen's murder trial began on January 5, 1932. A police officer took the witness stand and stated that when Peter first reported Chrissie's death in the police station, he had said, "My wife is dead. I think I have killed her."

The Johnstons were the last people, other than Peter, to have seen Chrissie alive. Mrs. Johnston told the court that in her opinion, when they left the house on Dunbarton, Chrissie had been totally intoxicated. Mr. Johnston didn't quite agree. He thought she was only slightly drunk.

Unfortunately, the pathologists who performed the autopsy neglected to examine the stomach contents or blood for alcohol. The evidence concerning Chrissie's condition was of prime importance to the Crown, who were attempting to prove that the woman was so helpless she could have been strangled without offering any resistance, which would account for the undisturbed state of the death scene.

Peter Queen testified in his own behalf. He stated that he and Chrissie had chatted for some time after the Johnstons departed. Chrissie had been extremely worried whether her brother Bert had swallowed the story about her being a domestic for Peter's aunt. Because Chrissie had been so weak from heavy drinking, he told her he had called a doctor who would be visiting with her the follow morning. Chrissie had told him to fetch their very best pillowslips in anticipation of the doctor's visit.

Peter said he went to fetch the pillowslips, but couldn't find them. He called out to Chrissie. When she didn't reply, he figured she had slumbered off. He sat down and smoked a cigarette. After about 15 minutes, he prepared to go to bed. It was then that he re-entered the bedroom and found Chrissie with the rope around her neck.

Peter shook Chrissie and then rushed from the house to the police station. He disagreed as to what he had said to the police officer. Peter swore he had said, "My wife is dead. Don't think I have killed her." Peter's statement is only one word different from the police officer's version, but the one word makes a world of difference to the meaning.

An expert testifying for the defence stated that Chrissie had definitely managed to strangle herself. He had examined the rope and said that because of its texture it would have stayed firmly fastened around Chrissie's neck even after she lost consciousness and her hands had fallen away.

It was the defence's contention that Chrissie had strangled herself while Peter was out of the bedroom searching for the pillowslips. The Crown believed that Peter had wrapped the rope around Chrissie's neck, thereby ridding himself of a woman suffering from both depression and alcoholism.

After two hours' deliberation, the Scottish jury found Peter guilty of murder with a recommendation for mercy. Peter was sentenced to death, but three days later this sentence was commuted to life imprisonment.

Peter spent over 20 years in prison before being released. He returned to Glasgow and created a new life for himself. None of his new friends knew his true identity.

Peter Queen died in May 1958. To this day, many believe that he was wrongfully convicted.

# Peter Reilly
# UNTRUE CONFESSION

This is the story of a mother and her son.

Barbara Gibbons was born in Berlin, Germany, on November 20, 1921. Her father, Louis, was in the import-export business and travelled a great deal.

The family moved to England when Barbara was still a child, and later, when the family business failed, to New York City.

Barbara eventually went to work for an insurance company. The family maintained a cottage in Falls Village, Connecticut, and for several summers Barbara would escape the city and make her way to her parents' summer retreat.

On March 2, 1955, Barbara gave birth to a baby boy. For no apparent reason, she called her baby Peter Reilly. No one other than Barbara was ever to know the identity of Peter's father. Barbara and her baby came to live in her parents' cottage.

As Peter grew up, it became apparent he was a good student and altogether a typical teenager, although there were those who may have thought him overly quiet. Eventually, Barbara and Peter moved into a small cottage that had once been a diner located near the village of Canaan.

Barbara and Peter got along well enough, but Barbara did have the habit of leaning heavily on her son when she thought he was in the wrong. Barbara often entertained rather un-savoury male companions, and thought nothing of drinking heavily in her son's presence.

Friday, September 28, 1973, should have been an ordinary day for Barbara Gibbons. Instead, it was to be the last day of her life. Barbara went shopping in Falls Village. She purchased some groceries and a wallet before returning to her cottage. At two o'clock, after school was dismissed, Peter joined his mother. They played a few hands of gin rummy.

That evening, Geoff Madow, a school chum of Peter's, dropped by in his car. He and Peter left Barbara watching Walter Cronkite on TV and headed for a teen centre meeting in North Canaan. Geoff drove his own car, while Peter, 18, drove Barbara's 1968 Corvette.

At 9:30 p.m. Peter left for home, arriving between 9:50 p.m. and 9:55 p.m. He entered the cottage, but his mother didn't respond to his greeting. He then went into her bedroom. His mother's nude body lay sprawled on the floor.

Barbara's eyes were blackened and her nose was broken. Both thighs were broken, and later it was discovered three ribs were fractured. Her stomach and back had been savagely slashed. Her throat had been cut in such a way that she was nearly decapitated. Barbara's blue jeans and panties were lying near her body. It appeared that she had been sexually attacked.

Within minutes police converged on the murder scene. This was really something. It wasn't every day that the peaceful little village had a homicide. That same night police read Peter his constitutional rights. They took a statement from him describing his activities up to the time he walked into his mother's bedroom. They also had Peter sign a waiver allowing investigating officers to question him without the presence of a lawyer. Peter's clothing was examined but no sign of blood was found on them. Stripped naked, his body revealed no scrapes or scratches.

Next morning, Peter was taken to Hartford and advised he was a suspect in his mother's murder. Peter may have even suggested a polygraph test would clear up the entire matter. Whoever first suggested the idea, the police were all for it. Once again, Peter was read his constitutional rights. He initialled each paragraph.

Sergeant Timothy Kelly was an expert at asking questions and operating his lie detector machine. Kelly and Peter came to an understanding that if Peter told all, the machine would effectively clear him of any suspicion in his mother's murder. Slowly the questions turned to the possibility that Peter may have killed his mother, but no longer could remember. Here are a few examples extracted from tape recordings of the interview.

*Kelly: Now is there any possibility that you came in that yard like a bat out of hell last night and hit your mother?*
*Peter: No.*
*Kelly: And you became frightened and you said, 'Holy Christ, what do I do now?'*
*Peter: No, I'm positive.*
*Kelly: Accidents can happen.*
*Peter: Right.*

A few minutes later.

*Kelly: From what I'm seeing here, I think you got doubts as to what happened last night, don't you?*
*Peter: I've got doubts because I don't understand what happened.*
*Kelly: Are you afraid that you did this thing?*
*Peter: Well, yes, of course I am. That's natural.*

Slowly and methodically, quiet, passive Peter Reilly was led through hypothetical situations illustrating that it was just possible he was the killer. More questions.

*Kelly: Remember you and I were talking and we were talking about your mother's legs. Remember?*
*Peter: Yes.*
*Kelly: What did you do to her legs?*
*Peter: I jumped on them.*
*Kelly: And what else did you do? What's really burning inside of you that you don't want to tell us about, that you did to your mother?*
*Peter: I'm not sure.*
*Kelly: What do you think you did?*
*Peter: Did I—I think I raped her.*
*Kelly: Okay, why do you say that?*
*Peter: I mean, that's what it seems like I did. That's what everything looks like I did.*

After 25 hours of questioning, Peter Reilly signed a statement confessing to the murder and mutilation of his mother. When news of Peter's confession spread through Canaan and the surrounding area, citizens were shocked. No one could believe Peter could harm anyone, let alone brutally murder his mother.

Peter was formally charged with his mother's murder. Bail was set at $50,000. Six thousand dollars was raised by concerned citizens, who formed a Peter Reilly Defense Fund. He was invited to stay with Marion and Meyer Madow, the parents of his friend Geoff.

Peter Reilly's trial began on March 1, 1974. Soon it was established that the police had acted fairly. They advised him of his constitutional rights. He had been fed and had been given time to sleep. At no time had he been threatened. As a result, his confession was admitted as evidence. A doctor took the stand and testified he thought Peter could have inflicted the wounds to his mother without getting blood on his clothing.

The jury was told that it had a choice of three possible verdicts: guilty of murder; not guilty of murder; or guilty of manslaughter in the first degree. After deliberating for several hours the jury found Peter guilty of manslaughter in the first degree. Later he was sentenced to 6 to 16 years in prison. Bail was raised to $60,000 pending an appeal for a new trial.

Again Peter's legion of friends came through with the extra money and again Peter was released from jail. By this time the dogged efforts of the local citizens had come to the attention of famous and influential people willing to assist the Peter Reilly Defense Fund in a material way. Among others, luminaries Arthur Miller, Mike Nichols, Dustin Hoffman, Elizabeth Taylor and Candice Bergen all took an interest in the case.

While his friends fought for a new trial, Peter returned to high school. He managed to graduate while still out on bail.

Finally, the court consented to a hearing in order to ascertain whether there were grounds for a new trial. With a new lawyer and funds to hire a private detective, this hearing progressed very differently from the trial that had preceded it.

During the course of the hearing, it became clear that while police had acted fairly on the surface, at no time did they direct a question towards Peter with the idea of clearing an innocent boy who had just found his mother's mutilated body. Instead, the questioning officers found themselves with a quiet, unsure, exceptionally pliable youngster, who would eventually agree to anything in order to please his interrogators. Doctors testified this extreme pliability was an outstanding feature of Peter's personality.

Peter's lawyer produced another suspect who had the motive and opportunity to murder Barbara. She had taunted him at every opportunity concerning his homosexual tendencies. In fact, the questioning of this witness became so critical that the presiding judge had to warn the lawyers that no one was on trial during the hearing.

On March 25, 1976, the court ruled: "After a long and deliberate study of all the transcripts of the original trial and the present proceedings, together with the pleadings and exhibits in both cases, this court concludes that an injustice has been done, and that the result of a new trial would probably be different."

Peter was not to stand trial again for the murder of his mother. On September 27, 1979, six years less one day from the time he walked into his mother's bedroom, the court ruled that "There was insufficient evidence to warrant prosecution."

No one has ever been convicted of murdering Barbara Gibbons.

# Alice Rhodes
# LOCKED AWAY

It has been said that all killers are despicable, but even in the murder business there are degrees. The nasties described in this piece rank right up there with the most reprehensible of all time.

The curtain of our horror story rises on the not-so-happy occasion of the marriage of 24-year-old Lewis Staunton to 36-year-old Harriet Butterfield. The nuptials took place on June 16, 1875, in London, England.

Lewis was small, cunning and totally bored with his occupation of clerk in an auctioneer's office. Harriet was a dumpy, ugly creature who, in the language of the day, was considered an imbecile. A year before her marriage, her mother had attempted in vain to have her certified as a lunatic.

One might wonder why Lewis Staunton would marry such an unappealing woman. The answer was cold hard cash. Harriet came complete with £4,000, a veritable fortune in those long-ago days.

The unlikely pair set up housekeeping in Loughborough Road, Brixton. Things didn't go well from the very beginning. A few weeks into the marriage, Mrs. Butterfield visited her daughter. She was coolly received by Lewis and left the Stauntons quite disturbed that all was not right with Harriet and her husband. Next day, she received a letter from Lewis, accompanied by one from Harriet. Both missives contained the same message. She was told in no uncertain terms that she wasn't welcome in the Staunton home and never to call again. I suppose mothers-in-law are accustomed to such treatment, but it still must have been hard to take.

Lewis retired from the clerking business and invested his newfound wealth. He also took up with a former girlfriend, Alice Rhodes. Alice was everything Harriet was not. Besides, she was sort of family, being the sister of his brother Patrick's wife, Elizabeth.

In March 1876, Harriet gave birth to a boy, Tommy. Rather than being pleased, Lewis found the child almost as obnoxious as he found Harriet. He had Alice Rhodes move into his house, ostensibly to look after his wife and his new son. Alice didn't do any of those things. She looked after Lewis.

Two months after Harriet gave birth, Lewis wrote to his brother Patrick relating how repulsive Harriet was and how she didn't take care of her personal hygiene. Patrick responded by suggesting that Harriet might find it pleasant to spend some time at his home, The Woodlands, in Cudham, Kent. The country air would do her good. Lewis shipped off Harriet and Tommy to his brother's home, where mother and child were given a room upstairs in the attic. Initially, Harriet took her meals with Patrick and Elizabeth, but it wasn't long before her meals were delivered to her in her room. Gradually, Harriet and her son were ignored and neglected. The one window in the room was boarded up. Harriet, who hadn't washed herself in the best of times, now totally disregarded cleaning herself or Tommy.

In October, Lewis and Alice Rhodes took up residence about a 20-minute walk from The Woodlands. Alice posed as Lewis's wife. No one had the vaguest idea that a few miles down the road his real wife and son were virtual prisoners, slowly starving to death.

Tommy grew so weak from lack of nourishment that Patrick took him to Guy's Hospital, where he died the following day. The death did not arouse any undue suspicions. When Lewis was notified of his son's death, he was somewhat less than distraught. He told hospital authorities his name was Harris and that the little boy was the son of one of his farm employees. He passed over 25 shillings for the child's burial. In Lewis's warped mind, that was the end of the matter.

By this time, Harriet was being fed leftover scraps from the Stauntons' table. When there were no leftovers, she wasn't fed at all. She had no washing facilities and grew so filthy that the other members of the family avoided the odour when they passed her door. Because she had no shoes, crusts formed on the soles of her feet. In time she lost the power of speech and made only guttural animal-like sounds.

As the months passed, Harriet was something that lived upstairs. She didn't exist to the outside world and was almost nonexistent to the Staunton clan. No great plan was hatched, but individually all three Stauntons and Alice Rhodes were waiting for Harriet to die.

Two things happened. Alice became pregnant and Lewis came to believe there might be an investigation if Harriet died at home. The four schemers decided to move Harriet out of Patrick's house. Lewis located a bedroom and sitting-room arrangement at 15 shillings a week, operated by a Mrs. Chalkins in Penge, London.

Harriet was in terrible shape. After all, she had not left her room all winter. The Stauntons knew they had to come up with a story for Mrs. Chalkins. They told her that the facilities were for Lewis's mother, who was basically healthy, but refused to eat. The concerned Stauntons asked Mrs. Chalkins for the name of a doctor. She recommended a Dr. Longrigg.

Harriet arrived at the rooming house on Forbes Road. Lewis and Patrick assisted her into the house. Mrs. Chalkins was shocked at her new roomer's appearance. She reeked of neglect. That night, Alice and Elizabeth stayed with Harriet. The two men took rooms at a nearby hotel.

Next morning, a Friday, the two women informed Mrs. Chalkins that Harriet had spent a difficult night and appeared to be very ill. Dr. Longrigg was summoned. He examined Harriet and told all concerned that she would be dead within 24 hours. She was placed in a nurse's care. The nurse was startled at the emaciated condition of her patient. At one-thirty that afternoon, Harriet died in her bedroom, while the Stauntons relaxed in the sitting room. No one shed a tear.

Within the hour, Lewis had an undertaker in the house. Dr. Longrigg signed the death certificate and left instructions with the nurse to lay out the body. Lewis attempted to have the burial take place that day, but the undertaker couldn't do the job until Monday.

The Stauntons returned to Patrick's farm. On Monday the annoying Harriet would be nothing but a memory. They would take the boards off the window and give her attic room a thorough cleaning.

Had the Stauntons displayed some emotion at Harriet's death, there is little doubt they would have gotten away with murder. Their callousness caused the nurse at Penge to wonder about the emaciated woman who must have been so neglected in life. She told the undertaker of her suspicions. He in turn spoke to a friend, who happened to be acquainted with Mrs. Butterfield. The acquaintance thought the dead woman might be Harriet. When Mrs. Butterfield learned of the death, she notified police. As a result of her complaint, the funeral was delayed and a post-mortem conducted. Dr. Longrigg immediately withdrew the death certificate.

The post-mortem indicated protracted undernourishment and protracted neglect. At the time of her death. Harriet weighed 70 pounds. A coroner's inquest was conducted. As a result, all four conspirators were arrested and charged with Harriet's murder.

Their trial was closely followed throughout England. Rarely have defendants been more despised by the British public. All four were found guilty of murder and sentenced to death.

Three days before the sentences were to be carried out, Alice Rhodes was given a free pardon. The sentences of Lewis, Patrick and Elizabeth Staunton were commuted to life imprisonment.

# Jimmy Riva
# DEVIL MADE HIM DO IT

Jimmy Riva was a bright little boy, but even as a preschooler he displayed tell-tale signs of being disturbed. He hurt animals and had an abnormal interest in blood. Later, in school, he showed flashes of brilliance interspersed with periods of depression. His grades suffered. In his early teens he let his hair grow to below his shoulders and wore a necklace of garlic.

The Riva family lived in Marshfield, Massachusetts, about 30 miles south of Boston. Many people in the town knew that Jimmy was one deeply troubled youngster. Sometimes, at night, he prowled the streets. Like some parents of disturbed children, Jimmy's thought that he might outgrow his aberrant behaviour. Several psychiatrists shared their optimism.

By the time he was 18, Jimmy had run away from home several times. Once, his parents found him in Florida. He had little regard for his appearance and rarely bathed. Away from home he lived off the land and broke into unoccupied homes for shelter.

Jimmy received psychiatric counselling and spent several short periods in mental institutions. Despite his history of irrational behaviour and his scrapes with the law, he had never displayed any physical aggression towards members of his family.

On April 10, 1980, Jimmy's grandmother, Carmen Riva Lopez, 74, was found dead in her burned-down bungalow at 19 East Street. Although Mrs. Lopez used a wheelchair, she was able to live alone and take care of her everyday needs. Her grandson Jimmy dropped in every so often to help her with heavier chores around the house.

Grandmother and grandson didn't get along. Mrs. Lopez

couldn't stand Jimmy's long hair and dirty appearance. She constantly berated him to cut his hair and bathe. Jimmy didn't take the verbal abuse well. He usually said little, quickly completed his chores and left the house as speedily as possible.

Authorities were at a loss as to the origin of the fire. Initially, they felt that they were investigating an accident caused by an infirm elderly woman. However, an autopsy revealed that the horribly burned Mrs. Lopez had died as the result of two stab wounds to the heart. Her lungs bore little evidence of toxic fumes, indicating that she was dead before the fire started.

In addition, two bullets were found in her body.

Both bullets had been painted gold.

A search of the cooled-down ruins of Mrs. Lopez's house uncovered a tin box that had escaped the ravages of the intense fire. The box, which belonged to Jimmy, contained several bullets covered with gold paint.

Jimmy was now the major suspect in his grandmother's murder. Brought in for questioning, he admitted visiting her on the day of the fire. He even admitted that he had argued with her as usual regarding his appearance, but vehemently denied having anything to do with her death or the fire. When Jimmy was searched at the police station, detectives found a bloodstained fishing knife in his back pocket. There were some hairs adhering to the blade. Jimmy was held in custody and charged with his grandmother's murder.

The case against Jimmy received a severe blow when laboratory analysis of the knife indicated that the blood on the blade was not the same type as Mrs. Lopez's and that the hair was not human hair. Police wondered if they had fallen into the trap of concentrating on one suspect to the exclusion of all others.

The murder investigation was at a standstill, but took a dramatic turn on June 14 when Jimmy's mother walked into the Marshfield Police Station and told detectives that she had just visited her troubled son. He had confessed to the murder of his grandmother in detail. The confession amounted to a horror story.

Jimmy told his mother that he was a vampire. He had shot his grandmother with bullets painted gold because he had been told to do so by voices that had total command over his actions. He had stabbed her with a kitchen knife and had attempted to drink her blood.

The voices of the devil and the vampires had urged him to drive to his grandmother's home. He had taken her washtub to the basement, but all the while had known that he would kill the elderly woman. Acting under the voices' instructions, he had previously painted his .38-calibre revolver with gold paint and had hidden it in the basement. His shots had not been fatal and his grandmother had begged for her life. That's when Jimmy had stabbed her with the kitchen knife. He explained that the voices had insisted and that he had been forced to comply with their wishes.

After Jimmy was sure his victim was dead, he had tried to drink her blood, but found this too difficult to do. He had doused the body with gas and had set it on fire.

Jimmy explained that after the killing he had contemplated suicide, but the voices had told him that would be the act of a coward. He had to obey the voices. Jimmy went on to tell his mother that he knew his grandmother hated him and the only way to satisfy the voices was to kill her and to drink her blood. They told him that he stood to gain many material rewards, such as cars and money, if he went through with his assignment.

Strangely enough, psychiatrists informed the court that Jimmy was competent to stand trial. On October 22, 1981, he was tried for arson and for the murder of his grandmother.

Defence attorneys logically pleaded that their client was insane, while the prosecution countered that Jimmy had planned, executed and covered up the murder knowing full well that what he was doing was wrong.

The defence presented a well-known psychiatrist who clearly stated, "He was insane at the time of the killing of his grandmother and is insane now. He was obviously not responsible for the murder by reason of insanity."

The prosecution scored telling points when their expert testified that Jimmy had taken a well-respected psychiatric test and had achieved marks indicating he was a "normal person." The prosecution agreed that Jimmy suffered from a mental illness, but argued that it did not diminish his capacity to recognize that he was doing something wrong.

A tape of Jimmy being questioned by police the day after the murder was played to the jury. The prosecution pointed out that the answers given by the accused indicated a normal, well-organized mind.

Evidently, this tape swayed the jury. Jimmy Riva was found guilty of second-degree murder and arson. He was sentenced to life imprisonment and must serve a total of 27 years before he is eligible for parole. After spending one month in prison, he was transferred to the state mental hospital at Bridgewater, where he is presently confined.

# Pauline Rogers
# POISON PAULINE

Morris Amos was a big healthy specimen, never sick a day in his life, until he took the miseries in the winter of 1977. Morris would bend over and complain that his bouts of cramp would be the end of him. On a good day, Morris could give Nostradamus a run for his money. He was dead on in regard to his future.

Morris's wife, Pauline, was a rock. Folks from Kentucky are like that. Whenever Morris complained, there was his Pauline with an encouraging word. When he began to lose serious weight, about 30 pounds in a few weeks, ever-loyal, ever-faithful Pauline was there at his side with piping hot chicken soup. It shouldn't have hurt, but it did. Morris complained of a burning thirst that wouldn't go away. Pauline brought him quarts of strawberry ice cream.

Louisville neighbours were amazed at Morris's rapid deterioration. He went from a good old boy with a substantial layer of suet cascading over his belt to a gaunt, feeble man, all in a few months. Diarrhoea on a daily basis will do that to a fellow.

Pauline insisted that Morris see a physician. The doctor took one look at him and agreed that something was drastically wrong with his 46-year-old patient. He prescribed vitamins and a high-protein diet. I would like to report that Morris's condition improved, but such was not the case. His condition worsened to such an extent that he had difficulty walking. The tips of his fingers turned blue and his face took on a grey, pasty look. On a second visit to the doctor, it was suggested that Morris reduce his workload, which was kind of redundant since Morris was now too weak to do much more than breathe.

A week after the doctor's latest advice, Morris was admitted to Suburban Hospital, where his illness was considered somewhat of a mystery. Physicians there couldn't figure out what was causing Morris to waste away to nothing. There were various suggestions, from muscular dystrophy to a virus, but all these conditions were ruled out.

On February 17, 1977, two days after being admitted to hospital, Morris died. Doctors believed that death had been caused by a heart attack, but weren't positive. They approached Pauline to suggest that a post-mortem would clear up any doubts and reveal the cause of her husband's rapid deterioration. Pauline wouldn't hear of it. She told the doctors, "My Morris would never approve of such a thing."

The death certificate was duly signed. Morris was laid to rest, accompanied by the usual formalities. It was sad. Pauline wept into a dainty handkerchief while her husband was lowered into his final resting place. Pauline received the proceeds of a modest life insurance policy as well as social security cheques. Life went on.

Five years later, when Morris's death was little more than a dim memory, Luther Rogers, an assembly worker down at the Ford plant in Louisville, was admitted to hospital. He complained of severe diarrhoea and a burning thirst. Luther tried every treatment his doctors recommended, but he went rapidly downhill. After several days in hospital, his health showed a marked improvement. In fact, Luther was so strong he was released into the loving arms of his wife.

Two months later, Luther, like a bad penny, showed up at the hospital again. He could hardly walk. Tests indicated a drastic decrease of white blood cells, but medics were stumped as to the cause. They met and discussed every possibility. Someone asked if Luther had ever been tested for poison. It was a long shot, but the doctors decided to conduct several tests. In the meantime, Luther's intake of food and drink was being carefully monitored.

Luther's wife visited as usual. She asked her husband's nurse if she could feed him some ice cream. After all, he complained constantly of his extreme thirst. The nurse could see no harm in ice cream. Luther looked up gratefully as his wife spoon-fed him heaping tablespoons of the cooling delicacy. It was strawberry, his favourite flavour. When Luther polished off the ice cream, his wife tossed the empty container into the wastebasket. After she left the hospital, Luther's lab tests were completed and given to his attending physicians. Normal urine tests contain 200 milligrams of arsenic. Our boy had 20,000 milligrams inside him. Someone was poisoning Luther. Doctors called in the police.

Detectives inquired about Luther's intake of food. They were assured that his entire diet was supervised and carefully monitored. Nevertheless, the nosy detectives wanted to question Luther's nurses. The nurses told the detectives that no one, absolutely no one, had fed Luther anything other than his prescribed nourishment, much of which was given intravenously. Of course, his wife was an exception. She had fed him strawberry ice cream. As a matter of fact, she had been there earlier in the day and had tossed the empty ice-cream container into the wastebasket.

The container was retrieved. Large traces of arsenic were found. Luther's home was searched for arsenic but none was uncovered. Finally, his wife's background was investigated. Well, son of a gun. Quicker than you could consume a mint julep, it was learned that Pauline Rogers's previous husband, Morris Amos, had died five years before under exactly the same circumstances that surrounded Luther's illness. Both had been healthy, robust mén who had wasted away in a matter of weeks for no apparent reason. In each case, Pauline had fed them strawberry ice cream. It was all much too much.

County coroner Richard Greathouse was made aware of the facts of Morris's death. Since arsenic remains in the hair and fingernails of deceased persons, he authorized the exhumation of Morris Amos's body. In June 1982, the body was transferred to University Hospital. A day later the results were delivered to the coroner's office. Morris had not died of a heart attack. Arsenic had been found in the body: 460 milligrams in hair, 470 in the stomach and 18,000 milligrams in the liver. From the hair it was ascertained that Morris had been systematically poisoned for over a year.

Pauline Rogers was taken into custody and charged with the murder of Morris Amos. Next day, she raised bail of $2,500 and was released from jail. That same evening, she was hospitalized with severe stomach cramps. Pauline had poisoned herself. She recovered, but the incident revealed that she was an avid gardener and had access to arsenic-laced pesticides.

In August 1982, Pauline Rogers was indicted on charges of murdering her previous husband, Morris Amos, and of the attempted murder of her current husband, Luther Rogers. Pauline was found guilty on both charges, although she never revealed the motive for her actions. She was sentenced to 20 years' imprisonment for murder and received the maximum sentence of 20 years for attempted murder. The sentences were to run consecutively.

Today, Pauline resides in the Kentucky Correctional Institution for Women. Officials there tell me she is a model prisoner and gets along well with staff and fellow inmates. She will be eligible for parole in the year 2000 at the age of 64.

# Timothy Roman
# THE TRAGIC LIFE OF SUSAN CABOT

When Harriet Shapiro's family moved from Boston to New York, they had no idea that little Harriet would become a Hollywood movie actress. Harriet, who was born in 1927, was an outstanding beauty with her olive complexion and flashing brown eyes. After graduating from Washington Irving High School, she was initiated into the acting profession, playing summer stock in Maine.

At age 23, Harriet changed her name to Susan Cabot and made her first movie, *On the Island of Samoa*, for Columbia Pictures. There followed a series of B-movies, such as *The Battle of Apache Pass*, *Flame of Araby*, *Tomahawk*, *The Wasp Woman* and many more. She appeared on the silver screen with the likes of Tony Curtis, Rock Hudson and Lee Marvin.

In 1959, at the height of her career, Susan made international headlines when she was romantically linked with King Hussein of Jordan. The unlikely pair dated and even arranged a rendezvous in New York before the romance fizzled, much as Susan's career faded, and eventually died. Susan was one of those beautiful women who had made a fine living for years as a budding starlet, but who never quite climbed the ladder to star status. She was quickly forgotten by the movie-going public.

Susan married businessman Martin Sacker, but eventually they divorced. She entered a second marriage to Michael Roman, bringing a son, Timothy, to the union. This marriage also ended in divorce.

Timothy had major health problems, having been born a dwarf, a fact that Susan could not accept. She spent thousands of dollars to save her son's life and to assist him in growing. As a youngster, Tim was subjected to growth-hormone injections over a period of years. While the experimental treatment succeeded in developing the lad's growth until he reached five feet four inches, the injections had severe side effects. When Susan was told that the injections threatened her son's life, she discontinued them, but immediately instituted other treatments. The large quantity of experimental drugs administered to Tim no doubt had a detrimental effect. He suffered from severe psychiatric problems and was considered to be emotionally immature during his teenage years.

Susan lived alone with her son in a luxurious home in the Los Angeles suburb of Encino, overlooking the San Fernando Valley. Years passed. Tim was her one consuming passion. Some said she was a domineering, obsessive mother who completely controlled the boy. Susan pointed out to her critics that when Tim was born it was estimated that he would grow to a maximum height of four feet. Because of her efforts, he was five feet four inches tall.

Acquaintances of Susan claimed that mother and son were emotional wrecks. She neglected her home to the point where they were living in abject squalor, with two large dogs as their only company.

In 1986, Tim was attending Pierce College, but didn't display any career direction. Although he had no friends, he did have a hobby. He was enthralled with the martial arts and read everything he could lay his hands on regarding the topic. In the main, his life revolved around his overprotective mother. Susan rarely let her 22-year-old son out of her sight.

On December 10, 1986, the strained relationship between the possessive 59-year-old Susan and her emotionally disturbed son burst into violence. Tim called police. They found him in the living room, sobbing uncontrollably. Susan Cabot, clad only in a purple negligée, lay dead on her bed. She had been beaten about the head. Tim told police that he had been attacked by a martial arts practitioner, who had overpowered him, cutting him on the arm and striking him over the head with some kind of blunt instrument. Tim said he must have been unconscious for about half an hour. When he regained consciousness, he called for help.

Paramedics attending to Tim noted that the knife wound on his arm was little more than a scratch and the bruise on his head had not even caused swelling. The first detectives at the scene listened to Tim relate how he was in bed earlier in the night, but was accosted when he got up to fix a sandwich. Police found it strange that there was no evidence of forced entry.

A search of Tim's room turned up a blood-smeared barbell, which proved to be the murder weapon. The many posters of martial arts films that adorned Tim's walls revealed the reason why he had picked a martial arts expert as his bogus attacker.

Tim was arrested and charged with his mother's murder. After so many years out of the news, the name Susan Cabot had made the headlines once more. Her old romance with King Hussein was again publicized with the additional juicy tidbit that Tim might have been sired by the king. It was rumoured that because Susan was Jewish, the romance was doomed and broken off by mutual consent.

Tim had more pressing problems. Several legal proceedings were conducted to ascertain if he was fit to stand trial. Eventually he was deemed to be capable. On May 1, 1989, over two years after his mother's death, Tim stood trial for her murder.

The prosecution painted Tim as a cold-blooded killer who knew very well what he was doing. He had planned the killing and had carried it out without hesitation or remorse. They also contended that he had inflicted superficial wounds to his own body in an attempt to invent an intruder. He had hated his mother for years for her domineering and possessive personality.

Tim's defence attorneys didn't see it that way at all, but before the defence had an opportunity to present its case, famed lawyer Chester Leo Smith took ill and could not continue. A mistrial was declared and a second trial set for October.

On October 5, the prosecution presented basically the same evidence as they had at the earlier trial. The defence leaned heavily on Tim's health problems. They pointed out that the boy had received hormone injections in his legs twice a week for 15 years between 1970 and 1985. In addition, they produced medical records indicating that Tim had been born with brain damage. Psychiatrists testified that his mental problems would have made it impossible for him to have formed the intent to kill his mother. It was a strong argument. There sat Tim in the courtroom, acting and looking like a boy of 14, although he had celebrated his twenty-fifth birthday in jail.

Tim took the witness stand in his own defence. He had drastically changed his story in the almost three years since the murder. From the witness stand he related that he and his mother had had a severe argument, which had culminated with her swinging the barbell at his head. Tim remembered trying to push his mother away, but nothing more than that. He admitted hiding the barbell. He admitted lying to police and making up the story about the man who had attacked his mother and himself.

Tim was found guilty of involuntary manslaughter, which carries a maximum sentence of four years' imprisonment. As Tim had already spent three years in jail, the judge sentenced him to a three-year suspended sentence. Because he had not been found guilty of the far more serious charges of voluntary manslaughter or murder, he was entitled to inherit his mother's estate of approximately one million dollars.

Timothy Roman walked out of court with his adoptive grandparents, a free man.

# Charley Ross
# THE KIDNAPPING OF LITTLE CHARLEY ROSS

Most of us are aware of the details surrounding the kidnapping of the Lindbergh baby from its nursery on March 1, 1932. The discovery of the child's body left the U.S.—indeed the world—in a state of shock. Bruno Hauptmann was eventually tried for the child's murder, found guilty and executed.

Far less is remembered today about the kidnapping of little Charley Ross, but at the time, his abduction caused almost as great an outcry as the Lindbergh tragedy. Charley was the first child kidnapped for ransom in the history of the United States.

Christian K. Ross lived in a large three-storey white house in the Germantown section of Philadelphia. Ross was a well-to-do businessman who devoted a portion of his time to politics and church affairs. He and his wife were considered to be pillars of the community. The happy, contented couple had seven children.

In the latter part of June 1874, Mrs. Ross departed for a vacation to Atlantic City with her eldest daughter, Sara. The two oldest sons, Stouton and Harry, left their home for a visit with their grandmother in Middletown. On Wednesday, July 1, the two youngest sons, Charley, 4, and Walter, 6, were at home with their sisters, Marian and Anne. Also about the home that day were two servants—a cook and a gardener.

Ross left for work in downtown Philadelphia. There was a sense of anticipation about the house, for the children were getting ready to celebrate the Fourth of July.

Charley and Walter went outdoors to play. No sooner were they outside than two men approached them in a horse and buggy. Both boys were unconcerned. They recognized the rig and the men. On the previous Saturday the two men had stopped and chatted with the boys, and had even given them some candy. The very next day the same thing happened. Now, for the third time, it looked as if the boys would get a treat. Incidentally, the familiar admonition "Never take candy from a stranger" is derived from this case.

Sure enough, the rig stopped and the two men offered the boys some more candy. When the men suggested they take the boys for a drive and buy them firecrackers, Charley couldn't wait to be lifted aboard the buggy. Walter scampered up on his own.

That evening, Christian Ross returned home from his business at six o'clock. His two sons were nowhere to be found. Accompanied by some concerned friends, he searched for the boys throughout the neighbourhood. As darkness fell, he was on his way to a nearby police station when he spotted Walter on the street. The boy was accompanied by a man named Henry Peacock, who had found Walter crying on a street corner some eight miles away and was delivering him to his home. Later, Peacock was checked out. He was exactly what he appeared to be—a concerned citizen delivering a lost, bewildered child to his parents.

Ross questioned Walter: "Where is Charley?"

"Why, he's all right. He's in a wagon."

After much questioning, it became apparent that little Charley had been spirited away by strangers.

On July 4, the Ross family received a ransom letter advising them that Charley was being held for a cash payment and that a more detailed letter would follow. With the receipt of the letter, the U.S. had experienced a new type of crime—money for the return of a child. Philadelphia police were at a loss for what action to take. They took none.

Analysts studied the letter and were convinced it was written by someone who was disguising his handwriting and purposely misspelling simple words. On July 6, another ransom letter was delivered, this time demanding $20,000 and warning the frightened parents not to let the police interfere with the drop off of the money.

All through July, the Ross family received notes from the kidnappers. They replied by placing advertisements in the local newspapers as instructed. It must be pointed out that, like the Lindbergh kidnapping, the Ross affair was public knowledge and received headline treatment across the country. The public thirsted for any new developments. Law enforcement authorities realized that if the ransom money ever changed hands successfully, there would be an epidemic of kidnapping throughout the country. All during July, Mr. and Mrs. Ross went through hell, for many of the kidnappers' letters contained details of what they would do to Charley if his parents didn't follow instructions to the letter.

Towards the end of July, the city of Philadelphia offered a reward of $20,000 for the arrest of the kidnappers and the safe return of the child. This reward attracted scores of crank calls and clues, all leading nowhere. Amazingly, the kidnappers kept up their correspondence with Ross.

Finally, the details of turning over the ransom money were worked out. Ross was to board a New York–bound train at midnight in Philadelphia. The kidnappers said contact would be made sometime during the trip. Ross boarded the train as planned, with two plainclothes policemen covering his every move. No attempt at contact was made. A further letter from the kidnappers made no reference to the aborted transfer.

On August 2, when Charley had been missing for a little more than a month, the first real clue to the mystery was uncovered. Ironically, it came from the New York Police Department. An old sea captain, Gil Mosher, went to the police with his story. He claimed his brother Bill had approached him the previous May with a scheme to kidnap one of Commodore Vanderbilt's grandchildren. He had turned down his brother, feeling the operation was too risky. The scheme was exactly the same as the plan actually implemented to kidnap Charley Ross. Gil figured it was too much of a coincidence. He was sure that his brother and a friend, Joseph Douglas, were the kidnappers. Gil's motive for coming forward was the reward money and a personal vendetta against his brother. He also stated that he could recognize his brother's distinctive handwriting, no matter what pains he had taken to disguise it.

When informed of this new development, Philadelphia Police Chief Kennard H. Jones, accompanied by Christian Ross's brother Joseph, rushed to New York. They heard Gil Mosher's story and had him describe his brother's handwriting before showing him the letter. Gil not only described the writing, but also pointed out his brother's habit of folding the letters in a distinctive fashion. Other minute details convinced the police that Bill Mosher had written the ransom letters.

The word went out to pick up Bill Mosher and Joseph Douglas. Both men were small-time thieves who had been in and out of jail for a number of years. Apprehending them was no easy task, for the police had made the decision to keep their search undercover. They feared for Charley's life if the kidnappers found out that their identity was known.

Abruptly the case took an unexpected turn. Judge Van Brunt owned a large modern summer home in Bay Ridge, Long Island. His brother, Holmes Van Brunt, lived in a large, gracious old Victorian home directly across the judge's lawn. When the judge returned to the city for the winter, he set up an alarm system that would go off in his brother's permanent home if anything was disturbed during his absence.

On the night of December 14, this alarm went off, waking up Holmes Van Brunt. Holmes, his son Albert, together with gardener William Scott and hired hand Herman Frank armed themselves and cautiously headed for the judge's house. They hid in the bushes waiting for the robbers to come out.

Finally the cellar door opened. Van Brunt shouted, "Halt, stop!" Two shots whistled past his head. The four concealed men opened fire. One of the intruders fell, shouting, "I give up," but the other man made it to a lane, where he ran into Albert, who swung his shotgun at the robber, breaking his arm. As the burglar raised his pistol, Albert got two shots away with his revolver, sending bullets into the robber's head and chest. The man fell but was still breathing. The shooting abruptly ceased.

Someone gave the dying man a drink of whiskey. Van Brunt bent over the critically wounded man: "Young man, your time is pretty short now. If you have anything to say, you had better be about it at once. Who are you? What is your name and where did you come from?"

The answer was barely audible: "Men, I won't lie to you. My name is Joseph Douglas. That man lying over there is William Mosher. Mosher and I stole Charley Ross from Germantown."

With a certain degree of desperation, someone asked, "Who has charge of the child now?"

The fallen man replied, "Mosher knows all about the child. Ask him."

The men, now joined by their wives and a few neighbours, huddled over Douglas.

"Mosher is dead," they exclaimed. "Can you tell us where the child is?"

"I don't know where he is. Mosher knows." Then Douglas added, "The child will be returned home safe and sound in a few days." Joseph Douglas closed his eyes and breathed his last.

The search for little Charley Ross continued. He was spotted in several U.S. cities, in Montreal, Toronto and Vancouver, as well as several Mexican and European cities. Over the years many adults have claimed to be Charley Ross, but all such claims have been disproved. Members of Charley's family continued to search for him for the remainder of their lives. When his parents died, his six sisters and brothers continued the search.

On July 1, 1924, the fiftieth anniversary of the kidnapping, Walter, who had become an extremely successful businessman, made a public statement concerning his brother's abduction. He stated that all the claimants to Charley's identity were cranks, but he still held out hope that the mystery might one day be solved.

To this day, no one knows what became of Charley Ross.

# Michael Sams
# HE PUT HIS VICTIM IN A COFFIN

This time would be different, thought Michael Sams as he meticulously planned the perfect crime. His previous attempt had been amateurish in its execution.

On July 9, 1991, he had plucked part-time prostitute Julie Dart off the streets of Leeds, England, and had killed her. A blow to the back of the head with a ball-peen hammer had rendered the girl unconscious. He had finished her off by strangling her with a ligature. Two days after Julie's disappearance, Michael had written a letter to police demanding £140,000 for her safe return. Police responded, but Michael pulled out of the complicated drop-off procedure before it was completed. A few days later, Julie's body was found in a field.

Michael now felt that the time had come to implement the perfect crime. He planned well. The victim was chosen, the plot perfected. Michael would kidnap a female and keep her hostage until the ransom was paid.

On Wednesday, January 22, 1992, Michael had an appointment to meet Stephanie Slater, a 25-year-old real estate agent employed by Shipways, a large real estate organization. Using the name Bob Southwall, he had phoned for an appointment to view a home at 153 Turnberry Road in Birmingham. He was waiting outside the door when Stephanie drove up in her company-owned Ford Escort.

Stephanie showed the house to her client. Without warning, in an upstairs bathroom, Michael pulled out a knife and a chisel. Stephanie couldn't believe this was happening to her. She lunged at him and the pair struggled. Stephanie felt the pain in her hand as the blade sunk into her flesh. Her attacker pushed her backward into the bathtub, helpless. The fight was over. She shouted, "Don't kill me, please don't kill me!" The man's voice rose, "Shut up, shut up. Be quiet. Don't look at me, don't look at me."

Michael knew exactly what he was doing. He tied, gagged and blindfolded his victim. Stephanie decided then and there to do everything this man asked of her. Her life depended on her wits.

Michael led Stephanie downstairs and into a vehicle. Twenty minutes later, they came to a stop. Michael assured Stephanie that she was not going to die unless she caused trouble. He informed her that she was being held for ransom. Michael had Stephanie make a tape recording for her employers. She repeated her captor's words, outlining her precarious position and advising them that they would be contacted again. Michael placed the tape in an envelope, which he had Stephanie lick shut. He told her if he licked the envelope, police would be able to obtain his DNA prints. Stephanie knew she was at the mercy of no ordinary criminal. This guy had thought of everything.

After driving for well over an hour, the pair arrived at their destination. Michael was alternately cruel and kind to Stephanie. He shared a pot of hot tea with her, but interspersed their chat with the threat that if she screamed while the gag was out of her mouth or if her blindfold slipped from her eyes, he would kill her.

Michael placed Stephanie in a coffinlike wooden box which she entered feet first. He undid her handcuffs in order to place her hands over a bar above her head before refastening the cuffs. Stephanie's hips scraped against both sides of the wooden box. It was pitch-black and bitterly cold inside Stephanie's coffin. She heard the sound of her captor's car disappearing in the distance. Stephanie Slater was so very alone.

Michael Sams drove the 15 miles from his workshop in Newark, Nottinghamshire, to his home in Sutton-on-Trent. His plan was now in motion. It would not only make him rich, but would illustrate his brilliance as a master criminal. He had come a long way since that day 15 years earlier when he had been imprisoned for car theft. While in prison, he'd contracted cancer. His leg was amputated and replaced with an artificial limb. All that was behind him now. He crawled into bed with his third wife, Teena.

Next morning, Michael drove to his workshop. Stephanie was in terrible shape. The blood had drained from her hands and arms. Her hips were scraped from rubbing against the side of the box. When her gag was removed, she had difficulty speaking. She had almost frozen during the bitterly cold night. Michael explained that he was demanding £175,000 from her employers, Shipways, which was owned by a large organization, Royal Life Estates. Once the money was turned over to him, he would set her free.

Letters received by Shipways were turned over to the police. From the misspellings, police connected Julie Dart's murder with Stephanie Slater's abduction. They realized they had a bona fide madman on their hands, and a clever one at that.

Four days passed. Stephanie was now following a regimen. Michael had improved the coffin so that her hips no longer scraped its sides and had provided her with blankets. When she awoke, she was allowed out of her capsule for breakfast and exercise. She was permitted to relieve herself, after which she was returned to her coffin. She talked to her captor, all the while being cooperative and complimentary to him. He in turn seemed to enjoy her company and appeared to be growing fond of her. At no time did he sexually interfere with Stephanie in any way.

Finally, the night of the ransom money transfer arrived. Michael gave Stephanie's superior, Kevin Watts, explicit instructions over the telephone as to how to proceed with the £175,000. Watts was to act as courier with the warning that police were not to be present. Police taped this conversation. Michael told Stephanie she would soon be home with her parents.

Kevin Watts started on his journey. He received written instructions at several phone booths, eventually finding himself on a lonesome road with instructions to place the money in a tray on the rail of a stone trestle. Watts did as he was instructed. Down below in the pitch blackness was Michael Sams. Attached to the tray was a length of thin cord. As soon as the sound from Kevin's vehicle faded into the distance, Michael pulled on the cord, causing the ransom money to tumble down at his feet.

Michael returned to Stephanie in his Newark workshop. She was elated. She realized that if he had failed to return, she would have starved to death in her cage.

Originally, Michael had planned to drop Stephanie off in an isolated area and let her walk to a phone. Now he felt some sympathy. He would drive her home. He knew very well her house would be guarded by police, but a block or two away would be safe enough. Michael pulled up near Hembs Crescent and let Stephanie out. His last words were, "Get back to your normal life as soon as possible. You may need some counselling. I'm sorry it had to be you." Stephanie stepped out of the car and removed her blindfold. The streetlights blinded her. She staggered as she walked.

Les Barnaby was up late that night watching a movie on the TV when he heard Michael's car pull up. He glanced out his window and saw an orange Metro speed away. An apparently intoxicated girl staggered down the street. Stephanie made her way to her home, knocked on the door and surprised her overjoyed parents. She had been held prisoner for eight days.

Police now had a description of the man who called himself Bob Southwall, as well as a tape of his voice. Les Barnaby came forward with a description of the suspect's vehicle. The case was featured on the BBC's widely viewed "Crime Watch" program. Police received more than 1,000 calls claiming to know the identity of the wanted man. One proved to be correct. Michael's first wife, Susan Oake, had no doubt about the kidnapper's identity. She immediately informed police.

Michael was arrested without incident and eventually the ransom money was recovered. He admitted to kidnapping Stephanie, but claimed to have no knowledge of Julie Dart's murder. However, an English jury found him guilty of murder, kidnapping and unlawful imprisonment. Michael Sams received three life sentences. Later, in prison, he confessed to the murder of Julie Dart.

# Ed Schroder
# HE DRILLED THE DENTIST

All the fellows at the London and San Francisco Bank couldn't understand the sudden change that had come over Ed Schroder. For years Ed had been a steady employee. Good family man, too. Salt of the earth. That was before June 12, 1880.

After that date, he hardly talked to anyone, was often absent from work and abruptly stopped playing poker with the boys. Ed just wasn't the same old Ed anymore.

The man his colleagues knew so well had been a career banker for eight years. He had been married for the same length of time to Mary Stebbins, the daughter of Reverend Horatio Stebbins. The reverend, who would later become regent of the University of California and trustee of Stanford University, was no small potatoes. He was furious when his daughter eloped with Ed, but, like many a father before him, resigned himself to the fact that foolish young girls marry boys they love rather than those their fathers choose.

The marriage was a happy one. Ed and Mary lived in a pleasant home at 1164 Alice Street. Two little Schroders blessed the union.

One fine day in 1878, Mary had a toothache. She paid a visit to Dr. Alfred LeFevre, a successful dentist who was well married to a sickly wife and was the father of four children. Mary didn't have a simple cavity. I know that for a fact because she continued to visit the 45-year-old dentist for the next two years. In case there is any doubt, we are talking hanky-panky here.

On the night of June 11, 1880, Ed was supposed to work

late, but packed it in around 9 p.m. He returned quite unexpectedly to his home on Alice Street. As he entered the front door, he heard someone rush out the back. His wife was upstairs in bed. Ed asked Mary who had been visiting. She told him that it was Sarah Gallagher, the family maid. When questioned further, Mary changed her story. She told her husband she wasn't a hundred percent sure it was Sarah, it might have been Sarah's boyfriend.

Mary had made the mistake of altering lies in mid falsehood. Ed was suspicious. He begged Mary to tell him the truth. Finally, she blurted out that the visitor had been Dr. LeFevre. She went on to say that the dentist had not only filled her teeth, he had also satisfied one of her more basic needs.

Ed was devastated. Next morning he advised Reverend Stebbins that his daughter was an adulteress. The reverend questioned Mary, who denied all. Folks, Mary lied through her teeth.

To prove his daughter had been visiting the dentist on legitimate dental business for the previous two years, the reverend, accompanied by Ed, paid a visit to Dr. LeFevre. They wanted a detailed accounting of her many visits. Regrettably, the doctor's accountant kept the books and he was not present. Ed said something about blowing the dentist's brains out, which was unfortunate. Such threats have a way of becoming evidence at murder trials.

The pair left the office without the bill for Mary's dental work. Later, Dr. LeFevre gave them a receipted bill in the amount of $83, which was kind of revealing, as it was later proven that Mary had never paid the dentist one penny.

Well, folks, it had been quite a 24 hours for our Ed. His wife had admitted to being unfaithful for two years and it appeared to him that her lover was paying him off with a receipted bill for dental work.

Ed took to the demon rum with a vengeance. It was as if he were attempting to drink the world dry. He became a close-mouthed, brooding man and often stayed away from the bank. His colleagues and friends had no idea what was causing his mental anguish until July 26. That was the day Ed drilled dentist Alfred LeFevre.

It was all very dramatic. The doctor had several patients with teeth just waiting to be drilled, cleaned or pulled. Seated on chairs, leafing through those months-old magazines favoured by dentists, were a Mrs. Spotts and a Miss Agnew. They would only be scared out of their wits. Seated in the dentist's chair at the time was a Mrs. Keeney. She would think the world had come to an end.

The doctor left Mrs. Keeney's side to fetch one of his hideous instruments. At that precise moment, Ed dashed into the office brandishing a pistol. He fired point-blank at the dentist, who staggered across the office to Mrs. Keeney's side before falling to the floor. Displaying a distinct lack of confidence in his aim, Ed fired a second shot at the fallen man. Dr. LeFevre was able to mumble that Ed had shot him in cold blood and without provocation. He died on the office floor. Mrs. Keeney had the dubious distinction of being the doctor's last patient.

A police officer summoned from the street was greeted by Ed with the great line, "Officer, do your duty. I have shot a man. No man can seduce my wife and live."

Ed was taken into custody and charged with the murder of Dr. LeFevre. His trial, which began on November 29, 1880, was the social event of the winter season in the Bay area. Little else was discussed. This one had everything: a backstairs romance between a banker's wife and a married dentist; the shooting beside that torturous chair; Mrs. Keeney's frightening experience. The Schroder murder trial was definitely not to be missed.

On the surface, it appeared as if Ed's goose was cooked. The victim had said he did it, even Ed said he did it. In addition, a gunsmith told the court Ed had purchased the murder weapon on the day of the fatal shooting.

As we all know, however, murder cases are not that simple. The jury was faced with a difficult decision. If they believed that Ed had planned the murder with intent to kill while in a clear state of mind, then he was guilty of murder in the first degree. If convicted, he would be sentenced to death. On the other hand, if Ed had been driven insane by the thought of his wife having sexual intercourse with Dr. LeFevre over a prolonged period, he could be acquitted.

Three days later, the jury returned a verdict of not guilty. Ed burst into tears and embraced the foreman of the jury.

Ed and Mary left the courtroom arm in arm to the cheers of the standing-room-only crowd. They remained in San Francisco only a few months. The notoriety of the murder case forced them to leave the city and they soon disappeared from public view.

It is not known whether his wife Mary required any further dental work.

# Chicken Stephens
# SENATOR'S DEMISE

John Walter "Chicken" Stephens was a sleaze. He was also a U.S. senator. Occasionally, the two go hand in hand.

Chicken was a good ol' southern boy who couldn't stay out of minor scrapes with the law. In 1849, while still a lad, he apprenticed as a harness maker, an honest profession if not one with a great future. When he stole a quantity of leather from his employer, his family made restitution to keep their boy out of the Leaksville, North Carolina, jail. Despite the occasional misdemeanour, Chicken became an official of the Methodist church in town and sold bibles on the side to augment his meagre income.

Let's take time out to relate how Chicken got his colourful nickname. This doesn't have much to do with the story, but it's so much fun that I can't pass it up.

A neighbour, Tom Ratliff, caught our boy red-handed with two headless chickens he had just stolen from Ratliff's coop. Ratliff was furious and had him charged with theft. When Stephens learned of the charge, he went after Ratliff with a pistol and a club. Two strangers separated the men and received superficial bullet wounds for their trouble. In the end, Stephens paid fines totalling $2,000 for the theft and the assault. The chicken story spread throughout the state, and forever after Stephens was known simply as Chicken. Years later, a local boy commented, "Mr. Stephens stole a chicken and was sent to the state Senate and if he'd steal a gobbler he'd be sent to Congress."

Undaunted by his unfortunate legal encounters, Chicken married a local girl, Nancy Waters, and after the prescribed nine months became the father of a healthy daughter. Seeking greener pastures, he and his family moved to Yanceyville, North Carolina. Once ensconced in his new surroundings, Chicken made the mistake of attempting to cook a crooked deal with Dr. Allan Gunn, a local man who was running for sheriff. He promised to deliver enough votes to assure Gunn's victory for the paltry sum of $4,000. Gunn was outraged and reported the offer to the Methodist Church. As a result, Chicken was excommunicated.

Once again, Chicken overcame a scandal. He ran for the position of state senator and won. Chicken saw the job as a licence to feather his nest. He immediately sought and obtained several minor posts, which enabled him to charge for favours. An unscrupulous judge issued Chicken a licence to practise law. That privilege cost him $20.

Now in high gear, Chicken, as a justice of the peace, reaped a percentage of every fine he levied. He also made a fortune selling political favours. By 1870, Chicken was a wealthy man with a fine family living in a large rambling home. There was one fly in the sarsaparilla: over the years Chicken had made many enemies. To protect himself, he carried several knives and a pistol.

Around this time, the Ku Klux Klan was a formidable force in North Carolina. When the members of that organization thought the legal community was lax, they were not above taking the law into their own hands. The Klan felt that Chicken had had his own way long enough. They would get rid of him in their own unique fashion.

On May 21, 1870, the Democratic Party was holding a convention in the Caswell County Courthouse in Yanceyville. The building was crowded with 300 delegates. Outside, in the town square, citizens came and went. It was a busy, exciting day in the town.

Chicken Stephens attended the convention. He listened to the speeches for some time before leaving with Frank Wiley, a huge man who had formerly been sheriff of the town. The two men were seen in the main lobby of the courthouse at a few minutes after 4 p.m. Wiley left the building alone. No one could remember seeing Chicken after that.

Back at the Stephens' residence, Nancy waited for her husband. He had told her he would be home by five for supper. When Chicken didn't arrive by 6 p.m., she contacted his two brothers, who went around town looking for the missing man. As night fell, they could only trace Chicken's movements to the courthouse lobby. They contacted county officials, who felt that it would be best to search every nook and cranny of the old building in the light of day. Several men were posted to guard the courthouse that night.

Bright and early Sunday morning, in a room used primarily to store firewood, the searchers came across the body of Senator Chicken Stephens. A rope was deeply embedded in his neck and his throat had been slit from ear to ear. He had also been stabbed in the chest with a pearl-handled pocket knife which lay on the floor beside the body. Chicken's gold watch and his money were intact, eliminating robbery as the motive for the crime.

An inquest into the death was conducted immediately. The jury concluded that Chicken had been murdered by persons unknown. That was the official stand, but many believed that the Klan was responsible. Everyone in Yanceyville knew that the leader of the Klan in that area was John Lea, a 27-year-old Confederate veteran. He had been in the courthouse on the day of the murder, as had several members of his organization.

Two months after the murder, Lea, former sheriff Wiley and two other Klan members, J.T. Mitchell and Felix Roan, were taken into custody. Although their guilt was strongly suspected, there was nothing more against them than vague insinuations. They were released from custody, to the elation of the townsfolk. In fact, a celebration parade was held in their honour.

The murder remained unsolved. As the years passed, John Lea was often asked if he had been involved in Chicken's murder. In 1912, he presented a typewritten sealed document to the North Carolina Historical Commission with instructions that it be opened upon his death.

Captain John Lea lived until 1935, when he passed away in South Boston, Virginia, at age 92. The sealed letter was opened. In it, Lea confessed that he had been the leader of the Klan and had organized and planned the murder of Senator Chicken Stephens. The three men arrested with him at the time of the murder were all involved, as were others. Lea named them: James Denny, Joe Fowler, Tom Oliver, Pink Morgan and Dr. S.T. Richmond. Lea had outlived everyone connected with the crime.

In his letter, he described every aspect of the murder in detail. Wiley had lured Chicken to the wood-storage room. The men had made their way singly to the room. When Chicken entered, he found himself staring into the barrel of a Colt revolver. He realized what was about to happen and pleaded for his life. As he pleaded, Mitchell placed a rope around his neck and drew it tight, forcing Chicken to the floor, gasping for air. Tom Oliver stabbed him in the chest and slit his throat. The men stepped back. Chicken Stephens was dead.

The conspirators left the room one by one and met that same night at the outskirts of Yanceyville. At Lea's suggestion they took an oath not to reveal what had happened in the courthouse wood-storage room. None of the men in on the execution-style murder of the senator ever came in conflict with the law during their lifetime. Many led outwardly exemplary lives and several held high public office.

# Antonio Strollo
# BEST FRIEND WAS A KILLER

Around the turn of the century, times were hard in Italy. For many, the United States was the land of opportunity. Construction was booming along the Eastern seaboard. Docks, railroads and huge buildings were being erected. Labour was in demand, and Italy provided much of the manpower to keep the construction industry going. From Italian stock would emerge names such as La Guardia, Di Maggio, Caruso and hundreds of others from all walks of life who would make their contribution to the development of the United States.

But all were not success stories. In the tiny town of Culiano, in the province of Salano, lived an elderly lady with her two sons. Her husband, after a lifetime of back-breaking work in the stubborn fields, had long since died. Now the widow Torsielli lived only for her two sons, Vito and Toni. For years she prepared their meals and washed their clothing while each day they worked the fields from sunup to sundown.

The years passed. Soon the old woman was confined to bed. She couldn't be left alone. The boys took the bulk of their meagre earnings and hired a woman to look after their mother. The situation looked hopeless. There was no way out. They would all live and die in Culiano without ever enjoying a moment's pleasure.

Other boys from the town were going to America. Some came back wearing bright socks and neckties. They gathered up their parents and took them back with them. Vito and Toni had a meeting. It was decided that they would live on practically nothing until they saved the fare for Vito to go to America. Then he would send money back to Culiano to take care of his mother. Who knows, maybe he would save enough for them all to end up in America.

Toni couldn't help being envious of his older brother but the scheme seemed the only way out of their predicament. Vito left for the New World. Toni and his mother waited for a letter, but no letter came. A month passed, two months, a year; still no letter came. God forbid, Vito might be dead, thought Toni. He and his sick mother might be waiting for nothing.

In the meantime, Toni was in love with Nicoletta Lupero, and had been since he was a child. Their situation seemed hopeless. Toni hardly made enough money to support himself and his mother, without taking on the added burden of a wife. Toni reached his thirtieth birthday. Nicoletta was 25. Some of their friends had been married for 10 years. From time to time, a former resident of the village would return from America. Some said that Vito was now rich, though no one said they had actually seen him. All tried to convince Toni that he was crazy if he didn't go to America.

Finally, he and Nicoletta decided that they would dismiss the woman who was looking after his ill mother. Nicoletta would move in with the aged Mrs. Torsielli and Toni would go to America, save enough money and bring them both to the New World. The day Toni left Culiano, the parish priest had to physically pull him out of his mother's arms.

Once in America, Toni met several other men his age from his home province. Through his acquaintances, he obtained pick-and-shovel work in Lambertville, New Jersey, 70 miles from New York City. Toni didn't mind the hard manual labour. It was no worse than what he had done back home. The big difference was that now he was getting paid good wages. Sometimes he made as much as $40 a month. Toni sent money home every pay day. Even after deducting his living expenses and the money he sent home, he still had some left over to put in the bank.

The months flew by. Toni made friends in Lambertville. Antonio Strollo was his best friend. It was Strollo who actually wrote Toni's letters to his mother and Nicoletta. He read the replies as well, for Toni could neither read nor write.

For three years, Toni worked and saved, always keeping an eye open for news of his brother, Vito. It was Strollo who got the bright idea that they should advertise for the missing man. Strollo was a true friend. Toni wouldn't listen when other men said Strollo was lazy and couldn't hold a job. Moreover, they said, he drank far too much Chianti. Strollo wrote and inserted the advertisement for the missing Vito in the *Il Progresso*, New York's Italian newspaper.

A letter came from Vito. He had seen the ad. He begged Toni to forgive him for not writing to their mother. Now that the ice was broken, he wanted desperately to see his brother. He told Toni he was prosperous, married and had children. He lived in Yonkers.

Toni was overjoyed. Vito was rich. Everything would still work out. Toni dictated a reply, which Strollo wrote and mailed to Vito. Several letters were exchanged by the brothers. It was decided that at the end of the month, pay day, Toni would leave his job, withdraw his savings of $300 and visit Vito. Toni would then continue to Italy, settle his family's affairs before returning to America with Nicoletta and his mother. Strollo would accompany Toni to Yonkers. As the great day approached, Toni's landlord, Sabbatto Gizzi, wrote down his name on a piece of paper and gave it to Toni. He wanted Toni to be sure to write.

On August 16, 1903, Toni and his friend Strollo boarded the train for New York. They transferred to a trolley. At the end of the line they continued on foot. Soon the pair found themselves in the country. Toni was hungry. He spotted a man digging in a field of mushrooms. He strolled over and asked where the closest restaurant was located. The man told him that there was a good Italian restaurant—The Promised Land—in Yonkers. Toni chatted for a while. Later the man was to state that the last he saw of Toni and Strollo, they were taking a short cut through some woods that adjoined his field.

Once in the woods, Strollo pulled a knife on Toni and stabbed him more than 30 times. Then he cleaned Toni's clothing of everything that could identify the dead man and took the $300. He had never seen so much money in his life.

In the ferociousness of his attack, he almost hadn't noticed his cut hand and knee. They didn't hurt. That night Strollo took a room at the Mills Hotel on Bleecker Street in New York City. He felt good, even though the cuts on his hand and knee got blood all over his bedsheets.

Next morning, Strollo ate a hearty breakfast, bought a cigar and a new suit. He bought a book, *Sua Maesta a Sua Moneta (His Majesty and His Money)*, to read on the trip back to Lambertville. Strollo was supremely confident that the body, if ever found, would never be identified. Back in Lambertville he would tell Toni's friends that he had left Toni with his brother in Yonkers. He didn't have to account for Toni's absence.

Toni's body was found the very next day by the mushroom digger. He immediately recognized the body as that of the man who had inquired about a restaurant the previous day. Police searched the body and found only one tiny piece of paper, which had obviously been overlooked by the killer. On it was written: Sabbatto Gizzi, P.O. Box 239, Lambertville, New Jersey. Detectives questioned Gizzi in Lambertville, and within 36 hours of the murder, they were face-to-face with Antonio Strollo.

The story of the lost brother was revealed to the police. Strollo told the whole story, but denied killing Toni. Soon the authorities located the store where Strollo had purchased the new suit. When they questioned the hotel clerk at the Mills Hotel, he told them of the bloodstained bedding. The mushroom digger identified Strollo as the man who was with Toni shortly before the victim was killed.

Strollo was taken into custody. Informers were placed in his jail cell, and soon the whole story came out. Vito had never been found. All the time it was Strollo who had written the letters to Toni, duping him into believing they were from his long lost brother. It was all an elaborate scheme to get Toni to withdraw his savings of $300, lure him to some isolated spot, kill him and steal his money.

On March 11, 1908, Antonio Strollo was put to death in the electric chair for the murder of Toni Torsielli.

Vito Torsielli was never found.

# Larry Swartz
# STABBING FRENZY

Robert and Kate Swartz met when both were students at the University of Maryland. Bob became a highly qualified electronic engineer, while Kate pursued a teaching career. They married and eventually settled in Annapolis, Maryland, where they purchased a suburban home at 1242 Mount Pleasant Drive.

The Swartzes had all the creature comforts, as well as the security that comes with two substantial salaries. There was one flaw in their apparently happy marriage. Kate couldn't have children. They decided to adopt a family.

Larry, the first child to be adopted, was a handsome six-year-old with a crop of jet-black curly hair. He had been shunted from foster home to foster home since birth, but seemed to be an appreciative, loving youngster who fit in well with Bob and Kate.

Michael, the second boy to be adopted by the Swartzes, was an angular eight-year-old. He too had been brought up in a series of foster homes. Unlike Larry, he didn't hit it off well with his adoptive parents right from the beginning. Although he had a relatively high IQ, his school work wasn't up to par. The Swartzes placed a high value on education and it rankled that their oldest son wasn't doing well in school. Michael was confrontational and seemed to be always at loggerheads with his mother and father. At times Bob would lose his temper with the boy and give him a sound thrashing. Larry didn't do that well in school either but he had a more placid, easy-going personality than his older brother. The two boys got along famously.

The Swartzes adopted a third child, four-year-old Annie, who had been abandoned by her South Korean parents. Annie soon became the star of the entire family. The two boys loved to teach her English and both Bob and Kate doted on her. As the years passed, there was still animosity between Michael and his parents.

One day, when Michael was 14 years old, he had promised his parents that he would stay at home. He disobeyed them and sneaked out a window. Meanwhile, Kate and Bob returned. It was a case of the straw that broke the camel's back. They locked the boy out and called his social worker. Bob and Kate made their views crystal clear. They simply didn't want Michael anymore. In their view, they had tried everything. Their lanky son, who had sprouted to six feet six inches, was more than they could handle. Michael moved out and for the next few years was transferred from one mental institution to another.

With Michael's departure, it seemed to Larry that all his parents' wrath descended upon him. True, his school work was deplorable, but nothing he did seemed to satisfy them. That's not entirely true. When he decided to become a priest and entered a high-school seminary in Pennsylvania, Bob and Kate were extremely proud. It didn't last. Larry dropped out of the seminary and returned home. The bickering continued, mainly over Larry's poor school work. When he turned 17, he told friends that he couldn't wait until his eighteenth birthday so that he could legally move out of his parents' home.

On the night of January 17, 1984, police were called to the comfortable home on Mount Pleasant Drive. A neighbour had summoned them. They were greeted by Larry Swartz and his nine-year-old sister, Annie. The boy was calm, considering the sight he had seen. In the study, police came across Bob Swartz's body. He had been stabbed many times. Furniture was overturned and there was blood on the floor and walls. Just outside the house in the snow, another officer found Kate Swartz's nude body. She too had received several stab wounds. The snow in the area of the body was soaked with blood.

Larry was able to answer the officers' questions. The

bodies were those of his parents, 51-year-old Bob Swartz and 43-year-old Kate. Larry told police that a noise had awakened him about 11 p.m. Annie was already awake and told him that their parents weren't in their bed. Larry looked out the kitchen window and saw his mother's body lying in the snow. He went on to tell detectives who were now at the scene that his brother, Michael, no longer lived at home. He was undergoing tests at the Crownsville Hospital Center, a psychiatric institution located only a few blocks from the Swartz residence. Larry explained that Michael was no longer welcome in their house because of the bad feeling between him and his parents. In fact, Kate had often mentioned to Larry that Michael was a mental case and that she was afraid of him.

An autopsy indicated that Bob had been stabbed 17 times from his neck to the pit of his stomach. He also had a number of defensive stab wounds to his hands and arms. Kate had been subjected to seven stab wounds, but had been killed by a blow to the back of her head that had caved in the top of her skull.

Michael Swartz immediately became the prime suspect in his parents' murder. Officials at the Crownsville Hospital informed detectives that the psychiatric dormitory where Michael was housed was totally secure. At the time of the murder he had been behind locked doors. Despite the hospital authorities' word that Michael had been confined, detectives tested the premises by having themselves locked in the dormitory. They found that other than the locked door, there was only one way out and that was through a heavily barred window, which proved to be impenetrable. It would have been impossible for Michael Swartz to have killed his parents. Police looked for another suspect, someone who hated the victims enough to stab them time and again after they were dead.

Three days after the Swartzes' funeral, Larry confided to his lawyer that he had murdered his parents. According to his statement, he and his father had argued that evening over one of Bob's computer programs which Larry had messed up. Larry went upstairs to his room and proceeded to finish off what was left of a bottle of rum he had hidden there. When he came downstairs, his mother started bugging him about exams he was then in the process of writing. Larry picked up an axe and struck Kate from behind. He then grabbed a steak knife and proceeded to stab her over and over again.

Bob must have heard the noise and suddenly appeared before Larry. Without a word, Larry spun around and plunged the knife into his father's chest. Bob staggered backward, but Larry was upon him like a wild animal, stabbing in a crazed frenzy until his victim lay still.

Larry dragged his mother's body outside into the snow and undressed her. He tossed the knife and axe into a swamp backing onto their property. Re-entering the house, he went upstairs and told Annie that everything was all right. She had just been awakened by a bad dream.

With Larry's assistance, the murder weapons were retrieved. His lawyers were able to plea-bargain the first-degree murder charges to two counts of second-degree murder in return for a guilty plea. Larry was sentenced to two concurrent 20-year prison terms with the rather lenient stipulation that eight years of each sentence be suspended. The sentence also stipulated that he receive psychiatric therapy.

Larry Swartz served his time at Maryland's Patuxent Correctional Institute, where he succeeded in earning his high-school equivalency diploma before being paroled.

# Kathy Telemachos
# BAD BLOOD

George Telemachos wanted the best for his only daughter. He tried his hardest, but it just didn't work out.

George and his wife moved from New Zealand to the United States because of their chronically ill baby son. The family settled on the southeast coast of Florida in Broward County, where Kathy, their second child, was born. Unfortunately, she suffered from the same serious liver ailment as her brother. Four years after Kathy's birth, her brother died.

George went into the restaurant business and prospered. No matter how hard he worked to make a living, he devoted much of his time to his sickly daughter. In hindsight, there are those who say she was his obsession. George flew Kathy around the country to consult with specialists. He opened more restaurants to defray Kathy's substantial medical bills. In the end, his devotion to his daughter affected his marriage. George's wife filed for divorce in 1977. It took two years before the decree was granted and another eight years for the courts to award shared custody of Kathy to her parents.

All the while, Kathy's health was failing. In 1981, at the age of 10, she underwent a liver transplant at Pittsburgh's famed Children's Hospital. A year later it was necessary to replace her rejected liver with another transplant. The second operation was a success. It was the first successful transplant of its kind to take place in the United States.

During Kathy's ordeal, George was constantly at her bedside. When she was well enough to travel, he brought her home to Florida. With the help of her father and mother, Kathy regained her strength. As the years passed, she was able to take part in normal everyday activities. During her last year in high school, she experienced a stunning setback when her kidneys failed. At age 18, Kathy received a kidney transplant with her mother as donor.

Upon Kathy's release from hospital, George gave her a car as a present. When she mentioned she didn't like the vehicle, her father bought her another. Whatever Kathy wanted, she got. George well realized he was spoiling his daughter, but he loved her so. After all, she had been seriously ill since birth.

Kathy was now a beautiful young woman. George wanted her to attend college against her wishes. Perhaps this was the turning point in their relationship. Kathy began to hang around with the wrong crowd. When George sold his restaurants and purchased the Baker Street Tobacconist Shop in the Hollywood Fashion Mall, he employed his daughter. George believed it would occupy her mind and keep her off the streets. The ploy backfired.

One day, Erik J. Delvalle, a high-school dropout, strolled into the shop to purchase a pack of cigarettes. Within weeks, he and Kathy were engaged to be married. To say that George was displeased with the match would be an understatement. He was devastated. In simple terms, he didn't believe Erik was good enough for his Kathy. He felt that Erik was a bum, which wasn't that far off the mark. By now George was well aware that Kathy had been introduced to marijuana. One day he noticed a .38-calibre revolver sticking out of her purse. When George discovered that money had been taken from his shop's cash register, he fired Kathy and ordered her out of the house. Kathy and Erik took an apartment of their own.

On July 23, 1990, after George hadn't been seen for almost two days, neighbours entered his home. They found George dead in his bed. He had been shot in the centre of the forehead with a weapon held only inches from his head. The entire house was in a shambles. Drawers had been pulled out and the contents of closets scattered about the floor. Detectives on the scene didn't feel that robbery had been the motive. It appeared to them that the murder had been a cold-blooded execution-style assassination made to look like the work of burglars.

It wasn't long before detectives learned of the bad blood that had existed between the victim, his daughter and her boyfriend. In addition, it was discovered that on the night of July 21, a police officer had questioned Kathy, Erik and a friend, Vince Magona, near George's home. The three were left to go on their way, but the officer had taken their names. Now that encounter took on a greater significance.

Kathy, Erik and Vince were picked up and questioned. Vince immediately spilled his guts. He told police that Kathy had led him and Erik on a dry run of the house a few days before the murder so that they would be acquainted with the layout. On the night of the murder, all three entered George's home. Vince and Erik made their way to George's bedroom, where Erik shot the hapless man as he lay asleep in bed. Vince told police he had been promised $300 by Kathy, but that she had only given him $100 from money she had taken out of her dead father's wallet. Kathy was definitely not a loving daughter.

When Erik heard that Vince had talked, he too decided to tell all. He added that he had tossed the .38-calibre revolver into a canal as they fled the murder scene in Kathy's car. Initially, Erik admitted that he had pulled the trigger, but upon learning of Florida's death penalty, he changed his story, stating that Kathy had fired the fatal shot. For her part, Kathy refused to discuss her father's murder.

Through questioning the young people's friends, detectives learned that the threesome had bragged about the murder before George's body was found. Kathy and Erik believed George to be worth close to $5 million. They had often mentioned that upon his death Kathy would be one rich girl. In reality, George had spent great amounts of money on Kathy's health problems. Although comfortable, he was worth considerably less than one million dollars. Ironically, it was revealed after the murder that George was suffering from heart and lung ailments and had only a few months to live.

Vince Magona was permitted to plead guilty to second-degree murder and conspiracy to commit first-degree murder in exchange for his testimony against Erik and Kathy. In this way he avoided the possibility of a date with Florida's electric chair. Hoping to be sentenced as a juvenile, Vince took the witness stand and told his story. He got off lightly. The presiding judge sentenced him as a youthful offender, imposing a prison term of three years, to be followed by two years' probation.

Erik pleaded guilty to second-degree murder. He was sentenced to life imprisonment with no possibility of parole for 25 years. During Erik's sentencing process, the direct motive for the murder surfaced. While it was true that the killers knew that Kathy would inherit her father's money upon his death, they had a more urgent matter with which to contend. They had stolen blank cheques from George and had forged his signature. In all, they had cashed $8,600 worth of cheques to purchase furniture for their apartment. George had to be killed before he discovered the theft.

Kathy refused to plea bargain. Vince and Erik both testified for the state at her trial. It wasn't pretty. Vince said that Kathy had insisted on being in the bedroom so that she could watch her father die. After deliberating for two days, the Florida jury found Kathy guilty of conspiracy to kill and first-degree murder. They recommended by an eight to four count that she be put to death. Despite this recommendation, the presiding judge overruled the jury's wishes and sentenced Kathy Telemachos to life plus 30 years' imprisonment.

Although the state of Florida is now executing male killers, not one woman has ever been put to death in the state. Since capital punishment was reinstated in the United States in 1976, only one woman, poisoner Velma Barfield of North Carolina, has been executed.

# Bill Thacker
# MOB LYNCHED THACKER

Our neighbours to the south take their politics seriously. Not only have they developed the distressing habit of assassinating their presidents, they are also not above killing each other over minor political differences.

Back in 1900, Bill Thacker lived, loved and drank locally brewed bourbon in his home town of Noah, Kentucky. Bill owned the general store and was one of the town's leading citizens. Yes, it's true, he slugged back that bourbon like it was going out of style. But say what you will about Bill, he was a good family man. He and Mrs. Thacker had five strapping children.

Bill hated Democrats. It is unclear why or how he acquired this abnormal distaste, but it was a well-known fact around Noah that when Bill was in his cups it was a good idea for anyone belonging to the Democratic Party to give him a wide berth.

On Monday, July 30, 1900, Bill was downing rotgut with a vengeance. He rounded up his 16-year-old son Robert and told him they were going hunting. Robert wasn't averse to spending a day in the woods with his dad. Who knows, if they were lucky they would bag one of those mean black bears. Bill explained that that wasn't the type of hunting he had in mind. He figured that they would round up a few Democrats and have some good old-fashioned fun with them.

Father and son mounted their horses and trotted off toward the nearby town of Foxport. On the way, Bill took long swigs from his bottle of bourbon. He didn't seem to mind telling everyone he met about his mission. He even told grocery-store owner Elijah Boling that he planned to hunt down a few Democrats. To emphasize his point, Bill flashed a pistol he was carrying in his coat pocket.

Out on the street, Bill met John Gordon, a strapping 21-year-old local farm boy. He asked John two questions—if he was a Democrat, which was answered in the affirmative, and if he wanted a fight, which was answered in the negative.

Bill strolled into Million's General Store. Inside were Homer Million, the son of the owner, and Miles Earls, another local boy. The two were discussing guns, as good old boys down Kentucky way are prone to do. John Gordon strolled in. So did Robert Thacker. Bill wanted to get things percolating. He suggested that his son Robert could beat the pants off John. John replied that he didn't know Robert and had no intention of fighting him.

Bill had tried, but there was no way to entice any Democrats into a friendly little scrap. In disgust, he and Robert mounted their horses and headed for nearby Mount Carmel. No sooner had they started off than they came upon Bert Wykoff and his two sons, Cleveland and Grosey. Bert and his boys were putting up a picket fence. Bill shouted, "Hurray for McKinley!" referring to President William McKinley. Bert replied, "We are going to beat McKinley this time."

Before you could say pork barrel, Bill and the Wykoffs were hurling insults at each other. As the men argued, John Gordon showed up to enjoy the fun. Robert Thacker shouted to his father, "Let's get away from these sons of bitches Democrats." John took exception to the remark and replied, "Who are you calling sons of bitches?" Robert answered clearly enough, "You." With that, John suggested they square off.

Robert pulled out a knife. John reached for a pole, but before he had it in his hands, Bill Thacker shot him directly above the left eyebrow. John slumped to the ground, critically wounded. Bill mumbled to no one in particular, "I hated to do that, but I had to."

Many of the good citizens of Foxport were attracted to the commotion. They stood around watching Bill Thacker, who was now acting like a madman, waving his pistol from side to side. Several men in the crowd attempted to reason with Bill, but he made it clear that he would only surrender to the justice of the peace, Squire Gaebke. Meanwhile, someone had fetched Dr. Emmet Pope, who examined the seriously wounded man and suggested that he be lifted out of the sun into the shade of some nearby trees. Soon after being moved, John Gordon died. Finally, Squire Gaebke showed up and took Bill into custody. He was lodged in the Maysburg jail to await trial.

In January 1901, Bill Thacker stood trial for the murder of John Gordon. Since several reputable citizens had heard all Bill's threats and had seen the cold-blooded killing, you would think that the results would be a foregone conclusion. Such was not the case. Bill claimed that John had picked up a large pole and would have killed his son if he hadn't shot him. In fact, Bill said that he had jumped between his son and John. It was only after John shouted, "I will kill you both" that he drew his weapon and fired. The bogus yarn did him no good. The jury quickly brought in a verdict of guilty.

Bill appealed on a technicality and won a new trial. All the same evidence was paraded before another jury. In addition, Robert Thacker was called on to verify his father's story. Robert made a major mistake by admitting he was carrying a knife when his father shot John. This pretty well destroyed Bill's story of shooting to save his son's life. Once again, Bill was found guilty and sentenced to life imprisonment. Once again, he appealed. The appeal was successful and Bill was returned from penitentiary to be lodged in the Flemingsburg jail to await his third trial.

That summer of 1903, rumours spread throughout the area. Bill Thacker would appeal forever and eventually would be freed. Was there no justice? John Gordon had been a gentle, well-liked boy who had never harmed anyone. He was dead. His killer showed no remorse. Stories about the murder were exaggerated. One such rumour purported that after Bill shot the boy, he sat on his victim's chest and smoked his pipe. Didn't such a man deserve to be punished?

On the night of July 15, 1903, the good folks of Fleming County gathered in secret by lantern light. Their purpose was clear. They fully intended to take the law into their own hands.

The mob met only minimum resistance at the jail. The keys to Bill's cell were handed over without too much discussion. Bill was dragged screaming and struggling from his cell. To quiet him, someone hit him over the head with a rock. The terrified man was taken to an orchard near Mount Carmel and unceremoniously hanged from a fruit tree.

Next day the town was quiet. It seemed no one had actually attended the lynching. A coroner's inquest concluded that Bill Thacker had met his death at the hands of persons unknown.

# Albert Tirrell
# SLEEPWALKING DEFENCE

Every so often the public is treated to a murder trial where somnambulism, or sleepwalking, is put forward as the principal defence. Somnambulistic behaviour was first used as a defence in North America by an attorney in 1845. Let's take a peek at the circumstances surrounding this most unusual murder case.

The Tirrell family of Weymouth, Massachusetts, was a proud, wealthy clan, big in the shoe business. They owned the largest factory in the area.

The patriarch of the family shuffled off his mortal coil in 1843, leaving control of his business and personal fortune to his 25-year-old son Albert. Al was a fine cut of a man, standing approximately six feet tall. He was well married to a gracious young woman who, wouldn't you just know it, answered to the name of Prudence. Al and Prudence had brought two little Tirrells into the world.

Al took to the shoe racket like a half sole takes to a brogue. For a year the entire Tirrell clan was ecstatic with the patriarch's choice. The shoe company prospered.

Then Al took a business trip to New Bedford. Old records indicate he was on the lookout for a good deal concerning the purchase of leather. He didn't find leather, but he did find a willing young brunette named Maria Pickford. Maria was a buxom, good-looking New England lass who was definitely tired of the rough whaling crowd she was accustomed to cavorting with around New Bedford. Al was more in keeping with what a girl had in mind when she thought of a good catch.

As for the conscientious shoe manufacturer, he fell about as hard as an ill-fitting, ankle-high reinforced work boot. Al simply forgot about Prudence, the shoe business and the two little Tirrells, pretty well in that order. He couldn't get enough of his Maria. To correct this situation, he installed his new love in a cosy little apartment in Boston. About the only time Al showed up at the factory in Weymouth was to collect his pay.

The entire family got on Al's tail. No Tirrell in the history of the Tirrells had ever strayed from the straight and narrow. In no uncertain terms, they told Al to smarten up. As for Prudence, well, Prudence cried a lot.

Brother-in-law Nathaniel Bayley was delegated by the family to have a serious chat with Al. Nat did the best he could. He pointed out that a man of Al's stature had a responsibility to the family business, not to mention his wife and children. Al agreed. But then the allure of that well-chiselled face and voluptuous figure drew him to Maria like a bee to honey.

One mustn't get the mistaken impression that all was roses with Al and Maria. *Mais non.* They fought like cats and dogs, but always ended up on the proverbial couch where, as we all know, much can be forgiven.

In September 1845, the lovers partied a tad too strenuously at the conservative Hanover House in Boston. They were unceremoniously asked to leave the establishment and seek accommodation in surroundings which catered to a more rowdy clientele.

The Tirrell family was astounded at Al's behaviour. More to teach him a lesson than anything else, they had him arrested and charged with adultery. Naturally enough, they soon relented and helped defend their wayward member. In the end, the court forced Al to post a bond promising to keep the peace for six months and not to associate with Maria.

Al pouted about the harshness of his sentence for an entire day before dashing over to Maria's new digs on Cedar Lane in Beacon Hill. The couple hit the sack with a vengeance. Al and Maria didn't surface for the better part of a week. Actually, Maria didn't surface at all.

On October 27, 1845, a fire broke out in Maria's room.

When firemen arrived, they quickly extinguished the small blaze in the mattress. On the bed lay the body of Maria Pickford. Her throat had been viciously cut with a straight razor, which was found on a table a few feet from the body. Al had left several items of clothing in Maria's room when he had hastily departed.

Police traced the wanted man. Hours earlier he had woken up Timothy Fullam, the proprietor of a livery stable. Fullam knew Al and had often rented him rigs. Now his customer appeared to be in a stupor. Al mumbled, "Someone tried to murder me. I'm in a scrape." Fullam thought Al was a bit tipsy.

Al drove to Weymouth, where he met with his brother-in-law Nat Bayley. He insinuated that he had spent the night with Maria, violating the conditions of his bail. Nat had no idea that Al was wanted for murder. He gave his brother-in-law some money and advised him to get out of town. Later, Nat would tell investigators that Al had appeared disoriented and confused.

Al made good his escape. He managed to obtain a berth on the freighter *Sultana* and remained at large for four months. Detectives traced the wanted man and took him into custody when the ship docked in New York.

On March 24, 1846, the apparently open-and-shut case came to trial in Boston. It appeared that Al didn't stand a chance. He admitted spending the night in question with Maria. He also admitted that he had sought help from his brother-in-law. Surely Al would end his days on the gallows. But such was not to be the case.

Al's wily lawyer, Rufus Choate, became intrigued with his client's confused state immediately after Maria's death. He dug deeper and learned that when Al was three years old, he had climbed out of bed and, while sleepwalking, had scrambled out a window to the edge of the roof. His father had pulled him to safety. Al had had no recollection of the incident the following morning.

Al's reputation as a sleepwalker grew as he reached puberty. To control his nocturnal wanderings, his parents locked him in his room at night. The boy chafed at this restriction until his parents relented. At age 16, Al left the house, clad only in his nightshirt, harnessed a horse and drove to an uncle's home some distance away. His amazed uncle discovered Al unhitching the horse in the bitter cold while completely asleep. Once awakened, Al had no idea how he had arrived at his uncle's home.

Prudence Tirrell took the witness stand in her husband's defence and related that she had awakened one night to find Al clutching her throat. She screamed and Al woke with a start. He apologized profusely, although he couldn't remember attempting to strangle her.

Lawyer Choate shouted at the court, "If Albert Tirrell murdered Maria Pickford, he was not responsible for what he did because he was asleep at the time and unaware of what he was doing." Choate went on to explain that on the morning of October 27, when his client reached the livery stable, "He was just awakening from somnambulistic sleep. He did not know where he had been or what he had been doing."

The Massachusetts jury deliberated for only two hours before returning a verdict of not guilty. Albert Tirrell left the courtroom a free man with the loyal and ever-loving Prudence at his side.

# William Udderzook
# WHERE THERE'S SMOKE...

I have often pondered why it is considered irresponsible to bet the coin of the realm on one particular horse on the assumption that the chosen steed will dash around an oval faster than its friends. Yet, if a person bets $50 that he, or she, will most certainly depart this world before the first snow falls, that's considered to be sensible, frugal and responsible.

This latter bet, or insurance, if you will, has given rise to a host of criminal activity, all designed to relieve those big bad insurance companies of their reported vast amounts of other people's money.

Everybody is fascinated by a spectacular, honest-to-goodness fire. In the more rural areas of North America, a respectable blaze is, in many instances, the only relief the agricultural set have from the excruciating boredom of just plain living. On many occasions, I have heard the good farmers mention one to the other, "No harm's been done. There was no one inside, and anyway, the insurance company will pay for everything."

Unfortunately, on February 2, 1872, there was someone inside. Four miles outside of Baltimore, on the York Road, a cottage owned by a Mr. Lowndes blazed merrily away. As the flames licked high into the crisp winter air, Lowndes twisted his handkerchief in anguish as one of his choice properties burned to the ground.

While thus engaged, he conversed for almost an hour with another spectator who had the unlikely name William E. Udderzook. You can imagine Lowndes's surprise when, after watching the fire for such a long time, his fellow flame watcher mentioned that he thought his brother-in-law, Winfred Goss, was still in the house.

Lowndes was, of course, familiar with his tenant, Mr. Goss. Now that he thought about it, he never did feel that Goss was the most stable character in the world. He particularly didn't like the idea that his tenant followed the rather precarious occupation of inventor. Goss had the habit of carrying around a ratchet screwdriver, his latest gadget. At the present time, he was working on inventing a substitute for rubber. It seemed right strange to Lowndes that an hour before, when the fire was just getting hot, Udderzook had not mentioned that there was someone in the house. At that time it might have been possible to attempt a rescue. Now it was too late.

As the fire cooled, the remains of what had once been a human being were removed from the blackened ruins. Later it was discovered that Goss had fortunately prepared himself for just such a tragic eventuality. During the previous four years, he had taken out four life insurance policies with a total payoff of $25,000. As recently as a week before the fire, he had the foresight to sign up for the last $5,000. The beneficiary of all four policies was his wife, Eliza Waters Goss, who it is my pleasant duty to report, was not in the house when it burned.

Now, this was all fine, but the police had one sticky question in search of an answer. How did healthy, 37-year-old Winfred manage to get himself trapped in the not-so-towering inferno. His brother, Campbell, could shed no light on the mystery, having only heard of the tragedy the day following the fire.

Our old friend Udderzook volunteered that he and the deceased man had been drinking whiskey on the afternoon of the blaze. Mrs. Goss was not at home. As suppertime approached, Udderzook left the cottage to eat with a neighbouring family, the Engels.

Later, when Udderzook and young Gottlieb Engels started off to rejoin Goss, they saw that the cottage was on fire. They assumed that a kerosene lamp, which had been giving Goss trouble, had exploded. The coroner was inclined to go along with Udderzook's story, but the insurance companies were another thing. They felt that where there was smoke, there was fire of quite another kind.

Those insurance companies had sneaky little investigators turning up all kinds of interesting bits of information. For example, despite Campbell Goss's solemn declaration that he had only heard of the fire the day after it occurred, the insurance men discovered that the very night of the untimely blaze, he had rented a horse and buggy from a livery stable where the chief subject of conversation was the spectacular fire. Not only that, he had galloped away into the country.

Those evil-minded insurance types were convinced that he picked up his brother and drove him to a nearby railway station. They believed Winfred was alive. Try as they might, the insurance operatives just couldn't get it through their heads that a man whose total income was $1,200 annually would legitimately fork over $500 for insurance premiums. Then there was the strange coincidence. You see, Winfred Goss had closed out his bank account the day before the fire.

All of this was reason enough for the insurance companies to hold up payment. Mrs. Goss was the soul of patience. She waited a full year before she brought suit against the companies. The insurance companies gained permission to exhume Goss or whomever, in order to examine his teeth. In this way they would identify the victim once and for all.

Mrs. Goss assured the investigators that her husband had had all his teeth. An autopsy revealed that the man found in the fire had only nine teeth. Based on this rather sound evidence, the insurance companies felt that Goss had not met his death in the fire. They decided to defend themselves against Mrs. Goss's suit.

Despite the evidence, Mrs. Goss was awarded the full amount of the policies, plus interest. It is difficult to reconcile the jury's verdict with the evidence, but suffice it to say, when it came to widows or insurance companies, juries always ruled in favour of widows. At least in 1873 they did.

Not at all discouraged, the insurance companies appealed

the verdict. This time it was rumoured far and wide that they would investigate until they turned up the missing W. Goss, assuming, of course, he was alive. These rumours came to the attention of our dear friend with the strange name, William Udderzook.

On June 30, a few weeks after the favourable verdict had been passed down, Udderzook took a little trip to Jennerville, Pennsylvania. He checked into a hotel with a middle-aged stout stranger, who never did give his name. Next evening, Udderzook rented a horse and carriage from a livery stable. He and the stranger drove away. At midnight, Udderzook returned the carriage and the following morning checked out of the hotel. He was alone.

The livery people were not that happy with the condition of the carriage. There were several large bloodstains on the interior walls, a floorboard was broken and two blankets were missing. Partial damages were recovered on the spot when the proprietor of the stable found a man's large ring under a seat.

A week later, a traveller was attracted by a group of buzzards making a racket just off the main road. Upon investigating, he found the head and trunk of what had once been a middle-aged, heavy-set man. Twenty-five yards away, partially buried, were a matching pair of arms and legs.

A coroner's jury identified the body as Udderzook's companion. On July 25, Udderzook was arrested and charged with murder. The insurance companies claimed that the body was that of Winfred Goss. If you have been keeping track, we now have two bodies thought to be W. Goss.

By the time Udderzook came to trial, the plot was clear. Some unfortunate soul, who was never identified, was murdered and placed in the Goss house before it was set ablaze. The real Winfred Goss went into hiding with Udderzook's help, who in turn was in cahoots with the widow and Winfred's brother Campbell.

When the insurance companies didn't come across with the $25,000 and threatened to find Winfred, the three conspirators decided to kill him for real. No one could prove that Mrs. Goss and Campbell were involved with Udderzook. If those blasted buzzards hadn't circled Winfred's assorted parts, Udderzook might have gotten away with it.

Alas, such was not to be the case. The prosecution was able to trace Winfred's activities from the time of the fire to the time he was murdered. Remember that ring found under the seat of the carriage? It was the property of Winfred Goss.

The jury must have studied the case at great length. They deliberated more than two days before finding Udderzook guilty of murder.

On November 12, 1874, in Westchester, Pennsylvania, Udderzook was led to the gallows. To the very end he insisted that all his troubles were caused by those vindictive big bad insurance companies.

# Helen Ulvinen
# THE PERFECT COUPLE

Carol and Dave Hoffman were the perfect couple. They owned a lovely home in Corcoran, Minnesota, and were the proud parents of two healthy children, Heidi, 3, and baby Bridgette. It wasn't unusual to see Carol and Dave lugging their small boat down to nearby Weaver Lake early in the morning to fish or scuba-dive.

The Hoffmans had been married for nine years when they realized that although Dave did quite well at his machine operator's job, they were regularly a bit short of funds. It was decided that Carol would re-enter the workforce at a factory in Golden Valley, a few miles from their home.

It was a great idea, but it didn't work out. Carol had to organize babysitters, rush home from work to prepare meals and take care of her two little girls. She was perpetually tired. The couple's social life suffered.

Dave had a solution. He invited his 65-year-old mother to live with them. Helen Ulvinen loved her grandchildren, and the thought of living with them held great appeal. She also felt she could be of help to her son and daughter-in-law. Helen closed her home in Minneapolis early in the summer of 1980 and moved to Corcoran.

There is something awkward about having the mother-in-law move in, isn't there? Sure, it works occasionally, but when things don't go well they tend to get out of hand. Carol couldn't stand having Helen underfoot all the time. It only took a few weeks before the situation became intolerable. Carol spoke to Dave. Naturally enough, he couldn't see anything wrong with his own mother. The subject became a bone of contention in the Hoffman residence.

On Monday morning, August 11, 1980, Dave reported his wife missing to police. According to Dave, he and Carol had a heated argument the night before. Carol had became furious and stormed out of the house. Because she was so upset, Dave wouldn't give her the keys to the family car. She left on foot. Dave waited for his wife to return, but she never did.

The police listened to his story, but thought that Carol Hoffman would return home on her own. Their attitude changed a few hours later when Carol's purse was found beside the highway just north of town. The contents of the purse, including a wallet containing money and credit cards, were intact.

A full-scale search for Carol was conducted by police and volunteers. There was grave suspicion that Carol had been abducted while walking alone along the road. Dave was inconsolable. He led search parties and appeared on radio and television, begging Carol's abductor to return the mother of his two children. Dave often broke down and cried.

Detectives questioned Carol's acquaintances in an attempt to find out more about the missing woman that could lead them to solving what they feared was now a murder case. In this way, authorities learned that she had often spoken to her friends about the deplorable situation in her home. Although Dave had advised them of the tension in the house, it appeared to be a much more serious problem than police had first realized. Evidently Carol had threatened divorce if her mother-in-law didn't move out.

Colleagues at Dave's place of employment were interrogated. Police learned that Dave was worried sick that Carol would take the two children if she divorced him. One employee told detectives that Dave had once insinuated that he would kill Carol by turning off her air supply when they were scuba-diving. Dave's colleague thought he was joking and dismissed the incident from his mind.

Police were now having second thoughts about Dave Hoffman. They decided to interrogate Dave as a suspect rather than as the grieving husband. He was asked if there was anything he was holding back, anything he wanted to get off his chest. Dave didn't hesitate. He told the stunned detectives that Carol had refused to have sex with him for weeks. He had come to think of her as an evil person and had decided to kill her for the sake of the children.

Once Dave was rolling, he couldn't stop. He told police that he had originally planned on killing Carol while they were scuba-diving at the lake, but on that occasion she was having so much fun he didn't have the heart to do it. On the Sunday that Carol supposedly disappeared, she didn't disappear at all. He simply strangled her as she lay in bed. Dave claimed that God had assisted him in removing an evil presence from his house.

Dave recounted that he had carried Carol into the bathroom, after which he had awakened his mother, who was pleased at what he had done. She agreed to guard the bathroom door against his young daughters disturbing him at his delicate work. Dave went on to describe how he had dissected his wife's body and had attempted to get rid of small portions by putting them down his garburetor, but the unit had seized, forcing him to abandon that method.

Dave had found an old duffel bag and gunny sack in the basement. All of Carol's body parts were placed in the two bags, together with some rocks from her garden. Mother was relieved of her guard duty, while Dave busied himself cleaning up for the next several hours. He went to bed, awoke at six-thirty Monday morning, had a bite to eat and placed the two bags containing his wife's parts into the boat, which he took to the lake. He rowed out to the centre of the lake and threw the two bags overboard. The rocks weighed them down nicely. For appearance's sake, cunning Dave did a little fishing.

Within hours, the Hoffman house was searched. Forensic evidence was found in the bathroom, garburetor and vacuum cleaner, corroborating Dave's fantastic story. His mother, Helen, was arrested. The two children were placed with county authorities and Dave was retained in custody.

On August 20, divers recovered the gunny sack and duffel

bag containing Carol's dismembered body. Dave, in his intense way, attempted to explain to detectives that he had really been successful in exorcising an evil presence from his home. He couldn't fathom why they didn't understand.

Detective Bob Salitros of the Hennepin County sheriff's department remembers the 13-year-old case vividly. It ranks as one of the strangest in his long career. During the initial investigation, he and his partner had a nagging feeling that Dave Hoffman was not the grieving husband he seemed to be. Salitros talked to Hoffman every day for 10 days before Hoffman revealed all the startling details of the murder.

Helen Ulvinen was found guilty in the murder of her daughter-in-law. On December 22, 1980, she was sentenced to life imprisonment. However, 11 months later, the Supreme Court of Minnesota overthrew the jury's verdict, claiming there wasn't sufficient evidence to warrant a guilty verdict. Helen was discharged from prison on December 22, 1981.

Her son Dave wasn't nearly as fortunate. On February 11, 1981, he was found guilty of murder and sentenced to life imprisonment. He is presently serving that sentence.

# Charles Walton
# CROSS SLASHED INTO VICTIM'S CHEST

Come along with me now to Lower Quinton, about nine miles down the road from Stratford, England. As everyone knows, this is Shakespeare country. What is far less known is that the area is steeped in superstition and witchcraft. Here you will be told stories of headless horsemen, of figures that are half man and half beast and of a black dog with luminous eyes who roams the countryside seeking victims. According to legend, he who gazes upon the black dog is doomed. To this day, it is believed that the close-mouthed inhabitants of the area practise witchcraft.

It was on Valentine's Day, 1945, that it happened. Seventy-four-year-old Charles Walton lived with his niece Edith in Lower Quinton. The old gent was a loner who did odd jobs around the tiny rural community. Because he was known never to part with a pence, Walton was reputed to be moderately well off.

At the time our story unfolds, Walton worked off and on trimming hedges for a local farmer, Albert Potter. On this particular day, he bade his niece goodbye at 9 a.m., and told her he would return for tea at four o'clock, as usual. Walton was a creature of habit. He always returned home at four and made himself a cup of tea when he worked for Potter.

Edith was employed in a nearby factory that manufactured war materials. Uncle and niece parted. Walton made his way to Meon Hill with the aid of his walking stick. He also carried a hay fork and sickle-shaped slash hood.

That evening, Edith returned home from her job at 6 p.m. fully expecting to find her uncle. Alarmed at not being able to locate the elderly gentleman, she called on a neighbour, Harry Beasley. Together they walked to Albert Potter's house. Potter said that he was pretty sure he had seen Walton from a distance up on Meon Hill shortly after noon. He had assumed it was Walton, but could not positively say it was him.

Darkness fell. With the aid of a flashlight, Potter joined the other two in the trek up Meon Hill. From time to time they called out Walton's name, as they felt that Walton's rheumatic legs may have given out.

Suddenly, Potter stopped short. "Stay there!" he shouted. "Don't come any nearer. You mustn't look at this."

The sight that greeted Potter was not a pleasant one, Walton's throat had been cut with a sickle. More hideous still, his body was held firmly to the ground by the prongs of the hayfork that had been plunged through his neck and into the earth. Walton's killer had slashed a cross into his chest.

Famed detective Robert Fabian of Scotland Yard was called in to lead the investigation. Torontonians may remember Fabian. He was brought to Canada in the summer of 1954 to investigate the riddle of the Marion McDowell abduction. Unfortunately, Fabian was unable to solve the McDowell case, which remains a mystery to this day.

On the morning of February 15, 1945, the colourful Fabian was at the scene of the crime in Lower Quinton. It didn't take the detective long to find out that he wasn't dealing with an ordinary murder, if any murder can ever be called ordinary.

Local police filled him in on the deep superstitions of the inhabitants. They even provided him with books on the subject. One such book described the case of an elderly lady, Ann Turner, who had been murdered in 1875 by a young lad. The motive for the murder had been the killer's belief that Ann had an "evil eye" that caused animals to die and crops to fail.

Fabian attempted to solicit the help of the locals in the area, but was met with a wall of silence. There were fewer than 500 inhabitants in Lower Quinton, nearby Upper Quinton and Admington. No one had seen or heard anything unusual, nor had anyone seen a stranger. In fact, no one even wanted to talk of the murder.

The tales of witches and evil spells was initially scoffed at by Fabian. He had investigated and solved scores of murder cases. Witchcraft was a phenomenon of years past. Then he heard that a few days earlier, a calf had been found dead in a ditch. Folks said it was an evil omen and the direct result of someone with an evil eye. They talked of little else.

Strange events hounded Fabian. While examining the murder scene, a large black dog ran down Meon Hill past the startled detective. When he told local police officers of the black dog he himself had witnessed, they recounted other tales of terror concerning the black dog. Eerily, within hours of Fabian relating his tale, a police car ran into and killed a black dog in Lower Quinton.

When the locals heard that Fabian had seen the phantom black dog, they ostracized the policeman. Pubs would empty when he entered. Citizens crossed the road when he appeared. Within days, another dead calf was found in the ditch. A dead black dog was found slung over a shrub near where Charles Walton's body had been found. In order to better understand what he was up against, Fabian pored over all available literature pertaining to the superstitions of the area. Despite the best efforts of Scotland Yard's most famous detective, Charles Walton's murderer was never apprehended.

As he investigated the background of the area, Fabian grew to respect some of the folklore of the region. He no longer scoffed at the strange tales and firmly believed that covens were meeting in Lower Quinton while the investigation was going on.

In all, Fabian and his assistants took over 4,000 statements, followed every possible clue, but did not make an arrest.

The detective did find out some strange and unusual facts. One such fact was that, in ancient times, in the month of February, bloodletting festivals took place. Blood was allowed to soak into the ground, supposedly to make the earth fertile. A few of the locals who did speak to Fabian claimed that Charles Walton's killing had been a fertility rite.

Fabian was told that the infamous black dog had once

appeared 60 years earlier, in 1885, which was within living memory of some of the natives. The dog had been seen on nine consecutive nights by a 14-year-old ploughboy as he headed home at night. On the ninth night, the boy witnessed a headless woman, which everyone agreed was a sign of death. The very next day, the ploughboy's sister died. She had been in the best of health.

After hearing this story, Fabian pored over a book entitled *Folklore, Old Customs and Superstitions in Shakespeare Land.* He came across the story of the ploughboy in more detail and was startled to read the lad's name—Charles Walton.

Detective Superintendent Robert Fabian died of natural causes in 1978.

# Nola Jean Weaver
# NOLA JEAN'S STORY

Long Grove, Illinois, is one of those tiny towns that makes city dwellers wonder what they are doing living in their crowded, traffic-choked metropolises. Now practically a Chicago sub-urb, the town has managed to retain a quaint tranquillity despite the large homes built at the edge of the community by wealthy Chicagoans who have found refuge from the city's high crime rate.

Nola Jean and Larry Weaver bought a home in a rather luxurious subdivision on the outskirts of Long Grove. They had been childhood sweethearts back in Camden, Arkansas. In 1962, the attractive, well-educated young couple tied the knot. Both pursued teaching careers. In 1976, after several transfers, they wound up in idyllic Long Grove, where Larry was appointed assistant superintendent of a large school district. Slim, athletic Nola Jean continued as a physical-education teacher. Their daughter, Tiffany, was eight years old when the family moved to Long Grove.

The Weavers had it made in the shade: a beautiful home, a lovely daughter and secure promising careers. On the night of December 4, 1977, their world crumbled. Two days earlier, Earl Goodfellow observed a pickup truck patrolling the neigh-bourhood. When the two occupants of the truck saw Earl look-ing at them, they sped away. Earl was suspicious enough of the strangers to mention the incident to his immediate neighbours, the Weavers.

On the night of the fourth, the Weavers followed their usual routine. Tiffany was put to bed. Larry and Nola Jean watched television before they too retired for the night. A little after 1 a.m., the stillness of the crisp winter night was disrupted by Nola Jean's screams. The Goodfellows were awakened by loud knocks on their front door. There stood Nola Jean, clutching Tiffany in her arms. Clad only in a nightgown, Nola Jean blurted out, "Call the police and fire department! There's been some shooting and a fire."

Earl Goodfellow responded to his neighbour's frantic request. In a matter of minutes the local fire department and the police were at the scene. The quiet winter night had been transformed into a beehive of activity centred on 99 Lincoln Avenue.

Initially, police were reluctant to enter the house as Nola Jean had told them that two men had accosted her and her husband. Slowly, armed officers advanced and entered. The house was empty except for the horribly burned body of Larry Weaver, which lay still smouldering on the bed. Firemen extinguished the last vestiges of the localized fire. A coroner would later confirm that over 90 percent of Larry's body had been badly burned.

Detectives questioned Nola Jean at the Goodfellows' residence. She told them that she and Larry were awakened a little after 1 a.m. by sounds in their home. Larry went downstairs to investigate. He returned in a matter of minutes, bent over her in bed and told her in a low voice to grab the .22 rifle they had in the house and get out of there. Nola Jean managed to gather up the rifle and make her way outdoors before being intercepted by one of the intruders. He disarmed her and called for Larry to surrender. Larry appeared with his hands over his head. The two men, now in full control, demanded money, big money. The amount of $750,000 was mentioned, which led Nola Jean to believe that the men had mistaken them for multimillionaires.

Larry pleaded with his captors, telling them that he didn't have that kind of money, but that he could obtain a smaller amount. The men agreed and one of them drove off with Larry in Nola Jean's car. Fifteen minutes later, they returned. Larry's captor growled, "He's lying." He then led Larry into his bedroom. Nola Jean heard one shot. Both men then ran from the house. Nola Jean rushed to Tiffany's room and frantically ran to the Goodfellows'. That in a nutshell was Nola Jean's story.

Detectives examined the interior of the house. Some things didn't jell with Nola Jean's story. There was no forced entry. All windows and doors, other than the patio door, which had been used by everyone, were securely locked from the inside. There was no physical evidence indicating how the men had gained entrance to the house. An examination of Larry's bed revealed that an accelerant had been spread over the bed. It was also ascertained that Larry had been under a sheet and blanket when he had been set on fire. Surely if he had been forced to lie on the bed, he wouldn't have gone under the covers. He had been shot in the head by a .22-calibre rifle. The Weavers' rifle was nowhere to be found.

Nola Jean was able to give such detailed descriptions of the two intruders that a police artist was able to compile composite drawings of the two men. Meanwhile, she was subjected to a lie detector test, ostensibly to remove her as a suspect. The test was inconclusive. When asked to take a second test, Nola Jean refused on the advice of her lawyer. That's when authorities decided the ideal life that the Weavers seemed to have led had to contain some secrets.

They were right. Close friends were questioned. It was learned that energetic Nola Jean was carrying on extramarital affairs with two men. One was her superior at the high school and the other was her brother-in-law. A student came forward with the startling information that he had witnessed his phys-ed teacher doing what comes naturally with her boss on a wrestling mat in the gym. Evidently Nola Jean had fallen out of love with her husband and was playing the field.

Homicide investigators kept digging and continued to come up with incriminating evidence. Although the Weavers' .22-calibre weapon was never found, it was proven that Nola Jean had purchased ammunition for the rifle on a recent visit to Arkansas. The two cars owned by the couple were checked when detectives first heard Nola Jean's story on the night of the murder. The engine of her car was warm and the seat was in the extreme forward position. Was it natural for Larry, a six-footer, to choose his wife's vehicle and not adjust the seat, when his own car was available? Police believed that Nola Jean had driven her own car that night in order to dispose of the murder weapon.

In addition, letters found in the house revealed that Larry had known of his wife's sexual activities. Nola Jean had responded to her husband's notes, describing her sex life with other men in minute detail. To add frosting to the layers of circumstantial evidence, Larry was heavily insured, both personally and through his employer. Nola Jean was the sole beneficiary of all the policies.

Nola Jean was arrested and charged with her husband's murder. All the evidence was presented in sensational detail. Nola Jean's married lovers were forced to take the witness stand and tell their lurid tales of illicit sex. After deliberating a full day, the Illinois jury found her guilty of murdering her husband. She was sentenced to 40 to 60 years' imprisonment.

While incarcerated, Nola Jean was a model prisoner. She taught several classes, all the while fighting for a new trial. On November 6, 1980, after Nola Jean had spent three years in prison, the Illinois Appellant Court overturned the murder conviction on a technicality and granted a new trial. She managed to stay out of jail awaiting the date of her second trial, which was scheduled to take place on June 27, 1983. She stunned the court by pleading guilty in return for a plea-bargain deal. Nola Jean was sentenced to 14 years' imprisonment with credit for time already served. After spending almost five years in prison, she was paroled at age 44.

Since that time, the former Nola Jean Weaver has changed her name, inherited a farm in Missouri left to her by a girl-friend and, in 1989, remarried.

# Joe Williams
# TRUTH REVEALED AFTER DEATH

Any criminal lawyer will tell you that you can never predict a
jury's decision. We must assume that in the vast majority of
cases their decisions are correct, but there are those occasions
where we have proof that juries have made terrible mistakes.

On May 21, 1939, Walter Dinivan awoke as he did each
morning of his retirement. Life was sweet. Walter had made
his money in the garage business and had purchased a sizeable
villa in Bournemouth, England. He loved to stroll through his
extensive gardens.

The villa was large and Walter had divided it into two flats.
Two elderly ladies occupied the top floor, while Walter, a wid-
ower, shared the first floor with his granddaughter.

On the day in question, Walter's grandson, who was a
member of the Royal Navy, visited his grandfather. Walter was
delighted and insisted the lad sleep over on the night of the
twenty-first. That day, the elderly gentleman enjoyed an out-
ing to Lullworth Cove with his two grandchildren. Upon their
return, they had tea. The two young people left the villa at 7:15
p.m. to attend a dance.

Walter Dinivan retired to his drawing room, sat in his
favourite chair in front of the fireplace and settled down to a
quiet evening at home. At 11:45 p.m., his two grandchildren
returned home from the dance. They were surprised to find all
the doors of the villa locked. Their grandfather had assured
them that he would leave a door open for them.

Finally, unable to get a response to his knocking, Walter's
grandson smashed the window of the front door and gained
entrance to the villa. He found his grandfather lying in a pool

of blood in front of the fireplace. He had been struck viciously about the head with a blunt instrument. Walter was alive, but he died the next day.

An autopsy indicated that ten blows had been inflicted to the elderly gentleman's head. There was also evidence that he had been strangled.

Scotland Yard was asked to assist in the case. The murder scene was straight out of a novel. The position and condition of the body indicated that Walter had not struggled, but had been surprised by his attacker. It was felt that, as there was no forced entry to the villa, Walter may have been acquainted with his killer and had invited him to enter the drawing room.

Walter may have entertained the murderer. On a table in the den was a bottle of beer, two large glasses and a small green glass containing whiskey. One of the beer glasses was over-turned, causing a beer stain on the tablecloth. The other large glass contained beer. The whiskey had been Walter's. His grandchildren stated that he never drank beer; he preferred whiskey, which he always drank out of the distinctive small green glass found on the table.

Detectives were able to lift a thumbprint off the beer glass that had been tipped over. There were also several cigarette butts in the ashtray. Since Walter didn't smoke, it was believed the cigarettes had been smoked by his killer.

Remember, this was 1939. Testing of saliva to identify blood type was not in common use, nor was it accepted as evidence in court. Despite this, Scotland Yard sent the cigarette butts for testing. In this way they learned that whoever had smoked the cigarettes had a rare blood type found in only three percent of the population.

On the drawing-room floor, detectives found a woman's hair curler, which did not belong to Walter's granddaughter. They also found a crumpled paper bag, which may have held the murder weapon, quite possibly a hammer. The motive for the murder appeared to be robbery. Walter was known to carry several pounds on his person. This was missing, as were his watch and rings. A safe located in the drawing room had been opened with a key always carried by Walter. The contents of the safe, believed to be several pounds, was missing.

Detectives took the fingerprints of everyone involved. None matched the fingerprint on the beer glass. Laundries were canvassed in an attempt to locate anyone who had brought in bloodstained clothing to be cleaned. Nothing pertaining to the murder was uncovered.

The massive investigation in Bournemouth was the chief topic of conversation in the community. Everyone was discussing the case. It was in this way that detectives learned of one man who was known to be broke the day before the murder and flush with money immediately after the killing.

Joe Williams was a crusty old retired soldier who had spent most of his soldiering years in India. The 69-year-old lived in abject poverty in an ancient dilapidated house that was heavily mortgaged. He had the appearance of Ichabod Crane and often acted in an irrational manner, particularly when provoked.

Joe was interviewed by Scotland Yard's finest and was totally uncooperative. He refused to allow his fingerprints to be taken and defiantly swore that the last time he had seen Walter was on May 17, four days before the murder took place. On that occasion, Walter had invited him inside the villa for a drink. Joe admitted that he had asked Walter for a loan, but Walter would only advance him five pounds, which he had taken from his safe.

Scotland Yard detectives were certain that Joe Williams was their man. They located Joe's favourite pub and dropped in to have a few drinks with their suspect. Surreptitiously, they gathered up Joe's cigarette butts and sent them for testing. Sure enough, Joe's blood type was the same rare type as that of the man who had smoked the cigarettes in Walter's drawing room.

Detectives searched Joe's filthy home. They found paper bags of the same type as the one left at the murder scene. These bags were traced to the manufacturer who had no trouble authenticating that their company had manufactured them. In fact, because the machine used on the paper was now obsolete, they were able to pinpoint the exact machine. Further, they were able to prove without a doubt that the bag left at the murder scene and the one found in Joe's house had come off this particular machine in consecutive order. The serrated edges at the top of both bags underwent scientific testing that proved this was the case.

The hair curler found in Walter's villa was thought to be a remote clue, but proved to be invaluable. The curler was old and was no longer being manufactured. Scotland Yard learned that Joe had been married years before. His wife had left him, but police were successful in tracing her. She had no difficulty identifying the curler as having once belonged to her. She still used the same curlers and willingly showed them to police. Detectives believed Joe had planted the old curler and the extra glass of beer to lead police to think that a woman had also been involved in the murder.

Four months after the tragedy, investigators felt they had an abundance of circumstantial evidence pointing to Joe's guilt. He lamely accounted for the large amount of money he had after the murder by telling his interrogators that he had been extremely lucky at the horse races. Joe's thumbprint matched the one on the beer glass, but Joe dismissed this as having been left there on May 17, when Walter had invited him in for a drink. No one believed him. Joe Williams was taken into custody and tried for the murder of Walter Dinivan.

In October 1939, Joe Williams was inexplicably found not guilty by an English jury. He smiled and joked with his guards as he left the courtroom a free man.

Joe Williams lived on for 12 years until March 1951, when he died peacefully in his sleep. The next day, crime reporter Norman Rae revealed in the *News of the World* what he had known for 12 years. Joe Williams had been guilty of the murder of Walter Dinivan. On the night of his acquittal, Joe had had a few drinks with the crime reporter to celebrate. He told Rae, "I did it. The jury was wrong. It was me." Joe even toasted the hangman, saying, "To the hangman who has been cheated of his victim."

Joe went through his every movement in the villa, revealing

details only the killer could have known. Nothing could be done about the confession. Libel laws prevented Rae from writing his story. Joe had been tried and acquitted. There were no technical reasons for a new trial and, having once been acquitted, Joe Williams could not be tried again on the same charge.

# James Wilson
# DID SHEEP FARMER KILL THEM BOTH?

When James Wilson left England in 1947 to seek his fortune in New Zealand, he had already formed very definite ideas as to how he would fulfil his ambition. His plans didn't include manual labour.

Within a year, James owned a prosperous sheep farm about 35 miles outside Auckland. He lived in a huge home and led the life of a country squire. And how did he acquire so much wealth in such a short time? Simple. Her name was Norah Harwood and her daddy was one of the most prominent landowners in the area. The day James married Norah, he was elevated from farm labourer to king of the castle.

In January 1964, after 17 years of married life, Norah died under mysterious circumstances. The attending physician refused to issue a death certificate. Norah was in good health one day and very dead the next. A post-mortem revealed that she had died as the result of strychnine poisoning.

When James was questioned, he confessed that he kept strychnine around the farm as a pesticide. Quite possibly, he and Norah had been careless. They stored the strychnine in a lemonade bottle in the kitchen. No doubt Norah had mistakenly mixed up the bottle with similar lemonade bottles she drank from each afternoon while watching her favourite TV program. Unfortunately, James had been in Wellington at the time of the terrible mishap.

Testing of the half-empty bottle of lemonade revealed large quantities of strychnine. Everything checked out, except for one thing. In the course of their investigation into Norah's death, police found out that James had been carrying on a prolonged affair with a younger woman, Freda Smart. Detectives were certain that James had murdered his wife. He had, in fact, committed the perfect murder. With Norah's death, James became the sole owner of the profitable sheep farm. Six months after Norah's untimely demise, James married Freda Smart.

Friends of the Wilsons were of the same opinion as the police. As a result, they shunned Freda. The new Mrs. Wilson had only one friend, Jessica Lacey, who owned a small grocery store and restaurant near the Wilson farm. The two women visited each other often.

Fifteen years later, Freda, now 53 years old, complained of pains in her stomach. She visited her family physician, Dr. Herbert Roventry, in Auckland. He prescribed painkillers, but nothing seemed to help. As the weeks turned into months and the pain increased, the doctor carried out a series of tests. Still, he was unable to diagnose the cause of Freda's discomfort. James was deeply concerned and spent much time with his stricken wife. So did Jessica Lacey. It was Jessica who called Dr. Roventry, imploring him to come to the Wilson farm. Her friend Freda was in excruciating pain and appeared to be near death. Dr. Roventry rushed to his patient's side, but he was too late. Freda Wilson was dead.

Dr. Roventry had no idea what had caused Freda's death. He called police and ordered a post-mortem. The post-mortem revealed that Freda's body was laced with arsenic. Arsenic in her hair indicated that she had been poisoned over a lengthy period of time. It was all too much. Two wives, both poison victims.

Auckland detectives were certain they would nail their man this time around. If James Wilson ran true to form, he would have a mistress stashed away somewhere. It didn't take them long to find beautiful 26-year-old Ivy Thomas. The pair had been seeing each other for about a year before Freda's death.

Investigators confronted James with their suspicions. He admitted to his affair with Ivy, but vehemently denied killing Freda. He claimed he had had no reason to harm his wife. He already owned the farm and was getting all the sex any man could want from Ivy. He simply had no motive to kill Freda. When questioned, Ivy told police that James had never broached the subject of marriage. She added that James wouldn't have been stupid enough to poison Freda, knowing full well he would be suspected of her murder. Police had to agree that her reasoning made some sense. To further complicate matters, James swore he had never kept arsenic around his home, nor had he ever purchased it.

James was interrogated extensively, until finally he confessed, but not in the manner police expected. He told them that when he had fallen in love with Freda, he had risked all to be with her, knowing full well that if Norah found out, she would divorce him. As the farm was in her name, he would lose everything and be reduced to a common labourer. Freda had wanted him to seek a divorce, but he wouldn't hear of it. Gradually the idea of poisoning Norah formed in his mind. Freda was privy to his thoughts. She implored him not to do it, not because it was wrong, but because she was afraid he would be caught. James went through with the scheme and it had worked out just as he had planned. As for Freda, James claimed he was as puzzled as the police. He definitely had had nothing whatever to do with her death.

Despite having confessed to poisoning Norah, James was brought to trial for Freda's murder. The prosecution theorized that Freda had found out about her husband's affair with Ivy. She may have asked for a divorce. James wouldn't hear of it. After all, Freda knew the details of Norah's murder. She had to be killed to silence her. Although James claimed throughout that he was innocent of Freda's murder, he was found guilty and sentenced to life imprisonment.

When sentence was pronounced, James suffered a heart attack. He was rushed to hospital, where he recovered. After being transferred to prison, he suffered a second, fatal heart attack. Between his first and second attack, James insisted that he had been convicted of a murder he had not committed. He continued to tell doctors that he was innocent of Freda's murder right up until he breathed his last.

As soon as James's death was announced, police received a visit from Jessica Lacey. Freda Wilson had confided in her that she had once followed James and had discovered his affair with Ivy Thomas. Freda was devastated. She was well aware that years earlier James had killed his first wife in order to marry her. The two women talked. Jessica suggested that there were two avenues open to her friend. She could let the affair run its course or she could obtain a divorce. Freda rejected both ideas. She revealed to Jessica that James had killed Norah. Maybe he would kill her. Jessica told Freda that James wasn't that stupid. He wouldn't kill her because no one can simply go around killing wives and get away with it. Freda looked at her friend in a strange way and abruptly terminated the conversation.

In the weeks that followed, Freda fed herself arsenic. Jessica had taken a vow not to reveal her friend's secret. She watched as Freda suffered excruciating pain. Unbelievably, Freda Wilson had poisoned herself so that her husband would be convicted of her murder. The scheme had worked perfectly.

# Marie Witte
# BOILED BODY PARTS

Even as a pre-teenager, Marie simply adored nudist camps. There was something about the fresh air, the freedom of movement and the volleyball. There were also members of the opposite sex. Marie enjoyed the latter most of all.

At age 14, Marie met a young serviceman at a nudist camp. His rank has always been something of a mystery, probably because he hardly ever donned a uniform. Despite her tender years, Marie married her lover. The wedding was a gala affair, covered by many of those magazines that feature nudist camps. That was the only thing covered; Marie took her solemn vows clad only in a wedding veil. The marriage ended in divorce a few months later.

Undaunted by this unfortunate union, Marie continued to frequent nudist camps. It was while sashaying around in the Florida sunshine that Marie met the vacationing Paul Witte. By now, Marie was a mature 16 and had been kissed many times. Paul was 26 and wanted more.

After vacationing in Florida, he returned to his mother, Elaine, in the tiny hamlet of Trail Creek, Indiana. But darn it all, Paul couldn't get his mind off that cute little Marie. He phoned in a proposal. Marie caught the next bus to Trail Creek.

Mummy Elaine didn't exactly take Marie to her ample bosom. After all, the girl was only 16, but who was she to stand in the way of her son's happiness? Within weeks, Marie and Paul tied the knot.

Surprise of surprises, the Witte marriage appeared to be a happy one. Two sons, Eric and John, blessed the union. Years passed. The boys grew up to be strapping teenagers. Everything appeared normal in the Witte household until September 1, 1981. That was the day of the tragic accident. Eric, 17, was fooling around with his father's gun when it discharged. The bullet plowed into the back of his father's head, killing him instantly. Sometime later, when Marie's house burned down, Elaine invited her daughter-in-law and her two grandsons to move in with her.

That was a mistake. The two boys turned out to be undisciplined hellions. Their grandmother couldn't stand them and they couldn't stand her. The tension was relieved somewhat in 1983 when Eric joined the navy and was stationed in San Diego, California. A few months later, Marie told anyone who inquired that her mother-in-law had gone away on vacation to visit relatives. She was a little vague as to when Elaine would return. At the same time, she and John took a trip to San Diego to visit Eric.

Nine months passed. No one had seen hide nor hair of Elaine, Marie or John. When a relative from out of town came to Trail Creek and found Elaine's house devoid of furniture and to all intents and purposes deserted, she went to the police. An inquiry at Elaine's bank revealed that her social security cheques were no longer being deposited there, but were being sent to General Delivery, San Diego. A further inquiry disclosed that the cheques had all been signed by Elaine Witte and endorsed by Marie Witte. A handwriting expert was brought in to examine Elaine's signature. He felt that someone had traced her name from an authentic signature.

The FBI located Marie and Eric, who had cashed some of the cheques. They were taken into custody in San Diego and charged with forgery and conspiracy. But where was Elaine Witte? Marie said she had no idea and could care less.

Back in Trail Creek, a relative of the Wittes went to authorities and, for the first time, police heard that Elaine had been murdered. The relative told a wild tale of murder and intrigue. Detectives were amazed at the horrific nature of the story they were being told. They approached the two Witte boys with the relative's incriminating statement.

John decided to talk. He told detectives that he and his grandmother had argued constantly. Marie had been using Elaine's bank card to withdraw funds from her bank account. When Elaine suspected she was being systematically robbed, she informed Marie that the very next day she was going to her bank to check on her affairs. Marie told John that Elaine would throw them all out of the house. Something had to be done post-haste.

Marie awakened John in the middle of the night and ordered him to kill his grandmother. John took his brother's crossbow and shot Elaine in the chest as she slept. Marie instructed him to clean up, before leaving the house for a few hours. John shoved his grandmother's body into a garbage can. When Marie returned, she called Eric in San Diego, asking his advice. Eric told her to put the body into the family freezer located in the basement. She and John spent three days hacking and chopping Elaine's body so the parts would fit in the freezer. The job became somewhat easier when Marie purchased a chainsaw.

Eric flew home on a 24-hour pass. He assessed the situation and suggested Marie install a garbage-disposal unit and a trash compactor to get rid of the body. The appliances didn't do the job. The garbage disposal unit clogged and burned out the motor, while the trash compactor wasn't capable of accommodating large bones. It too broke down.

Marie spent a full week boiling the body parts so that she could put them into freezer bags and store them easily in the freezer until Eric returned from San Diego and told her how to get rid of her mother-in-law.

Once police informed Eric of John's statement, he decided to confess as well, confirming everything John had already related. In addition, he dropped the bombshell that his father's death had not been an accident. His mother had commanded him to shoot his father. According to Eric, his father had abused him, his brother and his mother for years. After the shooting, Marie had rehearsed her sons on what to say to the police. Everyone had believed Paul Witte's death had been a tragic accident.

When Marie had wanted to stage another accident to get rid of Elaine, Eric had argued with his mother not to do it. He figured police would never fall for two tragic accidents in the same family. That was the reason they so desperately wanted to dispose of Elaine's body.

Eric had finally done the job. He threw the boiled body parts out of a car across three states on his way from Indiana to California. If anyone came across the boiled meat, it would be doubtful they would recognize it as human.

And what happened to the members of this joyous family? Let's see. John was not charged with any complicity in his father's murder. He testified against his mother in exchange for the right to plead guilty to involuntary manslaughter in the case of his grandmother. He was sentenced to 20 years' imprisonment.

Eric was given immunity from prosecution in the case of his grandmother in exchange for his testimony concerning his father's murder. He pleaded guilty to murdering his father and was sentenced to 20 years in prison.

On November 4, 1985, Marie Witte stood trial in Michigan City, Indiana, for the murder of her mother-in-law. All the gory details came out. With her two sons testifying against her, the outcome was a foregone conclusion. Marie was found guilty of murder and conspiracy. She was sentenced to the maximum allowed by law—60 years and 50 years to run consecutively. She was also charged with the murder of her husband. Once again, her sons testified for the state.

During her trial, it was revealed that Marie had attempted but failed to poison her husband with rat poison before eliciting the assistance of her son. She was found guilty of murder and attempted murder. On top of her previous 110-year sentence, she received a further sentence of life imprisonment. Marie Witte will most probably never be set free.

# William Youngman
# SON FROM HELL

We have in this volume presented for your enjoyment and revulsion some of the most hideous ladies and gentlemen ever to take human lives.

Now allow me to showcase William Godfrey Youngman, definitely a contender for the number-one villain of all time. William's father was a tailor in London, England, over a hundred years ago. The Youngman family, consisting of William Sr., his wife and three sons, lived in the top two floors of a three-storey home.

It was a foregone conclusion that William would take up his father's profession, but after a short while as an apprentice to the senior Youngman, he let it be known that the cut-and-sew game was not for him. William became a footman for a well-known physician, but soon managed to get into trouble. Evidently some of the doctor's belongings found their way into our William's possession. He wasn't prosecuted for this indiscretion, but he was fired.

William returned to his parents' home, where he displayed an aversion to any sort of exertion. He moped around the house all day thinking of ways to make money without indulging in the disagreeable act of manual labour. He mulled over the obvious, such as armed robbery and mugging, but dismissed these activities as far too dangerous. You see, William was not only a stupid oaf, he was also a coward. In his own dull way, he came up with a scheme never duplicated for its many cruel and heartless aspects.

Sly William made the acquaintance of Mary Streeter, the daughter of a farmer who worked his fields just outside the city.

Mary, who wasn't exactly rushed off her feet by eligible swains, liked William mainly because no other boy had ever paid her so much attention. When he invited her to London to spend some time as a house guest of his parents, she quickly accepted.

On a beautiful summer day, Mary arrived in London. William met her at the station. Together they started off for the Youngman residence, but because of the heat the young couple stopped off for a bit of liquid refreshment at a pub near London Bridge. While in the pub, an incident took place that would later assume some importance.

The owner of the pub, a man named Spicer, waited on William and Mary. When William let Mary pay for the drinks, Spicer sidled up to her and whispered, "That boy is an idler, a ne'er-do-well, and means you no good." Spicer had disliked William at first sight. When William turned his back, he again spoke to Mary. "I'd rather see a daughter of mine dead in her grave than married to a man as he."

Mary Streeter was in love. Who was this man who spoke so harshly against her William and what right did he have to say such things? She decided to ignore the man's warnings. That same day, William suggested that Mary take out insurance on her life in the amount of £100, a not inconsiderable sum in those days. William didn't let up. He pestered Mary so much that the next day, accompanied by William, she purchased the insurance policy, falsely listing her husband, William, as beneficiary. Mary shelled out the money for the first premium.

A week later, the stage was set for murder most foul. The young couple spent a day in the country, with Mary footing all bills for the day's activities. At 9 p.m. they returned home and ate a hearty meal prepared by William's mother.

One can only picture the Youngmans' satisfaction. Their not-too-ambitious son had met a lovely girl. It was obvious to everyone that it was only a matter of time before he and Mary would wed. The evening meal had been consumed with enthusiastic good cheer. William's two younger brothers, Thomas, 11, and Charles, 6, teased William about his girlfriend. All in all, it was a pleasant evening.

Mr. Youngman was the first to go to bed. He was accustomed to early hours, as he had to rise at 5 a.m. to travel to his place of employment some distance from his home. Mary and Mrs. Youngman shared a room, while William slept with his brothers.

Next morning, bright and early, Mr. Youngman got up and went to work, leaving his family asleep in bed, as was his custom. About 20 minutes later, the occupants of the first floor heard noises loud enough to cause concern. One of them put on his trousers and went upstairs. Halfway up he was met by William in his nightclothes. William was covered with blood. He screamed, "For God's sake, come up. There are several dead and dying. My mother got up in the middle of the night, just now, in fact, and attacked us all. I am afraid I have killed her in self-defence."

Upstairs, on the landing, just in the doorway of her bedroom, lay the bodies of Mrs. Youngman and Mary Streeter. Both had been stabbed to death. The two young boys were both dead in their bed. They too had been stabbed repeatedly.

Police were called and were at the scene in a matter of minutes. William gave them this fantastic statement, "My mother went suddenly mad and did it all. She attacked me with the knife after she had killed the others, and I wrested it from her and stabbed her to protect myself. I was entitled to do so. That's the law."

The officers looked at each other and shook their heads. Why had it been necessary for this strong 25-year-old man to kill his mother after he had "wrested" the knife from her? They pointed out this discrepancy to William, who doggedly stuck to his story.

Poor Mr. Youngman. That morning he had left his family sleeping peacefully. Now he was summoned home to find that they had all been murdered, with the exception of William. When questioned by police, he informed them that his wife had never been erratic in any way and for his son to insinuate that she was mad was in itself ludicrous. The authorities agreed with Mr. Youngman. William was arrested that very day. A search of his room uncovered the insurance policy. In Mary's trunk police found letters that Mary had received from William before her ill-fated visit to London. In these letters, William repeatedly asked Mary to insure her life.

William's trial lasted only one day. Despite the unbelievable nature of his story, he stuck to it throughout. No one believed it for a minute. The jury was convinced that they were staring at a bona fide monster, a man who could plan and carry out the murder of his unsuspecting girlfriend, his two younger brothers and his mother, all for monetary gain. One can despise William for the four murders, but in addition, his plan included another despicable element—he attempted to place the blame on his mother.

William Youngman was found guilty of murder and sentenced to hang. While in jail, he steadfastly held to his original statement and initiated a letter-writing campaign pleading with anyone who might help his cause, including the Queen of England.

All his efforts brought no results and William Youngman was hanged for his horrible crimes. While being led to the scaffold, he was heard to mumble over and over, "My mother done it all." Who knows, by then he might very well have believed his ridiculous story himself.